MASTER SPACE

Recent Titles in
Contributions to the Study of Popular Culture

MASTER SPACE

Film Images of Capra, Lubitsch, Sternberg, and Wyler

BARBARA BOWMAN

CONTRIBUTIONS TO THE STUDY OF POPULAR CULTURE,
NUMBER 31

GREENWOOD PRESS
NEW YORK • WESTPORT, CONNECTICUT • LONDON

Library of Congress Cataloging-in-Publication Data

Bowman, Barbara.
    Master space : film images of Capra, Lubitsch, Sternberg, and
Wyler / Barbara Bowman.
       p.   cm. — (Contributions to the study of popular culture,
ISSN 0198-9871 : no. 31)
    Includes bibliographical references and index.
    ISBN 0-313-28026-6 (alk. paper)
    1. Motion pictures — Production and direction. 2. Capra, Frank,
1897- —Criticism and interpretation. 3. Lubitsch, Ernst,
1892–1947—Criticism and interpretation. 4. Von Sternberg, Josef,
1894–1969—Criticism and interpretation. 5. Wyler, William, 1902–
Criticism and interpretation. 6. Cinematography. I. Title.
II. Series.
PN1995.9.P7B64   1992
791.43'0233'0922 — dc20   91-33480

British Library Cataloguing in Publication Data is available.

Library of Congress Catalog Card Number: 91-33480
ISBN: 0-313-28026-6
ISSN: 0198-9871

First published in 1992

Greenwood Press, 88 Post Road West, Westport, CT 06881
An imprint of Greenwood Publishing Group, Inc.

Printed in the United States of America

The paper used in this book complies with the
Permanent Paper Standard issued by the National
Information Standards Organization (Z39.48-1984).

10 9 8 7 6 5 4 3 2 1

Copyright Acknowledgment

Photographs courtesy of the Wisconsin Center for Film
and Theater Research in Madison, Wisconsin.

For my parents

Contents

PHOTOGRAPHS

ACKNOWLEDGMENTS

This book was written with the assistance, advice, and encouragement of many people and institutions. Steven P. Hill compiled and wrote the appendix on the four directors. He also went over the entire text in painstaking detail, offering numerous suggestions and corrections on matters of fact (dates, names, etc.) and clarifying the wording so that my ideas might be more clearly expressed. Hill also suggested the book's title.

I undertook this study originally during a summer seminar of the National Endowment for the Humanities. That seminar's leader, Charles Affron, gave me much help and encouragement in the first stages of my work, and subsequently as well. I also want to thank all the members of that seminar, especially Edward Benson, Steven Lipkin, and Samuel Chell, who continued to work with me for several years. Also formative were the film classes of Joseph Miller at the University of Maryland. Later, Illinois Wesleyan University provided a glorious sabbatical year; the members of its English department past and present and colleagues across the university have offered advice and friendship at all stages of the project. I also have every reason to feel grateful to the staffs and administrators of the film archives at the Library of Congress, the Museum of Modern Art, and the Center for Film and Theater Research in Madison, Wisconsin. While I have usually done my own typing, using a variety of Apple computers, Carol Finney and Barbara Maroules have pitched in at moments of crisis and brought computers, printers, prose, and bibliographies under control. Though not named here, my students have often asked the questions or made the comments that inspired my thinking.

Most sustaining for me have been three groups of friends — my women friends who are also professional mentors, Kathleen Hickok, Joyce Rothschild,

Kathryn Seidel, and Ellen Woodward; my siblings, Sandy and Peter Bowman; and my parents, to whom this project is dedicated, Ruth Anne Skinner Bowman and Bruce LeRoy Bowman, who taught me to question.

1

INTRODUCTION: SPACE IN CLASSIC AMERICAN FILM

In the 1990's, the younger generation assumes that one is speaking of outer space, when using the phrase "film space." This generation was weaned on movies such as the *Star Wars* series, the *Aliens*, and the *Star Treks*. Even more earthly films, such as those featuring the characters Indiana Jones or Batman, treat space as though it were "outer" rather than rooted firmly on a particular planet in a familiar human context. Directors have the freedom to manipulate the illusion of film space in this generation of films in a way that directors of the 30's and 40's, those with whom I'm concerned in this study, did not. Film-makers of the 80's and 90's do this by depicting a space that appears to be empty but dark, instead of most earthly films' depiction of a space that appears to be full but transparent. They also make us aware of the relation of space to time and motion. When ships flying through this space suddenly shift into "superdrive," still objects suddenly become dramatic slashes, as though time had really become a dimension of space for someone other than the physicist.

To bridge the historical shift for the young reader of this study between contemporary films and those I am studying, I will briefly describe the assumptions about space that characterize the films of Capra, Lubitsch, Sternberg, and Wyler in the 30's and 40's. Though employing very different sorts of settings, all of these directors endow the space in their films with great intensity despite spatial limitations. In fact, their creativity may be enhanced by these limitations, as a choreographer makes greater demands on dancers according to the size of the stage and the patterns of the music. These are limitations that an artist invites as they define his or her canvas and tools.

Both contemporary directors and directors of the 30's and 40's employ space so that it invites spectators into the scenes, but in the earlier films these invitations may depend more upon indirect means. For instance, Lubitsch will position the camera behind glass so that we can see the characters but not hear them. As spectators, we are asked to read their mime. Or Sternberg will partly obscure what we are looking at in order to inflate our curiosity about it. Likewise, the human bodies of the actors generally guide the narrative and focus the spatial effects in films of the 30's and 40's, whereas bodies in contemporary films compete or cooperate with machines to convey the stories. The spaceships, of course, are little bits of Earth in some other part of the galaxy, and contemporary directors must recruit our affection for them, as Capra never needed to promote his small towns.

The differing scales of films from each era also suggest why space has been re-formed: the configuration of space in films of the 30's and 40's suggested that the camera's job was to select from a limited space that was full, whereas the configuration of space in contemporary films suggests a largely empty but infinitely large universe in which the camera has found some point of interest. We look at an earlier film, thinking that the drama is a universal one. We look at a contemporary film, thinking that the drama is entirely unique, focused as it is on certain superheroes. (Granted, I am exaggerating the differences slightly to make my point.)

Two additional problems emerge when discussing space in films of the 30's and 40's. The first is the assumption that the word "space" means "something that is empty." The second is the built-in bias of language toward describing objects or actions as such, rather than the way in which these objects and actions cohere. Perhaps I can put aside the first of these problems merely by defining film space as the entire illusory volume before us as we watch a film, whether it be empty or filled by objects at rest or in motion. The second problem is more serious, since it demands that we attend to ambiguous, aesthetic, and intuitive issues rather than to clean-cut, logical, cognitive ones. Consider, for instance, territoriality, a major issue in the occupation of space in our daily lives.

In the space of films, territory lies under no particular "aegis" for spectators; we don't initially lay claim to territory or attach ourselves to it, unless we're invited to do so by the narrative.[1] (Paradoxically, though, we do feel a special power in relation to film space, which I will discuss shortly.) We do watch the drama of territoriality unfold among the fictional characters, and we certainly identify with their feelings about certain spaces, picking up on these usually unconscious feelings by understanding (at least subliminally) their relations with each other and the body language of an actor, which may convey all we need to know about a particular room, town, or environment. In John Ford's *The Searchers,* we may occupy such various spaces as the tepee of Cicatrice or the ranchhouse of Ethan's brother, and Ford may make us feel the impact of an entrance into or exit from these spaces by funnelling us through the second frame of a door or by inviting us to identify with a character's experience of intrusion. But both spaces are comparatively neutral until they are impressed by the director in these ways. Once they are "written upon," of course, we may feel comparatively at home in the ranchhouse and tense in the tepee.

Master filmmakers, then, begin with the knowledge that the space of film is initially neutral of any feelings on the spectators' parts that they possess it, sponsor it, gain power from it, or lend power to it. It is simply a container for activities.[2] As in most of our activities in life, space (either as a collection of volumes or as a consciousness of the interstices between volumes) remains invisible. We remain unaware of it; we simply proceed in a pragmatic way to act within it or upon it. But these filmmakers set out to alter our complacency and heighten our awareness of space — not space as a mere container (what is contained or does the containing), but rather space as everything within the frame. They may exploit a landscape or even a face. Sternberg writes in this connection: "Monstrously enlarged as it is on the screen, the human face should be treated like a landscape. It is to be viewed as if the eyes were lakes, the nose a hill, the cheeks broad meadows, the mouth a flower patch, the forehead sky, and the hair clouds."[3]

A master filmmaker's goal is to make acute what has been neutral, to intensify the total look of the screen, though these acute moments are necessarily of very finite duration. "Acute space" in film corresponds to a form of "elemental spatial thinking, shared by those in the visual arts."[4] And behind it lie certain assumptions that are foreign to the logical left-brain functions that dominate so much of our culture and so many of our daily activities.

It is often what we call the irrational activities in our lives that provide the clues to the spatial encounters that directors create on film. How often, for instance, does the arrangement of spaces and furniture in a house reveal the relationships between those who occupy that space? Whose music is housed in the communal spaces and whose television in private space? Who warrants his or her own study? Whose chair has the best view of the television? Who answers the phone and is it convenient to him or her? Usually these relations are unconsciously ritualized until some discontent disrupts or challenges the status quo. Then this "habitual space" becomes visible.[5] It becomes acute.

In one couple's household, this occurred when the husband abandoned "his chair" and started sitting on a sofa that the wife had habitually occupied. The wife had no particular claims to this sofa. (Property claims generally spring from furniture that is occasional in this family — given on a birthday or anniversary or holiday.) So the wife got rid of the sofa, and they went out and bought "her chair." The husband retreated back to "his chair" and, in addition, bought a new car and eventually a new chair as well. Because the wife was more aware of the drama unfolding, she had more control of the scenario. These were moments during which the habitual spaces of their lives became suddenly acute: the ordinary became extraordinary, and a qualitative shift occurred.

Unlike our most common response in our lives to tension — avoidance or an effort to minimize the tension—the master film director strives to exploit the tension of such moments. These qualitative shifts are the stuff of real drama, making what is neutral habitual and making what is habitual acute. But these qualitative shifts are not simply a matter of thinking more clearly about a situation. In fact, despite the cognitive jargon that tends to dominate our lives, I'm not sure that these shifts should be called "thought" or that they are "cognitive" issues. And I don't think that directors and their collaborators necessarily think about how they are going to arrange scenes spatially. They may have a sense of what they want or how they might achieve it. They may envision scenes. A director with his cinematographer may have strong feelings about shooting a scene from a certain distance or angle or in a certain light or with various properties at particular intervals. William Wyler, for instance, discusses all these intuitive choices as "certain habits," as part of his wish to achieve "an almost effortless flow of the scene" and "more interesting composition."[6] In the domestic drama described above, the wife felt the intrusion on the sofa long before she articulated it. Most decisions about film space, I would guess, are never understood in a fully conscious way; and exactly who makes the decision—or what combination of figures, such as director, cinematographer, writer, film editor, or set designer, makes the decision—may never be accurately recalled decades later for the film historian.

Being a spectator of film does exploit one aspect of territoriality that we also know in our daily lives: the establishment of territory through gaze projection. Unless we are terribly shy, we have experienced eye-holding space, the claiming of space through the intensity of gaze. In libraries, one can usually stare offenders against the peace into silence if they can be brought to notice the stare. Teachers hold their classes' attention through gaze projection,[7] and a teacher may experience a loss of attention or discipline on the day when glasses are forgotten. Once, having a teacher whose eyes focused in different directions, I found his gaze projection very disconcerting and diffuse. We have certainly all been held by a gaze and experienced its power—been intimidated by it or basked in its implied approval.

The experience of film spectatorship allows us to experience the possession of this one sort of power. No one will accuse us of staring during a film.[8] The darkness relieves us of even being seen clearly while staring. And the constancy and intensity of our gazes allow us to appropriate the space, neutral as it is, and what it contains on the screen. We are, in this sense, empowered. Whereas in daily life even our most powerful positions in our eye-holding spaces are challenged, in viewing a film we are not in competition with the other viewers unless the viewing conditions are inadequate or the other viewers obnoxious. But in these cases, the film viewing is interrupted by another drama. If spectators have a clear view of the screen in a completely darkened space and adequate space and comfort for their seated bodies, and if aural space is silent except for the soundtrack, their gaze projection creates a double spatial sense. Films depend upon "being here but also there,"[9] being safely ensconced in that dark, temperature-controlled state of relaxation in the theater while imaginatively entering and possessing that (neutral until created) narrative space of the screen.

Of course, a great deal has been said about the screen possessing or obsessing the spectator. A few years ago, any high school cheerleader could tell you about Hinckley, the young man who watched *Taxi Driver* and then shot the President. But, to be honest, I'm not interested in the behavior of madmen at the movies, though this phrase sounds suspiciously like a book title. It does seem plausible to me that we might understand abnormality better if we understood what happens to most film viewers. What we undergo in being spectators is certainly an exchange of some sort, but not a simple one. We do not simply attain space. We are not simply relieved of the need to be defensive. We do not become possessors of the screen world without a required return. The madman's response is imaginable, but it is an amputated version of what can be experienced by the film-goer.

The madman is empowered while being neither challenged nor inspired by the fictional world. The at first neutral space of the screen is never neutral for him; he never chooses to attend to its otherness. Instead, he surrenders his own sovereignty, and, in doing so, he diffuses the entire aesthetic process, which includes, for instance, the tension between the tenor (first term) and the vehicle (second term) of a metaphor or simile. For the madman, the symbol is impoverished and becomes boringly literal. For most spectators, though, the exchange between self and screen creates a pleasurable tension.

Observing the space of films can tell us a great deal about those who fashioned that space. Space invites and even demands certain responses. Don't apartments or rooms often reveal more about people than the people can articulate about themselves? Similarly, a study of the space of a film reveals how a master director and collaborators give body to a narrative, how they conceive of the interaction of characters. At times, the study of film space may provide clues to the collaborative work of director and cinematographer, or director and writer. Watching two Joseph Losey films, *The Go-Between* and *The Romantic Englishwoman,* the spectator experiences in the first film a brilliant collaboration between Losey's intuitive explorations of space and writer Harold Pinter's structuring of the narrative through the nuances of the characters' motivations, while in the second film the spectator experiences the narrative emptiness of the nevertheless aesthetically beautiful space.

In *The Go-Between,* the framing and double-framing of Leo passing through doors, standing against pillars and in windows and recesses, and climbing and descending staircases, with the camera following behind and seeing more than his preadolescent self sees, creates a visual correlative for Pinter's structuring of the film as an elaborate flashback — the narrator is the reluctant "seer" of "more" than his young self saw and, as a child, treated as merely utilitarian.[10] Like the narrator, *The Go-Between*'s spectators experience the complexity and richness of the space as we tunnel into its dark, woody recesses, pass a gold table service, and peer out at its denizens playing croquet on the lawn. Leo's tour is simply a preview of the space made more perverse by its inhabitants.

Usually, when film space has an aesthetically beautiful look while being empty of narrative resonance, we can make a fair guess (it is always speculation in a collaborative art like film) that the director lacks control or vision while the cinematographer, scene by scene, is lending the narrative a possibly irrelevant look — perhaps an interesting angle that's unrelated to the action. We'll never see it again, but it makes the space intriguing. Nestor Almendros's cinematography in *Sophie's Choice* struck me in this way, and farther back Haskell Wexler's cinematography in *In the Heat of the Night* fulfilled those physical aesthetic needs that are engaged simply in looking at something. But fully organic space,[11] rich in directional invitation, in human perspective that creates our identifications, and in movement or its promise, isn't realized without the overview inherent in film's fourth dimension: its persistence in time and its narrative control of the spectator's point of view. This overview is, of course, generally the responsibility of the director. At least, I find it convenient to explore the films of a single director and to use the director's name to describe the locus of creativity in those films. This procedure admittedly has an "auteurist" bias.

Film's magic is partly that the spectator seems always to have options, though this sense may be just a common aesthetic experience of space: to be in more than one place at one time.[12] We occupy a place as spectators and an imaginative place in the created world. It is not simply an escape, as has sometimes been charged, but it is an escape to somewhere,[13] into a fictional space where we participate in the film's fictionalizing and aesthetic powers. We move imaginatively, and our movement, when it is most rewarded, fills the new film space ideally with our projected identifications and our play. Like Uncle Toby in his garden in *Tristram Shandy,* we participate in the creation of a new emotional landscape.[14]

The director and his colleagues define the limits of this space, its enclosure and its ends; yet there is also offered a liberty of interpretation of space by the spectator that must remain undefined. E. H. Gombrich has studied the spectator's interpretation of space in paintings and found that "recognition of images is connected with projections and visual anticipations" by the spectator.[15] So space is not simply the enclosing horizontal and vertical planes but the physical being in that space, which is created between the director's three-dimensional vocabulary and the spectator's projected emotional occupation of that space.

Most of our interaction with space is unconscious, though it may demand of us very special skills. For instance, non-New Yorkers on midtown Manhattan's sidewalks during rush hour[16] will start muttering phrases they haven't heard for years, like "rat race" and "cog in the machine" and things about being "dehumanized." But if they were to look around from a vantage point above the crowds, it would be the rare native who is ever jostled. At a certain rhythmic pace with a certain lateral flexibility and an observance of traffic direction and pattern, the New Yorker maintains a personal space that is rarely challenged. After having adjusted to this definition of space in movement, I've been accused of bringing my "New York walk" to lazier and less structured streets. When I've done this, I have a tendency to collide with or brush Washingtonians and Chicagoans who haven't the sense to do their half of the dodging or don't do it at the proper rate to avoid my headlong progress. And they, no doubt, would like to confine me to the running tracks in their parks and open spaces.

The possessing of these unconscious spatial skills means that, when looking at film, we expect its illusion of space to have a visceral impact on us. Films made in the United States are especially noteworthy for their ability to satisfy this expectation of film-goers. I'm not just referring to the inevitable chase scene in certain genres of recent popular films, but also to their pacing. U.S. film of recent years varies the space, of course; it may use San Francisco and cars spinning down transmission-challenging hills or galactic space-scapes inhabited by warring vessels. But by referring to these films, I unfortunately make my point about space by exaggerating; in the films of the directors treated in this book — Capra, Lubitsch, Sternberg, and Wyler — the visceral impact is more subtle, more studied, and more cumulative. Interestingly, though, it seems unnecessary to orient my film students to these earlier U.S. films as I must orient them both to the narrative conventions of international film and to its aesthetic conventions regarding movement and space.

In our daily lives, we often create our environments, manipulating them to invite movement or equipoise, to encourage interaction or provide isolation and quiet. In these cases, we are often semiconsciously (intuitively?) attuned to space. We've all found ourselves changing the furniture around when we're vaguely dissatisfied — though probably not with the furniture. And we often have spatial rituals we perform and even joke about.[17] For instance, I must obsessively clean and stack before settling down to write. Certain spaces, we learn from experience, demand certain responses, though we probably had little to do with formulating the spaces that first imprinted these emotional reactions on us.

Directors probably can't influence our most primal spatial responses, but they can teach us how to respond to some of their most primal responses if they embody them spatially in the narrative. A director might choreograph that Manhattan sidewalk during rush hour and establish the rhythmic pattern of dodge-and-progress, manipulating the camera in such a way that the spectator comes to understand some of the joy of mastering that movement. A director might thus create a habitual space in which we feel comfortable even though in the real Manhattan we would be cowering rabbit-like in the nearest coffee shop.

To achieve the qualitative shift between habitual and acute space, a director and his colleagues must do more than just make us feel comfortable or make us fond of what we initially dislike. To make this shift, they must change some of our ways of categorizing objects in space. In ordinary discourse, we might speak of a character propelled by certain motives moving through an empty room. Certainly, a director might pragmatically instruct an actor to move in a certain way through space — to saunter or scurry. But were the director to embody characters' motives in the total scene, he or she might achieve "acute space." The actors still act, but the simple distinctions between characters, props, set design, and camera position and movement break down, and convey the same message in a more intensely realized manner.

Sometimes this means that the qualities that we conventionally attribute to character inform the environment as well; "motive" or "intention" (the inner state of the fictional character) would be apparent in the composition of the film space as well as in the actor's performance. This notion of a gestalt is certainly implicit in the term *mise-en-scène,* but it doesn't fully imply a psychological three-dimensionality as is implied in the way Freud imagined the dreamscape. That sort of displacement without any notion of space substituting for the actor's intensity is closer to what a director's acute space can accomplish.

On the other hand, acute space is not necessarily humanistic space. Certain properties of the environment might lend their nature to the actors' performances, as is often the case in horror movies. Some directors express visions in acute space that deny or short-circuit sentiment on the part of the spectator. Ridley Scott's films *The Duellists* and *Alien* disturbingly deny the human, as few films of the 30's and 40's do.

The directors studied in this book use space so that we, the spectators, feel it bodily. Even Sternberg's nearly static close-up of Marlene Dietrich's face evokes our experience of our own faces in space. E. H. Gombrich asks, "How does the baby which responds to its mother's smile with a smile translate or transpose the visual impression sent to its brain through the eyes into the appropriate impulses from the brain to move its own facial muscles in a corresponding way?"[18] Gombrich not only asks *how* we imitate facial expressions but also suggests *why* we do so, our earliest rewards being earned for these small muscular exertions. Doesn't a director exploit just these experiences of our bodies in space?

It should be clear that I am not studying decor or staging, though some of the basic lessons that a director learns may be those of the stage designer, who must, as R. L. Held explains, avoid "a picture-like relief" to achieve "the space of sculpture."[19] More particularly, I am not discussing space in every film during this historical period, as David Bordwell intends to do in his description of space in classical film. If I were, I would probably conclude as he does, that "the classical Hollywood cinema chooses to subordinate space" to narrative.[20] I am not surveying a historical phenomenon, though this use of space seems rooted in those decades when the big studios dominated production.[21]

I accept Bordwell's identification of three systems in any fictional narrative film: a system of narrative logic, a system of cinematic time, and a system of cinematic space.[22] My first concern is with the last of these, but I do make some effort to relate film space to narrative in chapter 2. Cinematic time is much less a concern of this study, except in instances where editing, pacing, or the timing of gestures or events necessarily interacts with the conjuring of film space.

In preparing this book, I have had to be selective in a number of ways. First, I have limited myself to the work of four major Hollywood directors: Frank Capra (1897–1991), Ernst Lubitsch (1892–1947), Josef von Sternberg (1894–1969), and William Wyler (1902–1981). It may be significant that these four Hollywood greats were all born in Europe; perhaps their view was all the more acute because they came to America as immigrants. But in any case, all four directors went on to achieve their greatest film success in the Hollywood studio system.

If I had studied the films of international directors — or even the large number of German silent films by Lubitsch before he came to the United States in 1924 — I would have ventured too far outside my area of competence, and I would have involved myself with too many variables (a different cultural background in the films, for instance).

That, in turn, led me to select for study only the films that these directors created in Hollywood's golden age, beginning with the introduction of sound just before 1930 — thus omitting a number of major silent films, which employ somewhat different spatial principles. I drew the outer limit at the decline of the studio-dominated era in the 1950's, when the spatial "look" of films became less consistent as directors relinquished their studio base and even particular sets (such as Preston Sturges's recurrent small town at Paramount). While I am not as conservative as Rudolf Arnheim when he protests against the increased size of the screen and the indiscriminate use of color,[23] I do feel that these technological developments have changed the spatial vocabulary of directors since the 1950's.

Leaving aside some significant silent films (Capra's *Strong Man,* Lubitsch's *Mme. Dubarry,* Sternberg's *Last Command,* etc.) and some relatively recent color productions by the same directors well past their prime (Capra's *Pocketful of Miracles,* Sternberg's *Jet Pilot,* Wyler's *Funny Girl,* etc.) in my attempt to work in a closely defined framework, I have also focused on main-line, fictional, "narrative" features. Thus, I have omitted the short and documentary genres, such as Lubitsch's episode of *If I Had a Million,* Sternberg's *The Town,* and Capra's and Wyler's World War II documentaries. All of these eras and genres are worthy of study, and no slights are intended. Rather, my selectivity was dictated by considerations of length.

In each chapter, I chose to illustrate the discussion of various treatments of space, and of other elements of each director's style, with no more than a couple of examples. In other words, the discussion is not intended to be an exhaustive examination of each sequence, or of each element of style or narration, in each film by that director. Thus, if I talk of Lubitsch's use of habitual space in *Love Me Tonight* or *Ninotchka,* but not in *Smiling Lieutenant* or *That Uncer-*

tain Feeling, may the devotees of the latter films not consign me to perdition.
Or, when I examine some of Sternberg's images with illustrations from *Shanghai Express* but not from *Dishonored,* or from *The Devil Is a Woman* but not from
The King Steps Out, or from *The Saga of Anatahan* but not from *Macao,* again, it is
not for lack of any interest, knowledge, or respect for those omitted films by the
master. The same goes for Wyler: my analysis of *Dodsworth* could apply equally
to *These Three* and *Dead End,* and of *Detective Story,* equally to *Desperate Hours.*
Would that one could write an encyclopedia on each film by each great director and his colleagues.

There is also a much more general question about my selectivity. Why not
Hitchcock, for instance, or Welles? First, many critics have exhaustively discussed their techniques. More importantly, these directors have demonstrated
a self-consciousness about their directorial choices that makes them less apt
subjects for me. While not necessarily seeking *unconscious* directing, I am
drawn to the problems of articulating the nature of a director's achievement.
The directors I have chosen to work on, with the possible exception of Sternberg, have often understated their achievements or distracted us from the full
import of their work. Wyler has been underestimated as not being an auteur,
Capra has been seen as a master of narrative but not as a stylist, and Lubitsch
and Sternberg have been seen as so dominated by stylishness or surface style as
to be lightweights in narration. In other words, I have been attracted to some
issue that I felt might be re-examined by considering their use of film space
and some of their narrative assumptions. Their presence in their films does not
register as a Hitchcock or Welles presence does. But it is recognizable. We may
feel less manipulated (Hitchcock) or less amazed (Welles), but the absence of
that self-conscious bond with the spectator creates a cooler invitation into the
film space.

Capra, Lubitsch, Sternberg, and Wyler also complement each other in the
ways they use space. Whereas Capra and Wyler use space in an overt manner,
making emotional and intellectual confrontations apparent in that space,
Sternberg and Lubitsch are masters of employing space covertly, always implying that the real story lies beneath some surface. Another pairing realigns
these four considerably. Wyler and Lubitsch share a certain neoclassical restraint and cleanness, practicing a more rigorous selectivity, while Capra and
Sternberg are Romantics. They have busier styles and are more concerned
with filling up the screen with a wealth of images. This last impression may be
based at least in part on Capra and Sternberg's concentration on the human
face.

NOTES

1. Norman Ashcraft and Albert E. Scheflen explore many of the issues of territoriality that I discuss and, especially, use the term "aegis" to describe the "system of conventional local, class, or ethnic customs" governing a space, in *People Space: The Making
and Breaking of Human Boundaries* (Garden City, N.Y.: Anchor/Doubleday, 1976), p. 74.

2. Glenn Robert Lym's study of architectural space has influenced me profoundly. His terms, neutral space, acute space, and chronic space, correspond to my use of neutral, acute, and habitual to describe film space. He discusses these concepts in *A Psychology of Building: How We Shape and Experience Our Structural Spaces* (Englewood Cliffs, N.J.: Prentice-Hall, 1980), p. 2.

3. Josef von Sternberg, *Fun in a Chinese Laundry* (London: Secker and Warburg, 1966), p. 323.

4. Lym, *A Psychology of Building,* pp. 2–6.

5. Ibid., pp. 8–9.

6. William Wyler as interviewed by Richard Koszarski in *Hollywood Directors, 1941–1976* (New York: Oxford Univ. Press, 1977), p. 112.

7. Ashcraft and Scheflen describe "the spaces covered by voice or gaze projection" (*People Space,* p. 7).

8. See Charles Affron's fascinating connection of the spectator's staring at a screen with an actor staring at a picture or mirror on that screen and the likeness of these acts to Lacan's mirror stage, in Affron's *Cinema and Sentiment* (Chicago: Univ. of Chicago Press, 1982), pp. 82–85.

9. Robert Harbison refers to "the simplest experience of being in more than one place at a time" when discussing "fictionalizing power" in *Eccentric Spaces* (New York: Alfred A. Knopf, 1977), p. xi.

10. Christian Norberg-Schulz's *Existence, Space, and Architecture* (New York: Praeger, 1971) develops a number of categories for classifying space, the most concrete of which he calls "pragmatic space" (p. 11).

11. Bruno Zevi uses the phrase "organic space" in *Architecture as Space: How to Look at Architecture* (New York: Horizon, 1957, 1974), p. 158.

12. Harbison suggests that the mind can be given "an existence outside itself" (*Eccentric Spaces,* p. xii).

13. John G. Cawelti discusses the idea of "escaping *to* somewhere" when he is defining formula literature in *Adventure, Mystery, and Romance: Formula Stories as Art and Popular Culture* (Chicago: Univ. of Chicago Press, 1976), pp. 15–20.

14. Harbison notes the creation of imaginary space in Sterne's novel (*Eccentric Spaces,* p. 4).

15. E. H. Gombrich, *Art and Illusion: A Study in the Psychology of Pictorial Representation* (Princeton, N.J.: Princeton Univ. Press, 1969), p. 228.

16. Ashcraft and Scheflen suggested this example of New Yorkers at rush hour (*People Space,* p. 5).

17. Lym suggests the relation of chronic space to ritual actions (*A Psychology,* p. 10).

18. E. H. Gombrich, Julian Hochberg, and Max Black, *Art, Perception, and Reality* (Baltimore: Johns Hopkins Univ. Press, 1972), p. 36.

19. R. L. Held, *Endless Innovations: Frederick Kiesler's Theory and Scenic Designs* (Ann Arbor, Mich.: UMI Research Press, 1977, 1982), p. 85.

20. David Bordwell, Janet Staiger, and Kristin Thompson, *The Classical Hollywood Cinema: Film Style and Mode of Production to 1960* (New York: Columbia Univ. Press, 1985), p. 50.

21. Ethan Mordden describes the studios' achievement of certain styles in *The Hollywood Studios: House Style in the Golden Age of the Movies* (New York: Alfred A. Knopf, 1988).

22. Bordwell et al., *The Classical Hollywood Cinema,* p. 6.

23. Rudolf Arnheim, *Film as Art* (Berkeley: Univ. of California Press, 1957), pp. 74–75.

2

FILM SPACE AS IMPLIED BY NARRATIVE: CAPRA'S
PROTAGONISTS LEARNING TO LOOK INWARD

Before I examine the space of the films of Capra, Lubitsch, Sternberg, and Wyler, I need to look briefly at the way in which film narrative implies space. To do this, Capra's films provide an appropriate sample. Secondarily, I am curious about whether one can speculate productively on the relation of film narrative to a biographical fact in the lives of these men: each came to the United States as an immigrant. It is impossible to extract this one influence from all the others in their lives, of course. If, for instance, an immigrant's consciousness could be described, couldn't any item in that description be attributed to some unknown influence or simply to variations of character? Probably. Still, I began this study without considering this biographical fact, and it seemed to insist upon its presence in some intriguing ways. The result is an admittedly speculative angle on the way in which Capra's most sophisticated narratives imply film space.

When speculating on the influence of the immigrant experience on the films of Capra, Lubitsch, Sternberg, and Wyler, one might be tempted to ask whether the settings of their films provide a clue. We remember easily the stories set in Europe, such as Lubitsch's *The Shop Around the Corner, To Be or Not To Be,* or *Ninotchka.* The settings of Sternberg seem by comparison even less familiar and far more exotic. Sternberg often finds his settings farther east — in Russia (*The Scarlet Empress*) or the Orient (*Shanghai Express, Shanghai Gesture,* and *The Saga of Anatahan*). The settings of Capra's and Wyler's narratives are far more often in the United States, though Wyler's adaptations sometimes require an England nearly as familiar. One might ask whether this contrast means that Lubitsch's and Sternberg's narratives are more deeply bound to an immigrant's experience. Do these directors challenge their spectators to explore an unfamiliar space because of their experience? More concretely, is Lubitsch nostalgic for European sophistication, or does Sternberg embody his own disorientation in his distant settings?

I am inclined to see all these directors as engaged in using their settings in a similar way — both as a familiar space in which spectators feel at home and as an alien space that challenges our assumptions. Consider Capra's Bedford Falls in *It's a Wonderful Life*. The spectator is not allowed to protest, "I've never lived in a small town," nor is someone who has lived in a small town allowed to declare, "Small towns are not like that."[1] The space is essentially free of associations for any spectator, no matter what his or her experience. From that beginning, the director can proceed to mythologize the space, building the narrative assumptions upon which his tales depend.[2] Capra, who needs for us to feel initially at home (before he plays cosmic games and turns Bedford Falls into Pottersville), creates the fantasy small town for us with a few visual and aural flourishes. Given the fact that every master director relies upon this process of de-familiarization, do Capra's settings or his narrative assumptions suggest his immigrant heritage, either through the great enthusiasm with which he embraces the United States or through patterns that we might indirectly associate with the immigrant's experience?

What is most basic to an immigrant's experience? And how would those qualities emerge in a story? In the narratives of Sternberg and Lubitsch, one is struck by the sophistication of their characters, often a sophistication that masks, at least temporarily, deeper feelings. I wonder whether the sophisticate isn't a locus for an immigrant's feelings of subordination, not subordination as weakness or passivity but as a learned talent for "reading" the native population. The cipher-like quality of a Dietrich or of Lubitsch's sophisticated observer (Belinski-Charles Boyer in *Cluny Brown* or Count D'Algout-Melvyn Douglas in *Ninotchka*) implies that they possess wisdom and that they understand how the socially dominant interact with subordinates. They are consequently elevated above this level of social interaction. They become classless in a class-conscious environment.

Whether Wyler uses a narrative dramatizing domination and subordination any more than any good story-teller is doubtful, though his plots specialize in this sort of confrontation. One only has to think of the marital confrontations in *Best Years* between Fred (Dana Andrews) and Marie (Virginia Mayo) or in *Dodsworth* between Sam (Walter Huston) and Fran (Ruth Chatterton) or in *The Little Foxes* between Horace (Herbert Marshall) and Regina (Bette Davis) to see a recurrent pattern of struggle in which the wiser subordinate male is the moral superior. This pattern implicitly seems to damn Leslie (Bette Davis) in *The Letter,* Cathy (Merle Oberon) in *Wuthering Heights,* and Julie (Bette Davis) in *Jezebel* as well. Among the films I will be concentrating on, only Catherine (Olivia de Havilland) in *The Heiress* seems to be an exception, succumbing, as she does, to her father's arrogant dominance. Ironically, though, even here Catherine turns into a stubborn figure very much like her father at the end.

She subordinates the lover who deserted her. Could Wyler have been attracted to these narratives because of the male's experience of subordination? Was that something he had experienced as an immigrant? (To rebut this supposition is *too* easy, as suggestive as the pattern may be.)

With Capra's films, I am in equally speculative territory. Yet the evolution of his film career suggests some grounds for considering his increasingly creative use of the immigrant experience. Moving as the earlier films are, Capra seems gradually to find spatial means to depict his central characters' inner states. In the later films, the psychological growth of these characters becomes more visible. Like Lewis Jacobs, then, I see Capra's intuitive understanding of film space in his best films as inextricably linked to his attitude toward a central character.[3]

NARRATIVE STRUCTURES IN CAPRA'S FILMS

Capra concentrates on three recurrent narrative structures in his career, yet only the last of these fully expresses the idea that an experience of subordination can lead to wisdom. The earliest structure that he uses in his Barbara Stanwyck films depicts her reformation. It features a woman somehow at odds with herself and others, playing out a role that at bottom is dishonest and painful. A loving man is traditionally the vehicle for her reform, which I have titled "the retrieval of Eden." The second structure that Capra exploits is the familiar screwball comedy, which in a melange of witty exchanges conceals the fundamental core of comedy — the maturation of its characters.[4] Unlike the Barbara Stanwyck films, which feature a certain heaviness of moral decision, these films proceed far more casually, relying less on human intent than on external circumstances and timing to complicate and finally to simplify the misunderstandings between two lovers. The lovers are characteristically too full of themselves to attend at first to one another, but the outcome of the vagaries assailing them is really a fortunate fall.

Though some critics consider Capra's last and best films to be screwball comedies, they constitute a much more complex quest than is implied by this genre. Capra's "Everyman Goes to Somewhere" films certainly share many of the assumptions of the Stanwyck films and the screwball comedies like *It Happened One Night*. All Capra films detail some development in a character who thoughtlessly or naively plays out a public role; and they all value the formation of healthy relationships in a couple or family. But the earlier two stages in Capra's career lack the cosmological perspective at work in these later films. Though it might appear that Barbara Stanwyck is implicated by her own guilt in the early films, Capra's assumption is that she is indeed innocent all along. She simply has to discover her own innocence. She is not responsible for the evil circumstances or for the con men with whom she is involved. Thus, Eden can be retrieved in these films. It was never altogether lost to begin with, but simply obscured by a facade.

In the middle stage, Capra's screwball comedies, while seemingly lighter, do require that characters mature. Characters are precariously poised on the edge of disasters that never materialize. Instead the final "fall" is a thoroughly comic one, imaged best by the blanket or "walls of Jericho" that come tumbling down between Ellie (Claudette Colbert) and Peter (Clark Gable) in *It Happened One Night*. This fall is indeed fortunate and applaudable, unlike the various earlier disasters that were barely avoided.

What comes into play in the later films—the Deeds/Smith/Doe trilogy and *It's a Wonderful Life* (minimally *State of the Union* might be added here too)—is sin, the genuine article, not the trumped-up Stanwyck sneer that needs wiping off. That's why I've called this third group of films Capra's "divine comedies." His heroes genuinely confront themselves, as well as false public expectations and complicated circumstances.[5] They experience both a fall (a real one this time) and a resurrection. Capra is very aware of his own mythologizing, for he often images the fall as a crucifixion and his heroes as Christ-like, performing a ritual of purification for the public. It may be the largely unconscious tapping of his immigrant experience that lends these late films their intensity, for the Capra heroes in these films are deeply and traumatically alienated from their earlier social complacency or laziness. And the confidence that they learn following their alienation is a far wiser one than they began with, one that is rooted in the utter psychological homelessness of their earlier subordination.

Retrieval of Eden: The Barbara Stanwyck Tetralogy

The Barbara Stanwyck character either has gone wrong or goes wrong in the course of these four films: *Ladies of Leisure* (1930), *The Miracle Woman* (1931), *Forbidden* (1931), and *The Bitter Tea of General Yen* (1933). But the wrong is curiously spurious; we do not feel it. Instead, Capra predicates each Stanwyck character as good-girl-misled. Her innocence is simply in remission, and film spectators' identification with her is like a miracle drug, a chemotherapy. Ritualistically, with the help of a loving man, we can reevoke that innocence and retrieve her former edenic purity. In *Ladies of Leisure*, Jerry, Stanwyck's painter lover (Ralph Graves), tries to capture in a painting the innocence of her face as she sleeps against his shoulder. He picked her up after she left a party, and she quickly identified herself: "I guess you were wondering what I was doing at that party. Well, brother, that's my racket. I'm a party girl. You know what that is?"

But part of the premise of these films is that the Stanwyck heroine sees less clearly what she is than does the man, who sees her with a lover's/artist's eyes. She is often seen as led into wrong by a con man or rake—like Hornsby (Sam Hardy) in *The Miracle Woman*—and led out of it by another man with special sight that transcends conventional standards, which Capra explicitly criticizes. For instance, the man of special sight in *The Miracle Woman* (David Manners) is blind, but he has a sardonic sense that allows him to hear the truth behind

Stanwyck's performance as a public healer. His blindness frees him from the false spectacle. *Forbidden,* perhaps the weakest of the four films, features Adolphe Menjou fulfilling both of these functions and thus confusing our identifications by making Stanwyck's self-sacrifices in her adulterous relationship with him less than successfully beatifying.

These three 1930–1931 narratives work on a simple premise. Capra seems most interested, not in the drama, but in the targets of the narratives — in the polemic, as it were. Capra seems to relish the confrontation of upper and lower classes in *Ladies of Leisure,* as upper-class men exploit the economic needs of lower-class women and Jerry's parents lobby for a suitable match for their son. These same tensions provide an undercurrent in *Forbidden,* but Capra exposes a range of oppressions here: the narrowness of small-town life, the boredom of marriage, the exploitation of women by men, by other women, and by themselves. Both *The Miracle Woman* and *The Bitter Tea of General Yen* attack the hypocrisies of religious leaders and their followers. But only in *Bitter Tea* is the polemic of the film developed progressively through the narrative. The spectator is drawn into the narrative by Capra, who insists passively on our identification with the Stanwyck character, Megan. But gradually it becomes apparent that Megan's perspective is skewed, that, in fact, she too is prejudiced against other races and other religions.

Unlike the other Stanwyck films, there is genuine complexity of character in *Bitter Tea,* a complexity that prefigures the third stage in Capra's directing. Its mastery of space suggests that Capra needed this greater narrative complexity in order to realize the story imaginatively in space. As is true of the narratives in Capra's third stage of directing, Megan is inwardly divided between a core of private intuitions, which emerges as her personality, and an outward collection of public roles, which must be progressively challenged by General Yen (Nils Asther). Yen is not, however, a zealous mentor. He sets challenges for Megan without preaching. Indeed, it is preaching and missionary zeal that have made her a racist and nationalist in the first place. So the subtext of the film is not about a woman in need of salvation by a good man, as is implicit in the other Stanwyck vehicles. Instead, the subtext of *Bitter Tea* looks forward to the maturation of the protagonists in the screwball comedies and the thorough realization of the flawed state of human existence in Capra's greatest films.

The drama of the immigrant's experience is best realized in *Bitter Tea,* where Megan eventually feels the full impact of being the outsider during another nation's political crisis. Here too, Capra continues to explore the false confidence of Barbara Stanwyck playing the party girl, the mistress, or the healer. In all four pictures, the Barbara Stanwyck character accepts a role in which she feels in control, but in which she is actually being exploited by a dominant male or by social stereotypes that she doesn't fully understand. Her naiveté may express some of the immigrant's feelings of being lost in a foreign land, where the natives dominate.

The Fortunate Falls: Capra's Screwball Comedies

Readers may have the impression that there is a neat boundary between Capra's Stanwyck tetralogy and his screwball comedies: *Platinum Blonde* (1931), *Lady for a Day* (1933), *It Happened One Night* (1934), *Broadway Bill* (1935), and *Arsenic and Old Lace* (1941–1944). This is not the case; instead, the two categories overlap sequentially, like hands clasped together from the middle finger on. In identifying these categories, though, I admit that certain films fit the pattern (intellectual and arbitrary as it is) more exactly than others. So I will set forth the basic pattern and then deal with the exceptions. *Bitter Tea,* as the last of the Stanwyck tetralogy (1933), already logically reflects the imaginative forces that Capra later put to work in his best screwball comedies. But *Platinum Blonde* (a 1931 screwball picture) precedes both Stanwyck films, *Bitter Tea* and *Forbidden* (1931). And very late, among the "divine comedies," occurs Capra's screwball comedy, *Arsenic and Old Lace* (1941–1944).

Having established my categories, I need to dispose of the exception presented by *American Madness* (1932). Like *Bitter Tea,* it is a time bomb ticking away early in Capra's career; its premises resemble those of Capra's great period—the premises behind the Deeds/Smith/Doe trilogy, *It's a Wonderful Life,* and *State of the Union.* The space of this film is rarely neutral, and its use of acute space intensifies the essentially personal struggle of a potentially great man. This is the struggle that James Stewart and Gary Cooper enact in the later films, when they are thrown into the macrocosmic arena of big cities or a wholly different time scheme and cosmos, as in *Wonderful Life. American Madness* is simpler, though, and in this sense resembles the early screwball comedies like *Platinum Blonde,* where only one member of the couple needs to mature. Walter Huston, the protagonist, is first chastened, and then his values are affirmed. The narrative pattern is of a too-public man needing to make more private family space for his wife. His self-questioning is not as personal nor as stygian as that undergone by Stewart and Cooper, but it might be seen as beginning to tap Capra's immigrant experience of subordination leading to insight.

We should attribute the great success of the screwball comedy, *It Happened One Night,* in part to its sexual vivacity and its exploitation of sexual difference. Both are the bread and wine of comedy—the need of one sex for the other and the jockeying of one sex against the other to assure each that this need will be met. At its best, both members of the couple learn something about themselves in the pursuit of this need, and *It Happened* has this balanced maturation at its center.[6] Ellie, the Claudette Colbert character, may be the spoiled brat ostensibly learning from the old-pro survivor, Peter (Clark Gable), but their East-Coast journey also brings into question all of Peter's egotistical assumptions. In one classic sequence, one of Capra's tour-de-force numbers, Peter arrogantly yet unsuccessfully demonstrates all his thumbing methods for hitchhiking, while Ellie stops a car instantly by raising her skirt.

The "fall" in all the screwball comedies is the sexual fall, a fall in the comic sense into a grace that allows two egos to meet amiably.[7] What is largely missing in these comedies, which is present in Capra's greatest films (the "divine" cycle), is the complexity of a thoroughly private dimension. The characters in screwball comedies, as in many comedies, lack the tragic potential that the characters in Capra's divine comedies possess. They lack an awareness of their own mortality, and consequently the fiction and the space of these films lack an existential depth that the later films possess. One transitional film, *You Can't Take It with You* (1938), has the macrocosmic view of the great films but lacks their tragic potential.

You Can't, like *It Happened,* poses male against female in the screwball proportion, which is an equilibrium, whereas the later divine comedies focus our attention solely on the developing, questing hero. In this equilibrium of male versus female, *It Happened* and *You Can't* both surpass Capra's lesser screwball comedies, which often feature less even-handed maturation. In *Platinum Blonde* and *Broadway Bill,* one feels rather impatient with the heroes (Robert Williams and Warner Baxter) for neglecting the heroines (Loretta Young and Myrna Loy) and succumbing to the distractions of, respectively, Jean Harlow and a horse.

The Divine Comedies: Capra's Greatest Films

What sparks great periods of productivity in any artist's career may always be somewhat mysterious. But Capra's Aha! occurred in a circumstance curiously ripe for conversion.[8] He tells the story in his autobiography, *The Name Above the Title,* of first feigning illness and then actually becoming critically ill at a point in his career when he felt he could only go down hill: "What *could* I do for an encore?" Capra confesses: "I had talked myself into a disease that baffled the experts." Then a little man appeared in his house, told him he was "a coward" and "an offense to God," and told him he could talk to more people than Hitler, at that moment being heard on the radio in another room. The little man disappeared. Capra cured himself, read Tolstoy and Dostoyevski, and then entered the next stage in his own career, which Capra in his autobiography calls "social-minded films": *Mr. Deeds Goes to Town* (1936), *Mr. Smith Goes to Washington* (1939), *Meet John Doe* (1941), *It's a Wonderful Life* (1946), and, partially, also *Lost Horizon* (1937), *You Can't Take It with You* (1938), and *State of the Union* (1948). Capra tells about applying himself more intensely: "From then on my scripts would take from six months to a year to write and rewrite; to carefully — and subtly — integrate ideals and entertainment into a meaningful tale."[9]

To make these new "divine" films, Capra needed to learn about Dante's *inferno.* Though too pat a model, there's a sense in which the Stanwyck films are about a *paradiso* — really about a nirvana that needs to be rediscovered within the woman's self; and the screwball comedies are about *purgatorio* — about learning and stretching toward an ideal. Capra's vision in his later divine films can even be called stygian, as we learn from this sentence in his autobiography: "When that unknown, faceless little man rescued me from the river Styx, the few calm words he uttered served as a chrism to totally commit my talents — few or many — to the service of man."[10] The treasure in each of these films is a journey to a river Styx by the hero and a striking parallel between the public and private dimensions of this journey. What in the screwball comedies could be called a happy ending is loaded in these divine comedies with a sense of having restored some essential balance to the universe that had been severely threatened.[11] The questing hero in the divine comedies overshadows an often sardonic woman, whose self-discoveries resemble, ironically, Stanwyck's in the edenic tetralogy. That is, these women simply need to peel off the outer sardonic skin to be revealed as inwardly idealistic and innocent.

Lost Horizon (1937) in some ways fits in with the Stanwyck tetralogy. The protagonist, here a male (Ronald Colman), succumbs for a time to earthly blandishments and cynicism, but redeems himself at the end in his titanic struggle to retrieve his "lost Eden" of Shangri-La. Unlike the heroes in the other divine comedies, Colman's Conway doesn't have to face particularly dark inner impulses or guilt. As the historical scene grows darker, the films do also — the lightest, *Mr. Deeds* in 1936, darkening to *John Doe* in 1941 and the perhaps even darker *Wonderful Life* in 1946. Though some of Capra's dark genius still informs *State of the Union* in 1948, his vision loses its confrontational tensions. His last films are light, spatially neutral dramas, somewhat reminiscent of the screwball comedies but without their great actors or their spatial acuity.[12]

IT'S A WONDERFUL LIFE: A CASE STUDY

The cosmology implicit in Frank Capra's *It's a Wonderful Life* is not unlike Dante's *Divine Comedy,* for it contains a *paradiso,* a *purgatorio,* and an *inferno.* Capra's *inferno* and *paradiso* are places (Pottersville and heaven); but they are also represented by characters (Lionel Barrymore's Potter and Henry Travers' angel, Clarence), and they correspond to states of mind for an everyman figure, George Bailey (James Stewart). Capra's *purgatorio,* on the other hand, corresponds to George's earthly existence. Capra creates a complex time sequence which begins in the middle of the story. George's state of mind, we find out later, suggests that he is in an inferno. Yet, unlike Dante's scheme, which takes his persona from a dissatisfied state of mind on earth consecutively through *inferno, purgatorio,* and *paradiso,* Capra presents us with paradise as a literal place very early in the film: after an initial shot or two of earth scenes with the voice-overs of children and adults praying for George, Capra cuts to a shot of stars, at the center of which certain clusters blink. The voice of a beneficent God talks to Joseph, the heavenly supervisor of second-class angels (like Clarence) who go off on earthly missions. At the very start of the film, then, the spectator's premise is an unearthly one. Capra provides the implied spectator with a larger cosmological frame, which is both supernatural and comic.

The film's representative of the inferno, on the other hand, is an earth-dweller: Henry F. Potter is Bedford Falls' resident devil. Predictably, God and the devil battle for men's souls in human territory. And the devil is inevitably more personal than the omniscient God (at least in Faustian versions of this battle). The battle, framed by God's distant beneficence, is also fundamentally comic: the spectator assumes that God won't lose, even though Joseph sends such a pitiful heavenly defender of George in the angel Clarence.

Heaven, or the film's paradise, is felt at the very start of the film and in the vision of love and goodwill at its close. Thus, heaven frames the other two perspectives. The hellish inferno of the film is George's journey through his own non-existence. While it is an imaginary hell (no one supposes that our non-lives run parallel in some other dimension to our lives), it intersects so closely with George's actual life that it is fearfully realistic. Interestingly, Potter does not appear in person in this hell, though his power and dominance are constantly implied. The purgatorial territory in the film is George's earthly life, marked by his frustrations and by the spectator's distanced perspective on them.

Clarence sets the comic tone of the film for the spectator; he is immune to some consequences and vulnerable to others. He can disappear suddenly by calling upon Joseph, as when he is biting the hand of the cop Burt (Ward Bond) to allow George to escape. But he takes his knocks when he and George are thrown headlong into the snow and when George shakes him by the lapels in the graveyard, Potter's Field.

Clarence is similarly both immune and vulnerable in his emotional relations with others. He seems completely immune to the opinions of others: he has a sort of social immunity, a blitheness, that suggests a discontinuity between his existence and the human lives around him. When he is in the engineer's house at the bridge after George has rescued him, he chatters lightly about being over two hundred years old and wearing the nightgown he had died in. And in Nick's bar, he sits speculating on whether he wants mulled wine or hot rum punch, oblivious to the annoyance expressed by Nick (Sheldon Leonard). But Clarence is definitely a go-between: he shares in the relaxed cosmic immunity of the blinking star clusters at the beginning of the film; but being also somewhat inept, he bridges the distance between the divine and the human.

Clarence is both divinely immune and humanly flawed. These are two important ingredients in comedy, and Clarence is a center of comedy in the film. He sometimes has laughter directed at him, especially George's skeptical gibes. For instance, George keeps calling Clarence "Gabriel" and suggesting that they fly somewhere, when Clarence has already explained that he must still earn his wings. Even the heavenly powers have some doubts about Clarence; Joseph says that he "has the I.Q. of a rabbit." But there is also a sense in which Clarence creates the comic solution for the film, the means by which George's inferno is inverted. He thus provides a vision nearing perfection of good neighborliness and friendship.

This inversion is what interests me in the film, for the scenes of George's nightmare journey through Pottersville juxtaposed with earlier scenes of George's day-to-day life in Bedford Falls generate the tension that must be resolved. And Clarence, for all his stupidity, hits upon the scheme of showing George what Bedford Falls and its citizens would be like if George had never been born. A comic premise thus informs the tragic nightmarish journey, and Capra images the film's cosmology in the iconography of George's two lives in the town.

Clarence's plan is both simple and elegant. He provides George with a vision of hell, but it is a personalized hell, one that disorients George and thus makes his reorientation possible. The structure of the film is a classically comic one: (1) the central character must be initiated; his ambitions are false ones, because he wants freedom without discipline; (2) in entering a stage of disorientation and madness, George (as Clarence points out) is privileged to see the suffering and servitude that he has averted through his sacrifices; (3) George's reorientation, which completes his initiation, contains his reaffirmation of the balance of discipline and freedom that his marriage to Mary (Donna Reed) has always represented (but that he has been unable to see); (4) finally, the last scene of the film dramatizes how George's restoration and rebirth bring about and are brought about by a similar renewal in the human community. The ending rejects the nightmare vision of a town run by an authoritarian tyrant. In fact, even the most limited characters, such as the bank examiner and the sheriff, participate in what Mary calls "a miracle." Society is traditionally renewed when the hero completes his night journey and brings back his new knowledge as a boon to the community.

The severity of George's madness, compared to the crises of Capra's other heroes, except perhaps for Gary Cooper's John Doe, is much greater. It is greater than the crisis of the Stewart characters in *You Can't Take It with You* or *Mr. Smith Goes to Washington,* or Gary Cooper's in *Mr. Deeds Goes to Town.* The purgatorial world in *Wonderful Life* is intriguing: George is punished and earns redemption during his earthly existence. About to choose hell by committing suicide, George is instead rescued by Clarence. But Clarence has to convince George he has made the right choice. Having snatched him from hell, Clarence ironically shows George a vision of hell on earth, a hell he can understand. The spectator understands this vision of hell by contrasting it with the illustrative (filmic!) history of George's life that was earlier shown to Clarence by Joseph in his orientation session. The earlier history depicts irreversible choices—usually between accepting and escaping responsibility. George's acceptance of responsibility in each instance is a redemptive act *before* he confronts the results of what he didn't do. Put in this way, the hell that Clarence invents for George to face seems a rather exaggerated response to George's one desperate wish to escape the life he has chosen.

But the life George has chosen was always purgatorial, a series of right choices made under stress. George chooses to save the druggist, Mr. Gower (H. B. Warner), from mistakenly putting poison in capsules, even though Gower smacks him for not delivering the capsules. Later, George's planned trip to Europe and his college education are sacrificed for the Building and Loan when his father dies. And letting his brother Harry (Todd Karns) settle out of town with his new wife, as well as falling for Mary, interrupts his more ambitious professional plans once again.

Capra poses these stressful choices as though we, the spectators, were looking in on the scenes from a distance. And this point of view effectively corresponds to the narrative scheme of God and Joseph giving Clarence a sort of guided tour of George's life, emphasizing those crises that defined him. For example, watching the confrontation between the druggist Mr. Gower and George, the camera is behind some shelves in the back room of the drugstore; we seem to watch the drama between the shelves, which form a tunnel-like frame for the action. This distanced point of view intrudes again when Capra inserts a freeze frame when George is buying a suitcase for his trip to Europe. It gives Clarence a chance to comment, "I like that face."

Other facets of the story make it seem as though George is being watched, and he sometimes protests against the watchers. The Bailey family cook, Annie (Lillian Randolph), comments on George's conversation with his father at dinner, and George says, "Annie, why don't you pull up a chair? Then you'd be comfortable and could hear everything that's going on." She comes back with, "I would if I thought I would hear something worth listening to." A whole audience of watchers later witnesses George and Mary doing a precarious Charleston as the gym floor opens up to reveal a swimming pool below. They don't offer any warning. Still later, a neighbor who listens to George and Mary's badinage from his porch finally stands up and yells, "Why don't you kiss her instead of talking her to death." All these witnesses, silent or vocal, contribute to the feeling that George is being both watched and coerced, gently or overtly.

In a simple Manichean scheme, heaven's forces posed against hell's, the forces coercing George would have to be seen as largely benevolent. But the moral universe in *Wonderful Life* is more complex than that. Consider, for instance, the fascinating ambiguity in the scene in which George and Mary become engaged. She has just returned from college and George has half-heartedly ended up at her house after escaping the festivities celebrating his brother's homecoming. In other words, George has just been royally coerced by his brother's defection. Then, his mother tries to steer him in the direction of Mary's house, though George insists on going off in the opposite direction. Finally, having succumbed to visiting Mary, George shares a phone with her when Sam Wainwright (Frank Albertson), a rival suitor, calls. They are doubly (or triply) witnessed: by Sam over the phone, by Mary's mother on the stair landing above, and by us, the spectators behind the camera. Much of the sexual tension of the scene is caused by the too-close proximity of George to Mary and of us to them. He looks at her hair, unsmiling. She looks at him and then away toward us (but not at the camera). They look at each other, and we see two profiles. Mary says: "He says it's the chance of a lifetime." George explodes, yelling: "Listen to me. I don't want any plastics, and I don't want any ground floors, and I don't want to be married to anyone ever. . . . Oh! Mary, Mary, Mary!" His denial has dissolved in the middle of this tirade. He calls her name tenderly as they embrace and kiss. Comically, Mary's mother screeches and runs away, for she has been rooting for Sam.

The narrative universe of the film poses both sympathetic and unsympathetic figures against George's ambitions, but intriguingly the sympathetic figures exert pressure more virulently. Certainly, both the bank examiner and Potter watch George malevolently. And Potter certainly suggests to George that suicide would be an appropriate escape: "You're worth more dead than alive." George confronts Potter before he goes to Martini's bar, where he is attacked by a relatively sympathetic character, the schoolteacher's husband. (George has lambasted his wife on the phone.)

The bar is usually an icon of refuge from tension in mid-forties films. In *The Best Years of Our Lives,* for instance, Butch's Bar is the place to which Homer, Al, and Fred retreat from their families. The neighborhood bar is imaged both as a place somewhat outside a community's institutions (and so an escape from public responsibilities) and as a masculine place where men can be more direct. In *Wonderful Life,* George retreats to Martini's when he believes he has nowhere else to go. In the bar, he is not manager of the savings and loan, father to his children, husband to his wife, or son to his mother. He prays to God as a lonely, frightened person.

It is when George prays that the space-time continuum of George's personal history is interrupted. We have gotten to the beginning of the film in its middle, though George has still to run to the bridge intent on throwing himself off. The hell that George's guardian angel dreams up is about as perverse a hell as can be imagined, though we never question why an angel would be the builder of a hell. In it, those whom George most loves and whose love he most relies on sequentially deny him, climaxing in Mary's and the town's belief that he is an insane man. His buddy Burt, the cop, even shoots at him as he runs off.

The key to this hell is that it consists of George's feelings of guilt and inadequacy projected outward and dramatized. What, after all, has haunted George in his life? I would propose that he is haunted by feelings that he is ineffectual, insignificant, and essentially a little, disposable man, who has never lived up to his dreams or his potential. Potter as devil has confronted George with this accusation before Clarence chose to make him live it. Potter says to him, "You once called me a warped, frustrated old man. Well, you're just a warped, frustrated young man." And there is truth in his words; George's purgatorial life has been a series of frustrations, each of which makes him feel more diminished and ineffectual, especially compared with his brother and Sam Wainwright. (These two figures interestingly resemble each other.) George is prevented from travelling, from going to college, from building great structures. Yet we know he hasn't stopped dreaming of these things: in his rage before his children and Mary, he kicks over models of a bridge and a skyscraper.

Ironically, the darkness of the anti-world that benevolent Clarence arranges for George corresponds to its devastating affirmation of all that George most fears—that he has accomplished nothing, that he is a nobody, that no one (even his mother and wife) really cares for him because he is so ineffectual. In a literal sense, of course, the narrative seems to be saying the opposite by demonstrating that George was essential in Bedford Falls' life, but that isn't why George is so horrified by the vision.

George's nightmarish misinterpretation of the hellish vision of his non-existence can be linked biographically to Capra's intense understanding of a subordinate's fears and guilt. One might connect it with the immigrant experience in particular by noting the way in which these fears and guilt are set in opposition to the traditional American ambition of leaving home and succeeding professionally. George feels himself to be competing with his brother, who has left home and entered the big city, and with Sam Wainwright, who has mastered American business.

From another angle, *It's a Wonderful Life* can be seen historically as an inverted version of *The Best Years of Our Lives,* made in the same year, 1946. Whereas *Best Years* dramatizes the anxieties of the returning soldiers, *Wonderful Life* dramatizes the anxieties and irrational guilt felt by the men and women who stayed home: the guilt of survivors. If *Best Years* is a film about coming home, *Wonderful Life* is a film about staying home under duress and watching a younger brother get all the glory and then return home a hero.

George experiences the unfavorable comparison with his brother's and Sam Wainwright's accomplishments throughout his life, not just during the war years. Even in winning Mary (as he thinks) from Sam, he is freeing Sam of an unwanted responsibility. Between Sam and his brother Harry, George watches others achieve all that he had wished for, and he ends up becoming his father— marrying, running the savings and loan, rearing children, and living in a small town. Though he occasionally kicks a car door after seeing Sam, and he wanders away from the merrymaking when his brother returns from college with an out-of-town wife and a ready-made job elsewhere, George "takes it." His heroism is intriguingly feminine in the way it emphasizes enduring and the nurturing of others. George enables others to fulfill their dreams—as when he distributes his honeymoon funds to those participating in the run on the savings and loan, or when he makes it possible for people to buy their own homes rather than pay exorbitant rents to Potter. Indirectly, his role in the film may be glorifying the women who remained at home during the war. But this subordinate role is also a familiar one to an immigrant, combining as it does both the immigrant's learned love of a new land and the immigrant's experience of starting at the bottom.

The implication of the last shot of the film — George, Mary, and their daughter Zuzu (Karolyn Grimes) are framed — is that they represent the community mythologized. They depict what the war was fought for. But George and Mary are also seen as warriors in a war at home: the battle is between heaven and hell, light and dark, Clarence and Potter, angel and devil. Such cosmological combat makes us nearly forget that George's brother is returning home having heroically fought against Germany. Those active in the world outside of Bedford Falls seem heroic for almost selfish reasons — Sam the capitalist is somewhat crass and exploitative, Harry the flyer is happy-go-lucky. (Consider the contrast between the flyer Harry in *Wonderful Life* and the Dana Andrews character, Fred, in *Best Years*.)

Still, preferable as George is to his rivals, his psyche is one peculiarly strained by guilt and anxiety.[13] George's father says simply that George was "born old." Because George strikes us as a worrier, it doesn't surprise us that the nightmare journey through his own non-existence should explore the fears that haunt him. This journey really has everything to do with George and little to do with his absence. For instance, early in the film George jokes about sitting down to his "last meal in the old Bailey Boarding House," and the joke is projected literally into his nightmare when his mother (Beulah Bondi) appears as the haggard manager of a boarding house. Of the old house that eventually is restored by him and Mary, he says at first, "I wouldn't live in it as a ghost." Of course, during his nightmare, he is a ghostly non-person searching it hysterically for his wife and children. Both these scenes suggest George's deeply felt guilt, first for not appreciating his parents sufficiently and second for denying his wife and children when he has run from them earlier. To Mary, he had complained, "Why do we have all these kids, anyway?" In the nightmare, children and families are absent: in Pottersville, Ernie (Frank Faylen) explains that his wife left him years before; and since George was not there to save his brother from drowning beneath the ice, their mother is childless and alone. A cemetery has displaced the housing development where Mr. Martini's and Ernie's families live in Bedford Falls. The remaking of history in the film interestingly makes Harry's war heroism dependent on George's earlier heroism in saving his brother.

The last scene of the film conceals some irony. While visually the scene seems to depict complete camaraderie, several narrative perspectives are represented. Mary and Zuzu with the citizens of Bedford Falls celebrate good neighborliness[14] and, thus, to some extent they celebrate themselves. The implicit presence of Clarence celebrates the divine perspective that cosmic balance has been restored. But George celebrates his release from a hellish confrontation with all his fears and guilts. The scale of the celebration fluctuates depending upon whose perspective the spectator adopts, George's expectations being so minimal as to inflate the others' into a beatific vision. After all, George has suffered so much that going to jail or whatever existence may demand is fine with him. His relief is confirmed by the presence of some of his earlier accusers in the crowd: Annie the cook, who accused George of not re-specting his father enough, deposits her savings in the collection; even the bank examiner contributes; and George's nemeses, his brother and Sam Wainwright, join in as Harry arrives with a telegram from Sam securing George financially. In fact, Harry proposes the toast to George, "To my brother, the richest man in town," and the celebration to welcome Harry home from the war is forgotten in the celebration of George's spiritual riches.

Capra's film, *It's a Wonderful Life,* sought to expunge the uneasiness of that part of the American public who stayed home. It does this by creating a mythic structure that images a war at home in cosmological terms. The protagonist George Bailey suffers, not death, but a hell in life as part of his heroic partici-pation in this war. Diachronically, the film, then, acted as an expiatory rite for 1946 Americans who remained at home. Synchronically, the film has become a Christmas Eve ritual. It functions as a purification rite before the new year, expurgating accumulated frustrations and absolving one's sins through the spectator's identification with George Bailey. In this more universal context, the film suggests that the subordinate's accomplishments will be rewarded and that his doubts and inner divisions can be dispelled. In relation to Capra's im-migrant background, it is also interesting that George is closely associated with and befriends the immigrants in Bedford Falls; in contrast, Potter calls them "garlic eaters." Capra and his co-writers, Frances Goodrich and Albert Hack-ett, defend all subordinates in their celebration of George.

If I were approaching Capra's films in a purely ideological way and allowing the intensity of his spatial images to recede, I might have a number of com-plaints to voice. In the best of all worlds, I would wish that Capra's heroines in the strongest of his films, the Deeds/Smith/Doe trilogy and *Wonderful Life,* might come to terms with themselves as dramatically as the heroes do. Yet there is also a somewhat uncomfortable realism built into the way that Capra imagines their development as related to their impulses to nurture the heroes.

Similarly, we live in a culture uncomfortable with all forms of sentimentality but, one might add, addicted in large numbers to soap operas and best-sellers that depict family sagas (and sin!) through several generations. Why is happy sentimentality suspect but sinful melodrama embraced? Am I simply identify-ing in our culture what Miltonists have been struggling with since Blake im-plied that Satan was the protagonist of *Paradise Lost?* If, though, it's true that we are drawn to the darker side of narratives, why do so few of Capra's spectators remember the dark, depressing center of so many Capra films?

Milton's Satan works hard at appearing to be a happy sinner, and most of the rich or powerful sinners in soaps and sagas possess similar arrogance or aplomb. Capra's heroes, though, step out of the melodramatic mode, as it has been defined by Robert Heilman. Heilman sees melodrama as depicting events that are externally motivated, unlike tragedy, which depends upon an internal struggle within the hero.[15] Capra's heroes enact an internal struggle that his spectators often manage to forget or ignore. That's not very different from what Miltonists struggle with—the readers who ignore Satan's "performance."

I am dealing in this book with two masters of comedy, Capra and Lubitsch. They cope very differently with this genre, especially with its chaotic center. Most comic protagonists face severe problems (perhaps a curtailment of their freedom or another injustice) in the narratives they occupy, but Capra's confront themselves and their deep feelings of failure in a way more reminiscent of tragedy than comedy. In Lubitsch's lighter comedies, the chaotic center is more often based on misunderstanding or misplaced power or mistaken identity, as in classic literary comedy. Perhaps the memories of Capra's spectators, when we forget the dark, suicidal struggles of his heroes, play a censoring role, attempting to simplify what he has made complex.

NOTES

1. Robert Sklar recognizes this talent when he explains: "The key to Capra's success, it was said, was his ability to convince audiences they were watching their own strengths and foibles, their own dreams and values, their own selves dramatized on the screen." See "The Imagination of Stability: The Depression Films of Frank Capra," in Richard Glatzer and John Raeburn, eds., *Frank Capra: The Man and His Films* (Ann Arbor: Univ. of Michigan Press, 1975), p. 124. Raeburn points out in his essay, "*American Madness* and American Values," that Capra creates an American society that is "probably mythical" (p. 62 in the same volume).

2. John Raeburn in his introduction suggests that Capra was not immediately accessible to the French *auteur* critics of the 1950's because "he was most obsessively concerned with scrutinizing American myths and American states of consciousness" and was consequently "not exportable" (Glatzer and Raeburn, *Frank Capra*, p. viii). Glatzer sees in *Mr. Deeds* Capra's attempt "to create an American mythology that might reinforce the nation in its time of financial and social crisis" (p. 140). William S. Pecter in the same volume compares Capra to Twain, saying in "American Madness" that Capra is a "folk artist in the sense of drawing imaginatively for his substance on some of the most characteristic matter of our national folklore" (p. 182). Richard Griffith connects Capra with "many of America's most popular writers" who have looked back to an epoch early in the twentieth century and created a "fantasy of goodwill," in *Frank Capra* (London: British Film Institute, n.d.), p. 3.

3. Lewis Jacobs remarks in his essay "Capra at Work": "What concerns Capra most in a movie is the story" (Glatzer and Raeburn, *Frank Capra*, p. 42).

4. Andrew Bergman offers an excellent definition of screwball comedy in *We're in the Money: Depression America and Its Films* (New York: New York Univ. Press, 1971), pp. 132–133.

5. Donald C. Willis in *The Films of Frank Capra* (Metuchen, N.J.: Scarecrow Press, 1974) asserts: "Capra's films were basically not political, but . . . they approached politics as possibly holding the answers to the questions they raised" (p. 9). Robert Willson believes that "most of the films move us to laughter instead of political action because of the presence of a comprehensive comic vision"; see "Capra's Comic Sense," in Glatzer and Raeburn, *Frank Capra*, p. 83.

6. Leland A. Poague puts it well: "Peter and Ellie learn about selfhood and about each other, and they learn to go beyond the false stereotypes that obstruct such self-discovery." See Poague's *The Cinema of Frank Capra: An Approach to Film Comedy* (South Brunswick, N.J.: A. S. Barnes, 1975), p. 156.

7. Andrew Bergman wryly explains: " 'Class' conflicts, in mid-'30s comedy, were really personality conflicts, and hence easily resolved by a good chat" (*We're in the Money,* p. 138).

8. Arthur Koestler identifies the "Aha Reaction" as one of three creative responses; see "The Three Domains of Creativity," in James F. T. Bugental, ed., *Challenges of Humanistic Psychology* (New York: McGraw-Hill, 1967), pp. 30–40. This one corresponds to "the flash of illumination" at the moment of truth. Koestler says that Karl Buhler first coined this term (p. 32).

9. Frank Capra, *The Name Above the Title: An Autobiography* (New York: Macmillan, 1971), pp. 172, 175, 176, 179, 182, 185.

10. Capra, *The Name Above the Title,* p. 185.

11. In Richard Schickel's book, *The Men Who Made the Movies* (New York: Atheneum, 1975), Capra explains: "I don't believe in tragedies. I'm not interested in them. I'm an optimist, and comedy to me is victory. Victory over anything. Tragedy is failure. I just don't believe in failures. . . . I think that the gospels are a comedy — good news. I think that the greatest comedy of all is the Divine Comedy — the Resurrection, victory over death" (pp. 87–88).

12. Robert Willson sees these final films as reflecting a "fairy tale fantasy" that was always present in Capra, but better controlled in the earlier films (Glatzer and Raeburn, *Frank Capra,* pp. 95–97).

13. Raymond Carney sees George Bailey as having "at least five partial or divided projections" of himself in other characters in the story; see *American Vision: The Films of Frank Capra* (Cambridge: Cambridge Univ. Press, 1986), p. 381.

14. See Jeffrey Richards's "Frank Capra and the Cinema of Populism," in Bill Nichols, ed., *Movies and Methods* (Berkeley: Univ. of California Press, 1976), pp. 65–77.

15. Robert Heilman, *Tragedy and Melodrama: Versions of Experience* (Seattle: Univ. of Washington Press, 1968).

3

———

Capra's Film Images: Ritualizing Habitual Space and Framing Acute Space

HABITUAL SPACE

Capra's creation of habitual space occurs primarily in his "divine comedy" films, but is occasionally apparent in the more complex films among the Barbara Stanwyck tetralogy and the screwball comedies. To identify habitual space, one needs to ask whether the space in a film is familiar. Do the characters seem to "belong" in the spaces where we find them? (This does not mean that they need to fit the spaces in a narrative sense. In fact, the character may feel "out of place.") These habitual spaces are not just functional; they are not just sets in which the characters move about. Nor are they in themselves intensely noteworthy; they don't demand our interpretation. These habitual spaces have an "unframed" quality, unlike acute spaces, which are framed and composed.[1]

One of the best examples of habitual space in a Capra film is the living space of the Vanderhoff-Sycamore family in *You Can't Take It with You*. We do not remember this space per se, but we remember it in conjunction with its larger context and the narrative consequences that develop here. This space accommodates the family's work and play in all their healthiness. The work and play activities are not simply instrumental. And the space does not simply contain them. It is not what Eliade calls "profane space," or what we might call utilitarian or neutral space.[2] The space and the activities within the space feel normal. Granted, this "normality" might seem farfetched for those who live in a relatively peaceful household. But Capra convinces us to suspend our disbelief, so that the ballet dancing, portrait painting, firecracker manufacturing, toy making, meal getting, and xylophone playing constitute a ritual normality here. And because film's first function is to de-familiarize space, we accept the subsequent re-familiarization as what it claims to be.

Occasionally Capra will push us toward a nearly conscious relation to this habitual space. But, for the most part, it does not make the demands on us as spectators that acute space does. As is true of most of us in our lives, we maintain an unreflecting relation to habitual space, a sort of unconsciousness that allows us to relax and to avoid analytic thought. In film, our slide into this undemanding spectatorship is like the comfort we experience in routines in our daily lives, a comfort that forms a kind of dialectic with the special circumstances of holidays, weekends, and having guests. The habitual space of Capra's films relaxes us partly in order to stimulate or even disturb us with later entries into the same space made acute.

Often the spectator's first encounter with a film space that will become habitual is acute, just as our first few days in a new house or apartment are fraught with conscious decisions about where to put things until easy routines relieve us of this consciousness. For instance, in *You Can't Take It with You,* at the first climax of all the living space activities, the camera spins and circles through the living room, following Essie Carmichael (Ann Miller) as she pirouettes around and between the other family members. This camera movement is highly self-conscious: it requires the spectator's engagement with Capra's methods by creating a visual echo of Essie's movement and by surveying the entire space. But Capra's ultimate purpose is that the film spectator feel at home in this space and accept what is probably not normal and certainly not ordinary as both normal and ordinary within this fictional context.

The above description identifies Capra's regular strategy for introducing habitual space. This strategy has several components: (1) plenitude, or filling up the space; (2) camera movement, or surveying the space; (3) familiarization, the return to the same space at regular intervals throughout the film; and (4) ritualization, or the acceptance of a daily order that depends upon a spatial order.

Plenitude

The packed screen is both an icon and a spatial strategy in Capra's films. And filling up an illusionary volume, filling all the niches in the available space, is one way in which Capra brings space to our attention. In *Wonderful Life,* for instance, the run on the Building and Loan, which becomes packed with panic-stricken depositors, brings this work space before us in a newly intense way, though we have seen it before. The space of the screen can be filled in an auditory as well as a visual way. When Longfellow Deeds enlists the help of his servants to test the resonance of his mansion, their chorus of hoots tests and fills this space.

Camera Movement

Camera movement through a screen space recreates the activity of characters in habitual spaces. It often, as in the spinning camera of *You Can't*, imitates
the activity we are observing. For example, the camera tracks with Walter
Huston's Mr. Dickson in *American Madness* through the work space of his bank
as he arrives in the morning. The camera penetrates to the bank's inner vaults
to watch the tellers collect their cash and retreats with them as the inner vault is
closed.[3] Camera movement is also an important element in ritualization, because it familiarizes us with the characters' routines.

Familiarization

The camera's track in *American Madness* recurs at the end of the film, mark-
ing off the film's structural boundaries and pointing out to us that we have witnessed an entire cycle in the life of the institution and the characters dependent
on it. The space in the old house that George and Mary renovate in *Wonderful
Life* is familiarized by constant returns to it in different stages of repair or dis-
integration. It thereby gives us a standard by which to measure George's inner
psychology. On his would-be honeymoon, the old house is decrepit in its disre-
pair, but cozy and inviting. Later during his nightmare of non-existence, its
space is hellish — cold, opaquely dark, and fenced by cobwebs. On his return to
life and family at the end, it is bright and filled to capacity with good neighbors, though its flaws (the loose banister knob) are not concealed. Part of the
familiarization process requires the humanization of that space, the relating of
space to a character's psychology. In *It Happened,* for instance, the slicing in
half of the space of the motel cabins by the blanket and the healing of this division at closure describe the progress of Peter and Ellie's relationship.

Habitual space in Capra's films is space with which Capra wants us to be
familiar. It is work space or play space, and it supports the narrative assumption that neither totally private nor totally public realities are particularly
healthy. Whether it is the space occupied by couples in most of the films or the
space occupied by the family in *Wonderful Life,* habitual space is often a measure of health in the films, healthy relations above all.

Ritualization

Ritual action takes place within habitual space rather than acute space, because ritual demands our expectation of a certain order and an unconscious
acceptance of the space by the characters.[4] The ritualization of these spaces en-
tails making them so familiar that they accommodate the repetitive behaviors
that form the texture of daily life. The nature of these daily rituals is such that
a correction of some aspect of the space can often correct one's mood without

ever identifying the cause of the annoyance. Much of the comedy of Capra's characters rests in their inadvertent or detached means of dealing with annoyances and making decisions. Most of the comedy in *You Can't* works in this way: Mrs. Sycamore writes plays because a typewriter was delivered at the house by mistake; Mr. DePinna was delivering ice one day some twenty years before and simply stayed; Kerenkov is a family member by virtue of being Essie's ballet teacher. These are not passionate or acute decisions. They are decisions into which characters slide, and which the habitual space supports. The space of Dave the Dude's apartment in Capra's *Lady for a Day* (1933), for instance, always centers Dave the Dude (Warren William) in the middle of a sunken living room, and we often see him dressing, preening, or being measured for clothes, surrounded by his underlings.

As we recall the habitual spaces in the great Capra films, they present clues to the narrative assumptions of those films. In *Bitter Tea,* there is Megan's bedroom, for instance. Is there any other Capra film so sensuous or so baroque, both ornamentally and psychologically mannerist?[5] In *It Happened,* the habitual spaces are the buses and cabins; each setting pairs up the two characters, and the latter artificially divides them. In *Mr. Deeds,* both the mansion and the courtroom are habitual, reflecting the sequence of Deeds's adventures and the spaces he manages to humanize. In *Mr. Smith,* the Senate chamber is the center of the film, with its levels (gallery and floor) and distances through which glances and speech (sometimes Clarissa's sign language to Jeff Smith) make their way. It also serves as a pragmatic habitual space at the center of more abstract sacred spaces in the film, the monuments and Jeff Smith's reverence for these images. *Wonderful Life* is the richest of Capra's films in habitual space; George and Mary Bailey's house, the Building and Loan office, and even Potter's office are realized spatially.

Meet John Doe is the sore thumb among Capra's divine comedies. Capra never returns to spaces in this film, at least not to exploit them as contexts for familiarization or ritualization. But this absence of chronic space also may explain Capra's inability to effect closure in the film: the sequential use of acute space leaves the film's narrative unanchored in relation to ordinary and normal human activities. In a sense, Long John has no "place" or home, no locus of friendship or family or romance, to which Capra can revert. The narrative's intensity resembles a tragedy more than a comedy. And Long John is more the outsider, wandering from place to place, than a comic prince, able to return to society with hard-won wisdom.

ACUTE SPACE

When Capra creates acute spaces, they have a distinctively framed quality, and they are bound by time, having a distinct beginning and end.[6] These intense filmic moments also have a more conscious and cognitive effect on the film spectator: they stimulate a kind of "spatial thinking."[7] These moments tend to correspond to equally intense moments in the narrative, though they often have no verbal signs, being, as they are, so intensely visual. These acute space moments often depict vivid or transfiguring feelings. To a large extent, they carry with them a resonance and a profundity that distinguish them from the habitual spaces of Capra's films. These spaces tend to be shared by the protagonist and the spectator but are simultaneously invisible to other characters, or they may depict an intense encounter between two characters to which the spectator plays intimate witness. Thus, they are intensely private and self-conscious moments for the film director, effecting a bond between characters and spectator. Though these acute space moments are often composed in a single take, the time that passes during them often feels timeless, so riveting is the image.

These acute space moments allow Capra's spectator to identify with certain characters. So much of our own early sense of our own identities is connected with the idea of place, of belonging to and possessing the one who nourishes us in a familiar dwelling space, of being inside and not outside. And these earliest ways of formulating our own sense of self are transformed in film into a way of formulating our sense of another self, rooted as film characters usually are in their contexts.

Jean Piaget identifies three spatial principles that children must learn: (1) proximity; (2) continuity; and (3) enclosure.[8] In learning about proximity, or the sense of how close or how far one object is from another, the child is learning about what in film is largely meant by composition. In learning the principle of continuity, or a sense of direction and of following regular paths, the child learns about the spatial principles that correspond to camera movement, kinesics, and depth of field in film. The principle of enclosure, or the setting apart of areas or domains, corresponds to the principle of framing in film.

Compared to William Wyler's acute spaces, Capra's are not subversive. In fact, nearly all of them are "on stage" instead of "backstage."[9] Like his narratives that feature forthright confrontations, his film spaces need not be read for their subtexts, nor the encounters of characters in these spaces for their withheld feelings or masked intentions. Part of Capra's skill as a director is his ability to make even acute space seem familiar to us, intensifying our images of what is an essentially sentimental relationship to space.

Such an orientation in the real world can be disturbing when, as young adults, we are often in rebellion against this sort of relation to space. We have broken from our hometowns, our parents, our schools, our churches perhaps. And most of us emphasize instrumental, territorial, or symbolic relations to space, rather than a sentimental one. In fact, a territorial relation to space, which determines our relative control over space, is in many ways in conflict with a sentimental relation to space. We may have played in a wooded space as children that is owned by a developer who subsequently bulldozes the land and obliterates even its physical contours. Our sentimental sense of belonging in the space conflicts with the developer's territorial rights to it, or perhaps our

owning of stock in his company or his paying of high property taxes to support
our local schools. Capra often poses symbolic and sentimental relations to
space against instrumental and territorial ones.

Capra creates acute space by composing and framing it with his characters.
He thereby humanizes it. Capra's spatial strategies are very much dependent
upon the configuration of space as a psychologically charged medium. Sometimes this charge can be almost tangibly felt, as when Capra creates "hallucinatory space" or when he "appropriates" the faces of his characters. Other times,
the character's glance, posture, or stance in relation to a secondary frame will
intensify the space occupied. Compared to Wyler, Capra seems less interested
in the tensions and confrontations between characters, except when a confrontation impinges on his protagonist. For instance, when George Bailey confronts Potter across his desk in *Wonderful Life,* he sits down only to find himself
unnaturally low in relation to the desk and Potter elevated in his throne-like
wheelchair. George's double-take evokes a laugh or smile from us, because
there's a too-fitting absurdity in the sawed-off legs of the chair: we've been
given an image of precisely how George feels, having to come to Potter for
help. It is an unrealistic image but a psychologically truthful one, and it reveals Capra's spatial bias. This instance is almost too self-conscious a technique, but Capra gets away with it, for self-consciousness lies at the heart of
Capra's creation of identifications with his central characters. It is an important element in Capra's creation of acute space.

Self-Conscious Space

Generally we associate self-conscious cinema with New Wave directors, who
deliberately call our attention to the processes of viewing and making films.
They make films that are "reflexive" or "self-referential" (not self-reflexive!).
This relatively modern group of films, occurring within the last few decades,
emphasizes various innovative, dissociative techniques. Such techniques de-
tach spectators from the fiction so that we might be more apt to treat it cogni-
tively as well as reacting on an affective level. Capra's films are also attentive to
spectators, though the self-consciousness that he advocates is integrated into
the fiction so as not to cause an artificial disjunction between form and content
(as Godard, for instance, deliberately effects in his films). Capra wants to define spectators' postures in relation to his fiction, not call into question the ver-
ity of the fiction itself.

The Penetrating Witness. One type of self-conscious space might be called the
penetrating witness. Though present embryonically in a number of Capra
films, the penetrating witness is most apparent in *Wonderful Life,* where we
spectators share this role with God, the angel Joseph, and at least one second-
class angel.[10] It's a very illustrious crew to be a part of. The spatial form taken
by this divine point of view is what we might call "specular shots," or shots that
imply an active penetration into the scene by an eye. This eye, really the cam-

In Capra's *It's a Wonderful Life,* the camera often peers into a scene, as it does here between the shelves in Mr. Gower's drugstore. We are made more self-conscious about our witnessing of this crisis between Mr. Gower (H. B. Warner) and the young George Bailey (Bobbie Anderson) and more aware that we share a divine point of view.

era's, becomes our eyes, so that we are made to feel that we are penetrating into a space formerly alien but now made accessible and familiar to us. One of these paradigmatic moments occurs when Joseph begins to show Clarence an episode from George's early life. We see only a blank screen. Then, remembering that Clarence is still only a second-class angel, Joseph adjusts the picture and the moving picture comes into focus for both Clarence and us. The penetrating witness is a prototype for the viewer of film. *Wonderful Life,* with its premise of divine intervention and an omniscient watching perspective (Clarence often looks up and over his shoulder to ask how he's doing), is rife with techniques that posit both this omniscient point of view and our own complicity with it.

As mentioned above, this technique is also implicit in some of Capra's earlier films. As far back as *Platinum Blonde,* Capra has the camera inflect the space of a black-and-white diamond-patterned floor in the entrance gallery of the Schuyler mansion. He does this by using this space repeatedly for confrontations between the aristocratic and pretentious Schuylers and Stew (Robert Williams) or his middle-class, fun-loving newspaper buddies. First Capra establishes the space of the gallery from the floor, looking up toward the landing on the next floor above. He has Stew play a bowing game with the family lawyer, Dexter Grayson (Reginald Owen) as he and the mother cross the landing and Stew mockingly bows to each in turn, evoking Dexter's bow. Later in the film, Stew stands on the landing where they have stood earlier and replays the same game, but this time Stew bows twice, evoking bows from Dexter each time and then bluffing Dexter into bowing a third time. Capra is inflecting this space with specular self-consciousness. Stew consciously manipulates visual cues and has consciously displaced the "higher" Schuyler dynasty in his physical position as he plays the game.

Finally Capra has the camera independently present on this landing looking down toward the floor and doorway in which first Stew and then Dexter were framed. But this time, the camera captures Ann (Jean Harlow) entering the gallery through the door on her way to a confrontation with Stew. The camera swings forward from the landing over the railing, pans to the right as Ann crosses the diamond-patterned floor and mounts the stairs, and then further circles to the right and pans to the left as she crosses the landing to Stew's room.

The elaborate movement of the camera, its mannerist watching of Ann's crossings and ascent, is enough to alert us to the showdown imminent between them. But it goes a step further. It aligns us with Stew's point of view, which has earlier claimed this space as his territory; and it aligns us with the implied omniscience of his game-playing strategies. The camera, Stew, and the film spectator are all complicit in the appropriation of this space and this fictional attitude. The narrative of *Platinum* even presents a strategy that complements this implied omniscience. Throughout the film, Stew, a newspaperman, has tried to write plays, but in the last sequence the Loretta Young character, Gallagher, suggests he use autobiographical elements instead of the far-flung exotic conflicts that have dominated his scripts. So with Gallagher's help, Stew in the last sequence of the film writes the script for the film, even adding his subsequent marriage to Gallagher, which has yet to occur when the film ends.[11] The characters with whom the camera has identified become the omniscient creators of the story in retrospect.

A similar reflexivity informs *It Happened,* because implicit in Peter and Ellie's journey from Florida to New York is the story that Peter will write about it. And, in fact, the camera plays with Peter's manuscript, which his editor first throws in a wastepaper basket and then retrieves. Where the penetrating witness technique is most apparent, though, is in the two motels where the couple rents cabins. It is the threat of *not* seeing — a threat depicted in the hanging of the blanket between them — that makes seeing so intense here.

Watching the "walls of Jericho," we become self-conscious because (1) the characters are made self-conscious by the semierotic position they are in; and (2) we are conscious that we are seeing what they cannot and so are voyeurs. Though the first of these two factors might be present in any love scene, the second makes this one unique. The eyes and the exchanged glances that usually inform such a scene have become ours: the film spectator becomes a mediator between Peter and Ellie. They stare toward each other even though the blanket is there. The camera flirtatiously shoots each in turn in one-shots, but from the other's side, as though peeking around the blanket, before returning to two-shots showing the whole space. We get to know the habitual space of the cabin from all angles spatially as they get to know each other. (Their relationship seems to require this diminishment of sensory stimuli to foster their concentration on each other.)

At other times, the camera acknowledges a presence before the narrative does. In a sense, the technique primes us for the coming narrative complication. Film spectators who are attuned to a director's use of space have the pleasure of their own omniscience in "seeing it coming." This is an embryonic sort of self-consciousness on the spectators' parts. For instance, in *Mr. Deeds*, consider the initial appearance of Babe (Jean Arthur) in the newspaper office. The editor, Mac (George Bancroft), sarcastically admonishes his reporters to get better stories on Deeds. The camera draws back from the editor at his desk to reveal male reporters clustered around him and a woman reporter behind him to his left: she stands by the door, playing with a piece of string. The camera movement is simple and expected. It is the arrangement of the figures in space, the isolation and gestural indifference of Babe, that transforms neutral space into acute space. Spectators are invited to wonder why she is set apart and what her motives are, for it quickly becomes apparent that the spatial arrangement depends upon her volition.

An impressive witnessing shot catches our attention in *John Doe*. Here, spectators are alerted to their role as seers by the elaborate crane shot over the black umbrellas held by the audience at the John Doe convention. Part of the self-conscious quality of this shot arises from its elaborateness. When a director like Capra, who generally chooses simplicity, instead chooses to complicate the screen both by filling it up and by moving the camera before this volume, the effect can be startling. Here it sets in motion an increasing sense of doom in the viewer. Already the narrative has asserted that nothing is going right. But then Capra's visual sense takes over and gives us a spatial confirmation of the dramatic message. He sweeps the camera over the black umbrellas. He uses the darkness and the artificial lights in the stadium against the rain-soaked crowd to create a crowd that looks like a negative image of themselves (as they, in fact, prove to be in the narrative — one of Capra's vicious mobs, prone to the influence of a despot). The black umbrellas, hiding the faces of the crowd and keeping them from seeing, and also keeping us from seeing them individually, are an apt spatial strategy. Part of the spectator's self-conscious witnessing in the scene consists of seeing the failure of spectatorship and of witnessing. The blind mob tries literally to blind Long John, as they throw tomatoes and newsprint at him.

The Implied Witness. In most of Capra's films, the witness viewing the scene is not explicitly present. Instead, he or she is implicit in a variety of ways: (1) the presence of surrogate witnesses in the narrative; (2) the use of double-framing, which implies the act that we are explicitly engaged in (looking into a frame); (3) the self-conscious behavior of the viewed protagonist, suggesting the presence of an audience, when none is present in the narrative. Like the penetrating witness, though, the implied witness technique locates the spectator in the film as an observer and a presence, if not as a participant.

Witnesses in Capra's narratives should not be confused with his mobs. Unlike mobs, witnesses are individualized, even if they appear in groups. They speak and react, not as a collective, but as a number of individuals perhaps surprised to find themselves in agreement. Their witnessing of the narrative action intensifies the film spectator's gaze, for to some extent they act as our surrogates inside the fictional space of the film. They stare as we do, but their witnessing is more potent. A group of street people in *Lady for a Day* acts as a social conscience for Dave the Dude, encouraging him to act as a fairy godfather to Apple Annie (May Robson), and they appear at crucial moments to help avert Annie's exposure as a street vendor to her daughter's prospective rich in-laws. They are like a Greek chorus but more effective, for the Greek chorus anticipates tragedy without being able to avoid it. Annie's friends are far more potent witnesses.

In both *Mr. Deeds* and *Mr. Smith,* witnessing involves a trial for the hero. Those who witness are like a jury watching the trial's progress. Deeds, for instance, is first tried on the newspaper's pages as "Cinderella Man." The headlines accuse him of being a fool. But the power of the surrogate witness occurs in the hearing room, when Deeds's sanity is put on trial. Here we have both the anonymous mob, functioning as a sort of audience, and the judges, who provide more significant witnessing. Capra establishes the importance of the latter spatially. The three judges sit on a diagonal in deep focus from over Longfellow's shoulder. Longfellow is in the foreground left. Though ready at one point in the hearing to commit him, the judges witness what amounts to his resurrection when he decides to speak up. And Capra invests them with the power to judge — in this case, to set Deeds free by pronouncing him sane.

Even better orchestrated is the gallery in *Mr. Smith.* Here the witnessing is by one of Capra's "good mobs" (they oppose his irrational "bad mobs"). But the power of group witnessing is led by the presence of Capra's main characters in the gallery and by the Senate president's awareness of this leadership. Like the central judge in *Deeds,* the Senate president here ultimately orchestrates the drama as a sort of benevolent, observing father.

One of the most dramatic of witnessed circumstances in Capra's films is Long John's sacrificial suicide at the end of *John Doe.* Capra lends witnessing a ritualistic significance, felt in *Deeds* and *Smith* but blooming in our mythic imaginations on the snow-swept top of this skyscraper. What have we witnessed, in fact, in both *Deeds* and *Smith* but the death and rebirth of a man and the principles he stands for? Capra's wish is to insert us in the drama by re-creating our role through the presence of surrogates. He forces upon us the terrible thing that we don't want to see. In film, witnessing is more powerful than the horror of isolation, or perhaps it is a necessary corollary to isolation. One thinks of the great confrontations with death in scripture — Job's suffering, Abraham's near-sacrifice of Isaac, Christ's nine hours on the cross — these figures are alone with their God. But scripture or any tale-telling always works in retrospect, whereas film's spatial premises require our "location" in the scene. A place is always present in the present if we see it before us. (This may be why the most literary of screenwriters, Harold Pinter, is always striving to displace us in time and space, in *The Go-Between, The French Lieutenant's Woman,* and *Betrayal.*)

In *John Doe,* Capra sets us in time — it is Christmas Eve — but it is a ritualistic time. In other words, it could be any Christmas Eve. "Silent Night" is on the soundtrack, but it functions less as a carol than as a mournful reminder of the silence that blankets the scene. The specific technique that implies our own witness, as well as that of the surrogates, is the use of a high-angle shot of Norton and his underlings, which shifts to a shot from the space outside the roof in midair. Norton and his underlings are not only witnessed by the John Doe club, which arrives later; they are pointedly witnessed by an omniscient eye. When the camera is poised outside the boundary of the roof, it frames Norton and his cohorts between the pillars that define this boundary, so that they are doubly captured by our view. And as in some of the other instances when self-conscious space is created, the camera behaves in an especially independent manner. It makes us more conscious of our spectatorship. At this point, after double-framing Norton and his crew, it tracks to the left, showing empty space beyond the building.

Still another technique at work in this scene making us self-conscious witnesses is synecdoche, the presentation of a part of a character's body that is made to evoke the whole. But the evocation of wholeness is in our witnessing. Capra is making special demands to involve us in the ritual action. His demands resemble the IQ tests we took in elementary school: the instructions read something like "tell what is missing from this picture," and we see a picture of the side of an automobile that has only one wheel. Capra, on the simplest level, is simply saying, "Guess who?" On a more atmospheric, intuitive level, he is working with a primitive threat as well. We are made more aware of our own witness when we are deprived of witnessing. And a lack of wholeness, when wholeness is withheld, threatens us as a mask or disguise might. Capra alternately uses synecdoche and deep shadows to cut us off from the Long John/John Doe who emerges onto the roof. Long John is thus effectively transformed into John Doe, a faceless, haunted man, who has come to represent something but has lost his own being.

In the many discussions of the relative ineffectiveness of this ending, a number of critics have asserted that Long John should have, according to the narrative's demands, committed suicide. Capra's spatial signals in this last scene

The dramatic ending of Capra's *Meet John Doe* silhouettes the main characters played by Gary Cooper and Barbara Stanwyck, creating what almost looks like a negative photographic image of them in this moment of crisis.

indicate that John Doe has committed suicide. Long John has been displaced by John Doe, and the narrative denouement is a waking up, a ritualistic resurrection, brought about as much by the collapse of Ann Mitchell (Stanwyck) as by the arrival and pleas of the John Doe club. Though perhaps a little mawkish, her fainting injects a less dream-like, hallucinatory reality into the action. As suicides go in Capra's films, jumping off a building (or off a bridge, as in *Wonderful Life*) detaches the spectator — who is always up on the height — from the naturalistic impact. Long John transformed into John Doe has lost touch with this physical reality. We know from the hallucinatory scene earlier that Long John is obeying the internalized insults of the mob. So part of the function of witness in this scene is the witnessing of identity. To see Long John is to give him back his self.

This technique can also be used to witness false authority and false configurations of self. To delineate false authority, Capra sometimes uses high angles, which is of note since he rarely uses angle shots. His departure from his own norm suggests a particular need to undercut the figures he diminishes in this way — especially Norton in *John Doe* and Kirby, Sr., in *You Can't*. Part of the premise behind the use of this shot, even more than to diminish the despots, may be to elevate the spectator into a judgmental position. Capra makes us aware of our witnessing role by giving us a special position in relation to the action, as was true at the John Doe convention. The particular shot might be called "a high angle of the subject's inevitable vulnerability." Capra chooses remarkably to double this effect in a mirror-like way in *Miracle Woman* when John is about to commit suicide. A tilt up to him leaning out the window is followed by a bird's-eye view of him drawing back into the room from the space in the alley. He has asked a woman in the apartment across the space to turn down her radio. When his musical compositions are rejected, he leans out again, but this time with suicidal intentions. Again the bird's-eye view captures his moment of decision, but the spectator now has the information to understand the camera's position. He has heard Florence Fallon's voice, paused, and withdrawn. The bird's-eye shot, preceded by the low-angle, postulates the spectator's witness but not without first imputing the responsibility for the action to John himself.

When Capra wishes to identify a false witness, he may withhold our sight of him. A dramatic example occurs in *Miracle Woman,* when Stanwyck's Florence and Manners' John meet on a beach and are interrupted by the con man Hornsby (Sam Hardy). Hornsby's voice precedes his image: "Am I intruding?" It startles the spectator out of the privacy of the moment. Then the camera pans to the right to reveal Hornsby. Our sense of him is based on our sense of him having invaded our privacy, as well as that of the lovers. His presence is a violation, and he is a voyeur. We have interestingly been aligned with the blind John, who would not have seen Hornsby's approach through this act of withholding on Capra's part.

The Standing-Men Frame

Capra uses the bodies of his actors to fill and define the frame. One technique, the standing-men frame, is most noticeably employed when Capra wants to enclose one of his protagonists in a claustrophobic way. Not only the protagonist feels trapped, but also the spectator, whose access to the protagonist is severely limited by the opaque bodies of the standing characters. Like Capra's use of high angles or a double frame to make the spectator more conscious of his or her own witnessing, the standing-men frame squeezes and directs our spectatorship. But we feel it as an overly static and enclosed configuration. And, indeed, Capra is usually identifying false or overly oppressive forms of authority or power with these frames.

Capra employs this frame comically in *Arsenic and Old Lace* when the two crazy aunts (Josephine Hull and Jean Adair) frame Mortimer Brewster (Cary Grant). He has just unsuccessfully tried to explain that murder is not an acceptable response to the pathos of an old victim: "It's wrong. It's not a nice thing to do. People wouldn't understand. *He* wouldn't understand." But the technique is versatile. It depicts Tony's boredom and alienation from his father's business cronies in *You Can't;* the oppression of Lulu Smith (Barbara Stanwyck) is shown in the adulterous relationship with Bob Grover (Adolphe

Menjou) in *Forbidden*—she is kissed by him on the stairs to her apartment and our view of her, except for her eyes, is altogether blocked.

In Capra's more complex films, the technique has deeper implications. Generally the protagonist who is caught between oppressive forces has in some way brought about his own imprisonment. And even when this standing-men frame is used for minor episodes, the import of the scenes is often twofold. Take, for example, *Bitter Tea*. Stanwyck's Megan has not yet arrived, and the bishop tells a story to illustrate his view of "the Oriental." He relates that when he told the crucifixion story to some Mongolian tribesmen, their eyes lit up, and he was sure they had been impressed. But when the next caravan of tradesmen passed through their territory, the tribesmen slaughtered them all by crucifying them. Though Capra's point is not clear at this point in the film's narrative, the bishop, framed as he is by a crowd of European missionaries, is revealed as culturally limited. And his limitations are Megan's. He tells the story to evoke horror from his audience and to convey his condescending disillusionment with Orientals. But Capra's spatial enclosure of the bishop should alert us to his recognition of the severe limitations in the bishop's perspective, especially his inability to communicate across cultural boundaries, which is the very next thing that Megan and her fiancé attempt.

Used often in *Mr. Smith,* the standing-men frame inevitably contrasts the protagonist's view of himself with the reality of his limitations. In one instance, reporters mock Jefferson Smith in the newspapers. They print photographs of him with snide captions that misinterpret his intentions. Jeff goes after the reporters, socking each in turn until he is restrained. Then he is framed between the reporters, who shoot questions at him: "What do you know about laws or making laws or what the people need?" He replies, "I don't pretend to know." And they shoot back, "Then what are you doing in the Senate?" Not being pretentious is not enough. Even being honest is not enough, as shown by the framing of Jeff between political boss Jim Taylor (Edward Arnold) and the boss's troubleshooter McGann (Eugene Pallette). In *Lady for a Day,* this frame is used to show Apple Annie's vulnerability before she is transformed into a "lady"; both Dave the Dude and the "artists" who effect the change tower over her.

When Capra frames his protagonist with his antagonists, as when Long John stands between Norton and his nephew Sheldon (Rod LaRocque) in *John Doe,* he is also prefiguring the end of this inevitable confrontation. For instance, in *State of the Union,* Grant Matthews (Spencer Tracy) is at first framed between Kay Thorndyke (Angela Lansbury) and Jim Conover (Adolphe Menjou). But his divided loyalties to them and the political success story they represent and to Mary (Katharine Hepburn), his idealistic wife, are inevitably tested and righted. In some ways, the narrative of this film resembles the Barbara Stanwyck vehicles: Grant Matthews is more the innocent misled than the hero confronting his own flaws and limitations.

The standing-men frame prefigures a belittlement of the standing men or women, and thus expresses Capra's intuition that the pompous, though redoubtable, standing figures must be confronted. When the protagonist stands between his foes, he often recognizes them for what they are and then faces the inevitable — that they must be fought.

The Devoted Heroine Posture

In Capra's films the devoted heroine at some point begins to look up at the hero in a somewhat surprised but pleased way. This posture signals her retrieval of innocence, brought about by her faith in the hero's authenticity. It often captures the moment when she involuntarily loses the veneer of cynicism that she has been wearing and accepts a lost part of herself by accepting the corresponding idealism in the hero. I am always tempted to think of this shot as a low-angle shot — I find my head inadvertently tipping to the angle of the heroine's — but in reality it is not. This shot carries with it a very strong invitation to identify with her point of view. The shot is usually an epiphanic shot that includes special lighting on the heroine's face — even more than on the hero's — and sometimes a soft backlighting on her hair.[12] This posture makes me very uncomfortable in my most feminist self, for it re-creates some of the more worshipful moments in my past when some male mentor inspired me. Has every professional woman had this experience, I wonder? Capra first creates the cynical professional woman and then delves into her hardened heart, finding a rich core of devotion. Inevitably its source is father-love. Father figures pervade Capra's fictions as judge-presiders.

Capra constructs an Electra complex for his heroines in *Mr. Deeds* and *John Doe*.[13] Both heroines think of their fathers, absent in the present, when they begin to idealize Longfellow and Long John. Jean Arthur's Mary Dawson (alias "Babe" Louise Bennett) says of her father to Longfellow, "Gee, that's funny. He was a lot like you." And she talks about fishing with her father, looking slightly up and into space — the devoted heroine posture. Stanwyck's Ann in *John Doe* uses her dead father's diary to construct the John Doe she wants, filling Long John's mouth with her father's words. But the Electra complex has gone somewhat askew here, because Long John protests to Ann's mother (Spring Byington): "I think she's in love with another man, you know, the one she made up, the real John Doe. Well, that's pretty tough competition. I bet ya he'd know how to say it all right. Me, I get up to it and around it and in back of it, but I never get right to it. You know what I mean."

Long John here has come smack up against Ann's idealized father, who never existed, of course, except in his daughter's imagination. And in admitting the essential flaw in the devoted heroine posture, Capra is less able to put over even a troubled romance in his narrative. Capra simply separates hero and heroine circumstantially and reunites them only briefly for closure, his heroine in a feverish and guilt-induced hysteria and his hero in a strangely hallucinatory state of imagining himself to be the John Doe she has created.

Capra seems to exhaust the premises behind the professional woman's Electra complex in this film. For his next dramatic film, *Wonderful Life*, the devoted heroine, Mary Hatch (Donna Reed), aspires only to motherhood (as her name suggests), and she is conveniently fatherless. The Electra complex is simplified when the father is distant: the hero fills a void rather than competing.

In both *Wonderful Life* and *Mr. Smith*, Capra's heroines mother his heroes as well as falling for them. In the former film, George's mother (Beulah Bondi) and Mary are accomplices: George's mother tells George that Mary is in town, pushes him in the direction of Mary's house, and calls Mary to warn her that George is on his way.[14] And in this film, as in none of Capra's others, except *State of the Union*, Mary is a mother herself, ironically protecting their children against even George when he cannot be a good father to them. In *Mr. Smith*, Clarissa Saunders (Jean Arthur), a bit maudlin after drinking with Diz, tells us, "You know how I felt, Diz? I felt just like a mother sending her kid off to school for the first time, watching the little feller toddling off in his best bib-and-tucker, hoping he can stand up to the other kids."

An earlier version of the devoted heroine posture, in *Lady for a Day*, takes the form of mother love itself. In this film, Apple Annie's adoration is for her daughter Louise (Jean Parker), and the goal of the film's elaborate charade is to preserve Annie's idealized mother role. Most intensely, the fragility of this goal is felt in the hotel garden, where the mother Annie (Robson) replaces the future husband (Barry Norton): Annie embraces her daughter under a flowered arch, before a waterfall, and in the same flickering light that romanticized the young couple's embrace earlier. In Capra's later films, the illusion of false idealization always gets punctured. Here it not only survives, but the young couple's future happiness seems dependent on its survival.

The women characters in the two later films *Wonderful Life* and *Mr. Smith* are more flexible and multifaceted than an Annie or a Louise; ultimately they are more equal partners to the heroes than the women in *Deeds* and *John Doe*, though they resemble these other heroines. When Jefferson Smith describes his national boys' camp, the land and its natural beauties, to Saunders, she is pictured in a back-lighted close-up with tears in her eyes. Her musical motif, "Jeanie with the Light Brown Hair," dominates the soundtrack, and her head nestles against her hand. This posture characterizes Mary in *Wonderful Life*, even in the sequence in Gower's drugstore when she and George are children: speaking into his deaf ear so that he will not hear her, Mary vows that she will love George forever. Thereafter, Mary's love for George is simply assumed.

This less troubled relationship in *Wonderful Life* may offset the more devastating inner voyage of the hero; the undivided heroine may counterbalance his severe dividedness. Mary functions more as a Dantean Beatrice than as a complex counterforce in the narrative, which was the heroine's role in the courtship trilogy, *Deeds*, *Smith*, and *Doe*. Donna Reed's Mary, then, becomes paradigmatic but not typical for the devoted heroine's posture. Capra uses this paradigm to invert George's security during his night journey. Mary, who has always acknowledged George lovingly, completely denies him here, projecting her vision of him as a deranged sexual maniac onto him through her scramble to escape and her terrified screams and wide eyes. She is the devoted heroine transformed into rape victim. The psychological truth implicit in this dualism, which Capra does not explore, is the uncomfortably close relation of victimization to devotion.

Historically Mary is also one of the prototypes for the predatory females in the domestic comedies and dramas of the 1950's, the woman whose main function is to capture a husband and cajole him into marriage and child-rearing. I think of these figures as "mother-women," though in the 1950's their bright red lipstick and nails, white skin, dark, short hair, and cat-like round faces suggest a subtext of vampire-animal aggressiveness.

Mary's underlying aggressiveness emerges when George tries to escape their inevitable marriage — long before they are married, when they both make wishes and throw stones at the broken-down house that will become their home; when they struggle on the telephone with George's reluctance;[15] and when George believes that all his life's devotion to his home and family and town will be rewarded by a jail sentence. At these times, the hard set of Donna Reed's face and her unsmiling concentration on the hero oppose the devoted heroine posture and give the heroine a more complex willfulness and identity.

The Appropriation of Faces

Seeing two of Capra's last films, *Here Comes the Groom* (1951) and *A Hole in the Head* (1959), was for me an extremely depressing experience. While the loss of quality in the performances might simply be attributed to the lesser acting talents of Bing Crosby and Frank Sinatra, as contrasted with James Stewart and Gary Cooper in the earlier films, I suspect that Capra himself was guilty of treating the faces before his camera differently. For just as space and objects in these films lack intensity, so also do the human bodies, especially the faces. Looking back at the earlier films, I realize that Capra's direction and the talents of his great actors combined to complement the difference between neutral and acute space in such a way that the spectator feels he has appropriated or come to possess the face of the actor in acute space moments.[16] The cool diffidence of Crosby and Sinatra does not create an equivalent identification with their fictional characters. We can appropriate Stewart's and Cooper's faces because they are vulnerable to us, open and readable. Even more significantly, their faces convey self-consciousness, a self-consciousness sometimes bordering on paranoia; it is as though they are invisibly in another space and time and on the other side of an invisible technology.

One of the most dramatic instances of our appropriating a face occurs in *Lady for a Day* when Robson's Apple Annie is remade into Mrs. E. Worthington Manville. Capra and cameraman Joseph Walker's shots of her new self approaching the camera recall earlier shots of a bedraggled Apple

Annie rushing toward a horrified desk clerk across a crowded hotel lobby. In contrast to the clerk's horror, Judge Blake (Guy Kibbee) graciously accepts his role as her husband. Appropriating Robson's face or Stewart's in *Wonderful Life* depends upon these wildly disparate moments, since we become complicit with the transformed characters.

Hallucinatory Space

One of the most powerful of Capra's techniques portrays the utter isolation of an individual from the public world. As one of Capra's least realistic and most expressionistic techniques, the creation of hallucinatory space can be either a threatening loss of connection or a renewing, inspired departure from the public space of performance. Capra's depiction of hallucinatory space always has an element of terror in it, for completely private space, while sometimes inspirational, is also uncontrollable and involuntary in its suddenness and its acuteness. It constitutes an invasion of the protagonist by a force greater than himself. For the spectator, these moments of hallucinatory space are intensely privileged. The film is approaching its limits by trying to approximate a state of mind.

These acute space moments arise more frequently as Capra's films darken, becoming more apparent in *Mr. Smith, John Doe,* and *Wonderful Life.* But a few prototypical moments occur in earlier films. For instance, in *You Can't,* Stewart's Tony walks into the gloomy, static space of the Sycamore living room after Alice has left; in a medium one-shot of Tony, he is isolated against a fuzzy background. At first no one acknowledges his presence, but then the mother tells him that he will only make things worse by trying to find Alice and by hanging around. Capra isolates Tony spatially by portraying him as unseen, though he walks among the others, and by limiting our sight of him briefly, taking him "out of context" with the selectively focused shot, which does not acknowledge actual space. Capra prepares us for this moment by earlier isolating Tony from his father's arrogance in the jail cell. In the Sycamore living room, Tony is isolated from the values that he has chosen but has managed also to sabotage.

An even earlier hallucinatory experience occurs in *Bitter Tea.* Megan falls asleep after witnessing the erotic play of General Yen's soldiers with girls trucked in for their amusement. She dreams first of her threatened rape by an Oriental in traditional garb with threatening elongated fingernails. Next, General Yen (Nils Asther) intervenes, dressed in a Western business suit but with a mask over his eyes. The dream space is marked by extreme tilts and ambiguous verticals and horizontals. When Yen strikes the offending Oriental, the latter seems to float through a gravity-less space. He disappears as he appears to hit the wall spread-eagled. And as the dream dissolves back into reality, the background space seems to spin around her face. As in the later instances when Capra creates hallucinatory space, this moment isolates Megan's suddenly acute sensitivity to her own inner division: she is both sexually attracted to Yen's personality and repelled by his race and culture.[17] These moments of acute sensitivity to the self are crucial in Capra's oeuvre.

In the later films, these acute space moments punctuate the narratives at moments of great decision or suffering or inspiration. The camera isolates Jefferson Smith's profile as he gazes entranced at the Capitol dome through a door of Union Station. The others initially in his frame leave it, and leave Jeff isolated and staring, with light falling directly on his face. Later, when Jeff is called to defend himself in a committee hearing investigating his ethics, Jeff rises into the camera's frame where he is isolated against the woodwork behind. The gaze of all in the room is on him. Still later, Jeff's face is isolated during the last moments of his filibuster. This moment immediately precedes Senator Paine's delivery of the letters that threaten to crucify Jeff on the cross of public opinion. These three moments seem carefully choreographed. They are all intensely private moments, but they also form a logical sequence that knits together the narrative spatially: the moment of dedication, the moment of accusation and inner doubt, and the moment of a final testing and proof of self.

In *John Doe,* these moments of hallucinatory space are interestingly divided between the active heroine and the much more passive hero. The moment of inspiration is Ann's as she sits down to write the initial John Doe letter. It is her moment of revenge for being fired and her ticket back into employment with a hefty bonus. As she sits at her typewriter, Capra and cameraman George Barnes collapse the space around her. The space darkens and becomes opaque, blending in with the black typewriter that separates us from her. Only her upper face, especially her forehead, glows above this black cloud. Following this shot is an extreme tilt with blurred background showing only her profile and her hands on the keys of the typewriter. The external context has been wiped out by the intensity of her private moment and her invention of the fiction that becomes the film's narrative. The reflexivity of the moment lends intensity to this hallucinatory moment.

Later in the film, after Long John has been chosen to play the protagonist in the drama, this acute space experience is transferred to his imagination. In the first instance, he relates to Ann a dream he has had about her. In the dream, Long John confuses himself with Ann's father, with whom, in fact, Ann has associated him in her construction of the ongoing fiction. The dream ends with a semierotic spanking administered by Long John/Ann's father/a priest to punish her for trying to marry Sheldon, Norton's rich nephew. In this moment of the dream's telling, Long John is all the figures who blend into one another. Ironically, she doesn't see that he has become what she has predicated. Spatially, the camera double-frames Long John sitting in the doorway to her room and watching her pack, with the door frame to his left and the figure of Beany (Irving Bacon) darkly framing him on the right. Capra contrasts his isolation with hers through a reverse angle shot from behind Long John's back into deep field where Ann packs her bag; her hair falls forward over her face, emblematic of her inattention to the authentic Long John.

This moment of transition, in turn, leads to Long John's loss of self in the intensely hallucinatory moment following the disastrous convention. Here, he walks toward the camera, replicating the backward track before him as he makes his way out of the convention stadium. But in this hallucinatory sequence, the mob surrounding him has been abstracted into the ghost images of severed heads superimposed on his space at oblique angles. These heads cry out insults in the black, opaque space around him. This black space recalls the blackened space of Ann's inspirational sequence as she types the initial story. The faces swirl as in a concentric watery medium around Long John, and the voices are disembodied, as though speaking out of his memory. The sequence of hallucinatory moments in *John Doe* resembles the sequence of moments in *Mr. Smith,* while emphasizing the complicity between the heroine and the villain, which causes Long John's black despair.

Linear Space

Linear space, like self-conscious space, is an umbrella term, covering several more specific techniques. All of these deepen and extend space so that the spectator is first drawn into the illusion of being in three-dimensional space, and then given the sense that the normal time dimension governing that space has been disturbed. Like Capra's creation of hallucinatory space, linear space constitutes extraordinary events and perceptions. What Capra does with linear space largely contradicts what André Bazin outlined as being true of deep-focus shots (one of the techniques that Capra uses to create linear space); Capra's linear space is fundamentally subjective and nonrational. It abrogates "realism" in favor of "perceptivity," the intensification of sight at the expense of the trivia and the full range of sensory data that realism implies. Linear space is space of intensified sight, which also implies insight or revelation.

The three particular techniques that often identify Capra's linear space are: (1) tracking behind a character into new space; (2) deep-focus, often complemented by a character moving through the space of the field or looking down a long table; and (3) a dialectic of deep and shallow shots or deep-focus shots with tracking.

Tracking Behind. When the camera tracks behind a character, there is generally some extraordinary reason for its movement. Capra, with his well-recognized genius for pacing a film, uses tracking in part to build up the tension in a scene: the distance through space implies a more lengthy treatment in time. Capra sometimes uses this lengthening of time to give a scene a chance to mature. For instance, when Tony (Stewart) is proposing to Alice Sycamore (Arthur) in *You Can't,* Alice's agitation leads them through the space of their offices. Tony follows her, and we follow him. We identify both with her agitation about Tony's lack of decorum in the office space and with his insistence that his love for her is appropriate anywhere. The camera's tracking and Capra's frequent reframings of the scene allow us the time for these identifications to develop, and they produce a spatial equivalence for the emotions of the characters we observe. Later in the film, the camera tracks behind Kirby, Sr. out the door of his office as he goes to finalize the merger that he has set in motion. But he is burdened by the earlier words of Grandpa Vanderhoff telling him that he can't take it with him, the words of the just-deceased Ramsey telling him the same thing, and the desertion of Tony from the family business. The track behind Kirby's stooped shoulders reinforces the burdens of conscience that Kirby carries. He is not allowed an easy escape from the camera. At another momentous time, the camera tracks behind Jefferson Smith as he walks for the first time into the Senate chamber. The tracking camera, as in the scene with Kirby, helps us to identify with the tension in the figure before us.

Deep Focus. More familiar in Capra's canon of techniques is the more static deep-focus shot. Here the character may move away from us into a new space, but the spectator watches from a stable position. This technique removes us to a more detached relation to the character, but it is also a more meditative stance. Often the deep-focus shot images depth of emotion: the character moves into space, as though requiring it for the extension of what he or she feels. The character's movement may depict this feeling, or it may relieve the character sufficiently so that the feeling can emerge in body language or words. Particular moments of disillusionment or despair seem to require deep-focus shots: when Deeds learns from Corny Cobb (Lionel Stander) that Mary Dawson is really the notorious reporter, Babe Bennett; when Saunders has just wised up Jefferson Smith about the graft in the Senate; when Kirby, Sr. spins Grandpa's harmonica down the long table in *You Can't Take It with You;* when Long John confronts Norton and Ann at opposite ends of the long table in Norton's office. In *Wonderful Life,* these shots characteristically exploit the topology of small-town life — the gate, the front walk up to the door, the frame house with its wide front porch. When George's brother Harry (Todd Karns) has married and once again left George in the lurch as manager of the Building and Loan, George faces his crisis at the front gate. In deep field behind, the newly wed couple and Mrs. Bailey can be seen framed by the front screen door. Later, George is framed by Mary's gate in deep focus down her walk, almost a reverse angle of the earlier shot, but one that watches George's movement into the house (and the domesticity of being contained in it) instead of away from the parental house. The corporate tables in *You Can't* and *John Doe* have given way to a different spatial metaphor in *Wonderful Life,* though Potter and familiar shots of George from over his shoulder still employ the surface of a table or desk as a means of separating the figures.

Dialectic of Deep and Shallow Fields or Deep Field and Tracking. Sometimes Capra defines and dramatizes depth in his compositions by deliberately posing it against shallowness of field (especially the dramatic close-up); or he may similarly oppose static depth to movement of the camera. Capra often uses the first technique as a spatial equivalent for the drama of conflicting impulses at a moment of decision. In *You Can't,* Kirby, Sr. goes up to finalize the merger in an elevator, which opens to reveal the corporate board table lined with executives, stretching deep into the field. Kirby remains paralyzed in the elevator. Capra cuts back and forth between close-ups of Kirby's face and deep-focus shots of the board table, either from behind Kirby or from before him representing his point of view. These sudden shifts of depth dramatize Kirby's inner division, especially his conflict between public and private realities and the great gap between them.

Perhaps intuitively recalling this scene when making *John Doe,* also with Edward Arnold as the representative of big business, Capra twice creates these dialectical moments with cameraman George Barnes. The first is Norton's moment of decision during Long John's first radio broadcast. In a beautifully choreographed long take, the camera first records Norton's deep-focus approach toward it down the hall from his office. The camera pans as Norton slightly opens the door to the servants' quarters and peers with him over his shoulder into their deep space as they listen enraptured to the John Doe address. Then, Norton closes the door and turns toward the camera into an extreme close-up. With a thoughtful look, he raises his hand into the frame; it is a gesture of having hit upon an idea. Norton smiles slightly and turns as the camera pans to the left to watch his transit back down the hall toward his office. On the soundtrack during this long take is Gary Cooper's voice appealing to his audience to help their neighbors and to tear down the fences that separate neighbor from neighbor.

Capra has intimately captured the moment when the fascist leader has seen his chance to exploit the public. He realizes this moment spatially by recording Norton's transits from his own isolation in elite office space to the shared space of his servants, and he prefigures Norton's manipulation of the public with his voyeuristic over-the-shoulder shot and his threatening extreme close-up. The close-up, in fact, is for the spectator's benefit, so that we might feel this threat. Later in the film, the focus of this dialectical shot shifts from Norton to Long John, who has recognized Norton's purposes to be self-serving. After a series of glance confrontations around the board table at Norton's home, medium shots of Long John and Ann alternate with deep-focus shots of the table with Norton standing at its end. The shifts in perspective, as was true in Kirby's confrontation with his own business cronies, vivify Long John's decision to oppose Norton and question Ann (though Capra aligns Ann with Long John and against Norton in the dialectic of his shots).

One has only to recall the decisive moments in George's life to locate these dialectical shots in *Wonderful Life.* At the moment following George's plea that the Building and Loan remain active following his father's death, Capra uses a continuous shot like the one dramatizing Norton's inspiration in *John Doe* to show George's first sacrificial decision. Coming into the outer office, he is pictured in deep field gathering up his suitcase. He moves toward the camera, though, as the board chairman emerges with their decision to keep the organization alive only if George will become its managing executive. Just as George swings into a close-up before the camera, the chairman says, "But George, they'll vote with Potter otherwise," and George freezes in that posture. The dialectical shot, which alternates between long shot and close-up or medium shot, is present when George and Mary are about to escape on their honeymoon. Here the close-up, though, is just a facsimile of a close-up: George and Mary's faces are double-framed in the rear window of Ernie's cab, and this static frame alternates with long shots of people running toward a mob in front of the bank and the Building and Loan. George leaves to see what is happening but Mary's face remains static in the rear window, dramatizing George's choice.

Unnatural Silence and Celebratory Sounds

Leaving those techniques I have grouped as linear space, we should consider Capra's innovation in auditory techniques; he knows, as a director, how to modulate presence and absence, whether it be light and dark, movement and stasis, or, in this case, noise and silence. In all these cases, Capra and his soundmen play against the spectator's expectations and thereby intensify the affective power of these techniques. Sometimes, they withhold, and thus titillate the spectator. Unnatural silence occurs in instances when the spectator expects or yearns for forthright speech, a scream, or a great noise. It is an auditory image for the muffling of the protagonist at a moment when he must speak or cry out to satisfy us. One has only to remember George Bailey's silent horror after his mother has denied his existence in *Wonderful Life,* or Mrs. Manville's silently suspenseful approach to the count when she intends to confess her identity in *Lady for a Day.*

Both silence and extreme noise oppose the celebratory sounds of song and of simple instruments. These celebratory moments are familiar to any viewer of Capra's films. His films often end with them: the wild dance to the harmonicas playing "Polly Wolly Doodle" at the end of *You Can't,* for example, and the communal singing of "Auld Lang Syne" at the end of *Wonderful Life.* The raucous, dance-like mobs that sweep Deeds off his feet and that dance in the Senate gallery at the close of *Mr. Smith* are part of the same impulse. Even the end of *John Doe,* gloomy as it is, resounds with the singing of Beethoven's "Ode to Joy" on the soundtrack. The celebratory moments in *Deeds* and *Doe* seem to come earlier in the films, when Longfellow still has his innocence unscorched and when Long John makes his one break for freedom before the ending. Longfellow on his tuba helps the town band play him off to the big city, and later he drums "Swanee River" on a garbage can during his courting exuberance. Long John plays a penny whistle in the door of a box car while the Colonel dances to the clack of the train on the tracks.

The Night Journey

Like hallucinatory space and linear space, the night journey is a composite of several techniques. But in this case, some combination of the techniques functions together to constitute this thematic sequence in the narrative. The night journey of the hero is a descent into a personal hell.[18] The paradigm for this journey is the time and space dislocation in *Wonderful Life* when George explores the contours of a world in which he never existed.[19] The premise, then, for this journey is the hero's sudden and terrible loss of identity and his Dante-like search for some new and renewing means to measure his worth.

The night journey is familiar in Capra's "divine comedy" films: Mr. Smith sitting in the shadows of the pillars of the Lincoln Memorial; Mr. Deeds shadowed by the bars on the window of the county hospital's mental ward; Long John walking through the hallucinatory space of his nightmare sequence. But Capra also constructs *Lost Horizon* and *Bitter Tea* around the loss of ordinary reality. In *Bitter Tea*, Megan loses the old sureties when her fiancé plunges her into the midst of civil war. The nightmarish realities of this war punctuate the rest of her initiation: the gunfire of an executioner's squad awakens her on her

The George Bailey character, played by James Stewart in Capra's *It's a Wonderful Life*, undergoes a trial of his own non-existence, a kind of night journey. His friends, played by Ward Bond and Frank Faylen, frame him here before he explores his dark house.

first morning at Yen's palace; she pits her own safety against Mah-Li's loyalty and is betrayed.

In *Lost Horizon,* the two journeys through the Himalayan mountains and the blizzards punctuate Conway's initiation into the nonviolent ethic of Shangri-La. These snow journeys look on the screen like negatives of the photographic images of Capra's other night journeys. Instead of black, chaotic compositions (the hallucinatory space of *John Doe,* the turbulent waters in which George plans to drown in *Wonderful Life*), the snow journeys in *Lost Horizon* are white and involuted, but they act in the same way: to disorient and displace the initiate. Like a Turner painting, in which the cosmos appears to be animate, all that the hero once took for granted as stable and benign assumes a malign will of its own. The animate cosmos about the hero is, of course, an externalized image of his own inner turmoil; its externalization depicts an essentially psychological threat for the film spectator.

Psychologically the night journey corresponds to an initiation rite, and to a ritual sacrifice that appeases an angry god. It has implications both for the individual and his personal growth and for the ultimate well-being of the community. At the beginning of this trial and sacrifice, the initiate thinks only of escape: Deeds wants to escape Mary/Babe's betrayal by retreating inside himself; Jeff Smith wants to escape back to the simplicity of his Boy Ranger life; Long John wants to retrieve the simplicity of being a bum riding the rails; George Bailey wants to escape his responsibilities to his family and town. They are all men in desperate pain from disillusionment or despair. Conway must escape Shangri-La to know its value, which is true of Capra's other heroes as well. In a mythic sense, they all must "try on" death in order to rediscover the value of life.[20] George Bailey's experience of this death and rebirth in *Wonderful Life* is a parable of the same mythic movement of the other Capra heroes. And *Lost Horizon* is a parable that, to me, does not work, because it lacks all but tenuous connections to ordinary reality.

The night journey defines one of Capra's recurrent visions of space. He intensifies space in these sequences by fragmenting it. One method he uses, the swirling vortex, has already been mentioned. In this vision of space, Capra abandons verticals and horizontals, and he wars with the squareness of the film frame itself. The image is circular, and it spirals outward from or inward toward the center. The second method that Capra uses to fragment space involves multiplying the verticals or horizontals to cut the space of the frame into bits or to darken it. The effect is to scatter and distribute the hero's image into these separate bits or shadows, as do the bars in *Mr. Deeds* and the pillars in *Mr. Smith.*

Also characteristic of these sequences are extreme angles. For instance, the camera from a high angle cranes behind the pillars of the Lincoln Memorial as Jeff Smith takes up his bags and sits in the shadows. Capra and cameramen Joseph Walker and Joseph Biroc are extremely expressionistic when they create George Bailey's night journey in *Wonderful Life.* They transform Main

Street during his loss-of-identity nightmare. With quick cuts that also fragment space, they flash the neon signs of nightclubs, bars, and dance joints at
odd angles onto the screen. The shots are also unnaturally close to depict
George's disorientation as he takes in the "Pottersville" version of Bedford
Falls. To portray the Chinese civil war in the opening sequences of *Bitter Tea,*
Capra and film editor Edward Curtis superimpose running mobs across each
other at angles, showing one darkened image dissolving into another.

Sacred Spaces

Capra establishes some spaces in his films as sacred by framing the space
and usually by double-framing it; he also expresses the hero's reverence for it,
usually through the hero's posture and tone of voice. *Mr. Smith,* Capra's film
most filled with sacred spaces, features the doubly framed shots of the temple-
like structures of the District of Columbia, especially the Capitol dome and the
Lincoln Memorial. Capra is not altogether sentimental here; he argues for the
sentiment and tests the reverential postures of his heroes in the most severe
way.

The focus of sacredness for Capra is on the worshipper, not on that which is
worshipped. It is a subjective state of mind, and it fluctuates with the hero's
imaginative and generative powers. Grant's Tomb in *Mr. Deeds* does not constitute a sacred space, but in Longfellow Deeds's telling of Grant's life he creates a
sacred space of belief for the heroine and himself. The devoted heroine's posture depicts Mary Dawson's reverence for Longfellow's reverence for a country
that would allow a farm boy to become the President. The layering of reverence, in each case for something immaterial in the object or the person re-
vered, characterizes these sacred spaces. This reverence, especially for some
specific person instead of a process, could become unbearably sentimental if
Capra were inviting it literally and directly. But he always approaches these
sacred spaces indirectly and leaves them lacking closure. The scene between
Deeds and Mary at Grant's Tomb, for example, loses its intensity when Deeds
becomes self-conscious. His sudden shyness reminds us of our spectatorship of
an intensely private moment, so that we excuse the sentimentality: we weren't
meant to witness the scene, but the fact that we did intensely privileges us.

Capra's technique in *Mr. Smith* can be compared with George Cukor's technique in the Judy Holliday vehicle, *Born Yesterday,* which features the same
Washington milieu and attends to some of the same Washington corruption.
But in Cukor's film, the significance of these spaces emanates from character,
especially from Holliday's innocent patriotism. Holliday's candor thankfully
tempers her patriotism, but the Washington spaces are still static and uncom-
plex. In *Mr. Smith,* the treatment of space is dynamic, changing registers with
the narrative's progress. Unlike the tourist point of view in Cukor's montage of
Washington's monuments, Capra always uses these sites as a way of measuring

the character's development. His characters see these sacred spaces differently when they gain more insight into themselves and others.

When Jefferson Smith returns to the Lincoln Memorial after his false accusation by Senator Paine, he no longer sees a black man gazing up at an idealized Lincoln statue or a little boy reading the Gettysburg Address. Instead, Jeff is alone on his second pilgrimage and the statue is father-stern. A point-of-view shot dollies forward to the last words of the Gettysburg Address: "That this nation under God shall have a new birth of freedom and that government of the people by the people for the people shall not perish from the earth." A new birth is precisely what Jeff needs himself, and he finds it, not in the public interior of the temple-like monument with its oversized proportions, but on the shadowy outer edge where the pillars shadow him and where Clarissa Saunders can approach him.

Capra's sacred space is symbolic space made personal. It is not worshipped for its own sake. In most of Capra's narratives, sacred space is subordinated to character. In *You Can't*, the suggestion that the Vanderhoff family lives in their house because Alice's grandmother lived there is displaced by the need of the family to be with the living Alice. And the sacredness attending Harry Bailey's return from the war in *Wonderful Life* is lent instead to the celebration of George's return to life.

Slicing the Frame

Capra occasionally slices the frame spatially into separate realms in order to dramatize a spiritual or emotional gulf between two characters. This spatial separation occurs in *Wonderful Life* when George and his guardian angel first confront each other in the bridge-control house. They are drying their clothes, and the clothesline slices the frame at a diagonal between Clarence in mid-field on the left top of the frame and George in the foreground at the bottom right. Clarence is just hatching his idea that George be shown what the world would have been like if he had never been born. Once this plan has been set in action, the boundary between them is breached. In fact, George, as a non-being, is part only of a spiritual realm. He has been forced to try out the omniscience of death and non-being that Clarence is a part of (having died some two hundred years earlier).

In *Lost Horizon*, Conway and the High Lama are similarly separated in the frame by the presence of a large candlestick and candle. Again, the implication is that the two occupy distinct spiritual realms. Conway's newly acquired peace of mind has not been tried either by emotional doubt or physical trial. An earlier prototype for these instances is present in *You Can't*, when Tony and his father stand back to back in the jail cell, son listening to but rejecting his father's arrogance toward the other men being held. Posture and the vertical bars of the cell slice the frame and suggest that the characters inhabit separate spaces.

Direct Look of Closure

In several of Capra's best films, a character looks us directly in the eye with a smile as the film ends. This character seems to acknowledge, welcome, and thank us for our presence as film spectators. It is also a look that acknowledges our complicity in the celebratory ending: the spectator has wished for it — the spectator has gotten it. This acknowledgment is not as extreme as the last shot of Haskell Wexler's *Medium Cool,* where the film audience feels that it is being sucked into the camera's eye as we move closer and closer to the camera, wielded by Wexler himself. But Wexler's use of this technique originates in the same impulse on the part of the director, namely to invite the spectators to participate. However, as in Wexler's finger-pointing closure, the narrative threatens to become brittle at this point. Its infrastructure becomes suddenly visible, and our extra-sight threatens to reveal more than we want to see. Wexler, in an elaborate parody of blindness, allows us a retreat into the cave-like eye of the camera, while continuing to inform us on the sound track of his fictional characters' fates. Capra's use of the direct look of closure is much more gentle. It is like the genial sideways glance of a professor at the especially bright student to see if the latter has made the connection or caught the humor.

In *You Can't,* the direct look is given by Grandpa Vanderhoff (Lionel Barrymore) as the camera watches him, seated at the opposite end of the dinner table (a familiar icon in Capra's films), framed by family members on either side. Grandpa has been a sort of Prospero/director figure in the film, so that this direct look comes as no surprise. His direct look acknowledges a certain arbitrariness about the ending as well. That the Kirbys should have joined the dinner table does not surprise or ruffle Grandpa; his final look and half-wink assure us of the ordinariness of the scene.

In *Mr. Smith,* the Senate president (Harry Carey, Sr.) sends us off with a smile. Here, more so than in most of Capra's films, closure has come upon us suddenly. Since Jeff Smith is buried beneath the letters and telegrams, we have only to witness Saunders and Diz's celebratory dance in the gallery and then the president's shrug when he cannot regain order. Here, the direct look is an invitation to us to join the celebrants, and again it is given by the benevolent father figure who so often acts as a surrogate for the film's creators.

In *Wonderful Life,* George Bailey (James Stewart) gives the final direct look. But throughout this film, we have been sharing the cosmic viewpoint of God and his angels. Clarence has made his omnipresence felt in this final scene by leaving a copy of *Tom Sawyer* among the gifts and by advertising his promotion to first-class angel when the bell rings on the tree. So when George winks and faces us, he acknowledges Clarence and our complicity with that divine point of view at work in the narrative.[21]

Capra's direction of films mobilizes his spectators so that the space he and his cinematographers create resonates, not only with the intense self-consciousness of his characters, but also with ours. It is certainly possible to resent those demands being made on us, because they assume a certain warmth and intimacy that we may not always embrace. If his heroes undergo trials, so do his spectators, due to the way he manipulates us as witnesses.

If Capra were a psychologist (not that he isn't!), he would not be a behaviorist. His model for human behavior implies deep sources of both suffering and inspiration. His creation of hallucinatory space and of night journeys attempts to embody spatially the most profound divisions and fears in his protagonists' psyches. These techniques often challenge what Capra would see as an artificial boundary between waking reality and dreams. By creating acute space moments in those techniques I have called linear space, Capra inverts what he has done in the highly internalized hallucinatory space and night journeys. Instead of projecting what is inside his protagonists' heads onto external space, he isolates his figures by deepening the space they occupy. By doing so, Capra often dramatizes a decision or moment of understanding rather than the suffering preceding them.

While I am reluctant to propose too schematic an analysis of Capra's film space, most of his techniques describe one or another stage in his protagonists' development. In his use of sacred space, for instance, what is sacred and how it is sacred varies with the complexity of the character's self-image. A simplistic idealism is transformed into something more complex, less self-righteous, and more pragmatic. Thus the definition of what is sacred and why it might be thought of in this way evolves in each film. Also, I tend to arrange some of Capra's techniques sequentially, matching them with phases of each protagonist's growth. While witnessing of various sorts spans the entire growth process, the oppressiveness of the standing-men frame tends to come early in a film, the devoted heroine posture to emerge in the middle, and celebratory sound and direct looks of closure to mark the end. While not predictable, the recurrence of these techniques lends a satisfying wholeness of vision to Capra's film space.

NOTES

1. Glenn Robert Lym, *A Psychology of Building: How We Shape and Experience Our Structural Spaces* (Englewood Cliffs, N.J.: Prentice-Hall, 1980), p. 9.

2. Ibid.

3. See Charles J. Maland's description of this scene in *Frank Capra* (Boston: Twayne, 1980), pp. 70–71.

4. Lym, *A Psychology of Building*, p. 10.

5. Leland A. Poague compares *Bitter Tea*'s look to the look of Sternberg's films (*Cinema of Frank Capra*, p. 138), as does Maland (*Frank Capra*, p. 75).

6. Lym, *A Psychology of Building*, p. 3.

7. Lym, *A Psychology of Building*, p. 4.

8. Jean Piaget and Barbel Inhelder, *The Child's Conception of Space*, trans. F. J. Langdon and J. L. Lunzer (London: Routledge and Kegan Paul, 1956), pp. 37–43, 76–79, as discussed by Christian Norberg-Schulz in *Existence, Space, and Architecture* (New York: Praeger, 1971), pp. 17–18.

9. Erving Goffman discusses a "back region" or "backstage" where, he says, "the

suppressed facts make an appearance," in *The Presentation of Self in Everyday Life* (Woodstock, N.Y.: Overlook Press, 1973), p. 112.

10. Poague comments on the new presence of a deified narrator in this film and its implications (*Cinema of Frank Capra,* p. 206).

11. Richard Griffith, in his essay "Capra's Early Films," asserts that Gallagher is "the prototype of the several Capra heroines, customarily acted by Jean Arthur or Barbara Stanwyck, whose whimsical tough-mindedness cures the hero of delusions about himself or others" (Glatzer and Raeburn, *Frank Capra,* p. 55).

12. Maland comments on Joseph Walker's lighting effects in *Mr. Smith* (*Frank Capra,* p. 108).

13. There may be a corresponding father/son theme in *You Can't, Mr. Smith* (Jefferson Smith and Senator Paine), and *Wonderful Life*. For an exploration of that theme in the latter film, see Robin Wood, "Ideology, Genre, Auteur: On *It's a Wonderful Life* and *Shadow of a Doubt," Film Comment* 13 (1977): 49.

14. Robert B. Ray discusses this sequence in terms of the opposition between adventure and domesticity in *A Certain Tendency of the Hollywood Cinema, 1930–1980* (Princeton, N.J.: Princeton Univ. Press, 1985), pp. 190–192.

15. See Capra's comment on this scene in the interview by Glatzer, in Glatzer and Raeburn, *Frank Capra,* p. 39.

16. In the interview with Glatzer, Capra discusses his attitude toward faces: "I love faces, I love to look at people, and I think others do too — all kinds of people, walking in and out" (Glatzer and Raeburn, *Frank Capra,* pp. 28–29).

17. See Poague's complex discussion of these ambivalences (*Cinema of Frank Capra,* pp. 138–144).

18. Stephen Handzo identifies the likeness of *Wonderful Life* to Dante's *Divine Comedy* and its inversion of the Faust myth in his essay "Under Capracorn" (Glatzer and Raeburn, *Frank Capra,* p. 175).

19. Maland contrasts Pottersville with Bedford Falls very effectively, considering lighting, sets, acting, composition, camera movement, music, sound effects, and editing (*Frank Capra,* pp. 148–150). Richard Griffith, on the other hand, feels that "the shifts of mood between the naturalistic and the fantastic are too abrupt, and there are too many of them"; see *"It's a Wonderful Life* and Post-War Realism," in Glatzer and Raeburn, *Frank Capra,* p. 162.

20. See Poague's discussion of "the mythological sequences of death and rebirth" in comedy and in Capra's films (*Cinema of Frank Capra,* pp. 27, 227).

21. Ray believes that the ending of *Wonderful Life* is only "superficially optimistic" (*A Certain Tendency,* pp. 182, 215).

4

Lubitsch's Film Space: Implying Space to Stimulate the Imagination

Considering Ernst Lubitsch, one inevitably begins with the "Lubitsch touch"—a phrase around which Lubitsch scholars congregate or come to blows.[1] Herman Weinberg defined this touch as both an attitude and a method, and that's probably why the richness of the phrase draws others back to it. Weinberg pointed out that Lubitsch could "reveal people to us," especially "their foibles and weaknesses, vanities, desires, dreams, illusions," but that Lubitsch did so gently: "he was content not to scratch the surface of his characters too deeply."[2] The "Lubitsch touch" stands for that focal point where one can no longer, even as an exercise, distinguish form and content (though we've always wondered why our mentors kept doing it anyway). It suggests Lubitsch's elusiveness,[3] his reflexivity,[4] his playfulness,[5] and his irony.[6] Perhaps it even suggests his sexiness,[7] though the indirectness of the sexiness in his films is not likely to satisfy everyone's taste.

I must confess that I'm enamored of Lubitsch's indirectness, perhaps for the same reasons I love Austen's ironies and Barbara Pym's layered social perspectives. Lubitsch sometimes employs the socially layered world of the comedy of manners, and he loves the interplay between the outright verbal messages of his characters and the underlying play of tensions and passions. The character with whom Lubitsch most closely identifies is often the most sophisticated or observant—the Belinski of *Cluny Brown* (1946), the Monescu/LaValle of *Trouble in Paradise* (1932), or Count Leon D'Algout in *Ninotchka* (1939)—though these figures often complement a more active and naive figure (Cluny, Madame Colet, or Ninotchka). Lubitsch likes the dynamic interplay between the worldliness of one character (often with an amoral flavor) and the empathy or naiveté of another.[8]

Lubitsch's creation of film space relies on the indirection characteristic of his narrative sensibility. Lubitsch is intent upon keeping us from seeing things so directly that we might take them for granted: this fear of making things too obvious or too routine causes him to adopt a teasing, playful, or ironic attitude toward us, his audience. His use of space often depends upon what we can't yet see or what we anticipate, what we see but don't hear, or what we infer from a fragment of the object or a symbol standing for it. Of course, Lubitsch is not above using well-worn techniques of farce. Certainly his timing, his use of repetitive comic actions, and his manipulation of props owe much to this most energetic branch of comedy. I don't find these spatial techniques to be in conflict, because they all draw upon a coherent response in the audience. They require, first, that we be uninhibited and, second, that we be imaginative. The more purely farcical techniques probably draw upon the first of these responses, though the physical quality of farce requires empathic participation. (Is there a physical kind of imagining that invites our participation in farce?) All of Lubitsch's acute space techniques rely upon what I will call implied space; they suggest that what we actually see is incomplete or that it stands for something else or something more.

HABITUAL SPACE

But Lubitsch also creates habitual space that is less intense. We find his habitual space in a greater proportion to acute space in his later films, such as *Heaven Can Wait* (1943) and *Cluny Brown* (1946). The larger proportion of habitual space to acute space in these films makes them, not just less sharply ironic, but also gentler and more narrative in a linear way. I can't bring myself to attach a favorable valuation to one of these groups or to exclude the other as inferior. They simply produce different aesthetic effects. The earlier films, such as *Trouble in Paradise* (1932) and *Design for Living* (1933), are more elliptical; Lubitsch takes greater chances with the narratives and with the spatial shifts from place to place. The resulting speed of the narrative complements the acute space techniques that follow each other so furiously in these films.

The gentler narratives of *Heaven* and *Cluny* may result, in part, from their concentration on the exploration of a single sensibility, Henry's in *Heaven* and Cluny's in the other. *To Be or Not To Be* (1942), coming just one year before *Heaven,* has excruciating tensions in the narrative that are often embodied acutely in the film space. Studios may be an important variable with Lubitsch and his writers, though he worked for nearly all of them — Warner Brothers, United Artists, Paramount, Metro-Goldwyn-Mayer. But he had never worked for Twentieth-Century Fox until those last two films.

In both of these final films, Lubitsch conveys his sensibility more through the scripts, especially in the mischievous energy of Henry and Cluny, than in spatial terms. When Henry, for example, is being questioned by the devil at the beginning of *Heaven Can Wait,* Henry believes himself qualified for damnation because "I can safely say that my whole life was one continuous misdemeanor." Cluny, who has an uncontrollable impulse to fix faulty plumbing, explains the failure of her engagement to the town pharmacist: "He said, with his standing in the community, he cannot afford a wife who is subject to impulses either to pipes or to himself." While Lubitsch's acute space is not altogether absent from these films, the narratives are less often punctuated by their surprising visual jolts.

ACUTE SPACE

Lubitsch's acute film space relies upon techniques that imply more than they show. It supposes that imagined space is more real than actual space (pragmatic or utilitarian space). Anyone studying aesthetics understands what lies behind this assumption — that Van Gogh's sunflowers capture more of the essence of sunflower than do real ones, which pale in comparison. A fear on the part of artists about too great a striving toward lifelikeness springs from the fear that this "realism" might distract them from grasping essentials or from attending to the unseen implications of an action. But in making a film, where an illusion of three-dimensional space provides the medium and where what is filmed *is* actual, the director faces a new challenge: how might he or she enhance reality when the medium is external? One means by which Lubitsch transcends the mundane is by inviting the spectator to create the transcendent reality. To do this, he provides us either with a surrogate screen or with a fragment from a larger unseen puzzle. We are asked to imagine the unseen.[9]

The Threshold Response

The threshold response is a familiar one in our daily lives. Don't we have an impulse to pause or change our pace as we pass through a door? Partly, this change is simply cautionary. We allow for the person who may be on the other side, passing by, or for our imagined mirror image opening the door from the other side. But thresholds, like doors and arches, are also charged with the tension between the territories that they separate, especially where each territory promotes different assumptions about behavior. There is, at my own university, a door that separates a hall with some faculty offices from a second hall lined with classrooms. On one side of the door, the system of conventions demands quiet, a hesitant pace, certain formal greetings when a faculty member passes, whereas on the other side of the door students scurry in and out, some sprawl outside classrooms, others make scurrilous remarks about a difficult exam just taken. The classroom hall is noisy and lively. The door partitions off the office territory, though it is open to anyone in the classroom hall, and a glass panel next to it even makes it somewhat visible from the classroom hall.

But students unconsciously observe this threshold, maintaining the privacy of the faculty hallway. To some extent, they feel themselves to be intruders in this space, just as I catch my breath with a "Here we go again" sigh as I move toward an early morning class through that door into "their" territory. Or, as a faculty member, I find myself looking away from those animated conversations as I leave class, feeling that my role excludes me from projecting my gaze into their space.

To create implied space, Lubitsch exploits these threshold responses. Whatever our feelings may be about being intruders in a space, about belonging in a space, or about defending the conventions that govern a space, Lubitsch magnifies them. His object is to make us at least semiconscious of these pauses, for he uses them to tap our fears and our confidence. He jettisons us out of habitual space and into the vividness of acute space.

One of Lubitsch's familiar strategies is to exploit the pause that often occurs at a threshold.[10] His focusing of the camera on doors reportedly led Mary Pickford to fire Lubitsch from his first American film. She is said to have exclaimed, "Doors! He's a director of doors! Nothing interests him but doors!"[11] Lubitsch does often seem to abandon the spectator at the door,[12] but he wishes to force the spectator to imagine the scene on the other side of that threshold. Part of his premise is that what is imagined is better than what is seen. In this sense, Lubitsch trusts that the spectator has just as vivid and probably as lascivious an imagination as he does. Lubitsch exploits the threshold's power to titillate. This power depends upon the pleasure of anticipating pleasure. There is a wonderful description of this state of mind in George Eliot's *The Mill on the Floss*. Eliot describes Stephen and Lucy's courtship and the pleasure they feel in not yet being engaged. Lubitsch wants to make these pauses both luxurious and frustrating, the combination of the two defining his use of our threshold response.

Lubitsch often uses the threshold response when a fuller development of the scene might spoil the tone of the comedy. For instance, in *The Shop Around the Corner* (1940), the camera tracks back through the furniture-draped office with Mr. Matuschek (Frank Morgan) after he discovers from a detective that his wife is having an affair. But it stops as he goes into his office. The pause and wait before Pepi (William Tracy) enters and prevents his suicide is ominous, because Lubitsch puts us through a second track back to his office door. But we don't enter the office; we only see the bullet hit one of the light fixtures, which is framed in the top part of the door. The comedy contains a suicide attempt, but the spectator of comedy does not participate in the physical preparations for it or in the despair that frames the action itself. Instead, we remain on the comic side of the door, anticipating the rescue and feeling frustration at Pepi's slow progress. Here Lubitsch exploits the tension felt at the threshold between wanting to enter the office and see what goes on and not wanting to enter and see.

In more lascivious contexts, as when the camera waits outside the bedrooms

In Lubitsch's *Ninotchka,* Greta Garbo's glum Soviet character watches as Melvyn Douglas's sophisticated European takes a fall. This occurs just before Garbo's famous laughter. Spatially the restaurant is divided by the half-wall behind Garbo, which creates a threshold for Douglas's character.

and office on the stair landing in *Trouble in Paradise,* or outside the royal suite when the Russians are receiving the attentions of cigarette girls in *Ninotchka,* Lubitsch more often frustrates our prurient wish to see. He thus inflates the sexual innuendo.[13] For instance, in *Ninotchka,* we hear the merrymaking as its volume and confusion increase from the hall, and we watch the first cigarette girl enter, leave, and reappear with two more girls. The restraint of the slight pan to watch them travel down the hall and joyfully enter reflects our feelings of restraint about being abandoned in the hall. We would like to sweep into the suite and join them, abandoning altogether our distanced positions as spectators.

Lubitsch frustrates us for several reasons: (1) to make us at least semiconscious of our role as spectators; (2) to stimulate our imaginations; (3) to implicate us in the less than admirable behavior of his characters. He relies on the fact that we will participate more in his fictional world through our unsatisfied desires than we will by being allowed to join the jovial crew, because we are made to admit the desires we have in common with the characters. Every child knows that what is forbidden must be worthy of attention. And Lubitsch calls upon this sort of logic in us. Often Lubitsch does not allow the frustration to go unrewarded. It almost immediately explodes into laughter in *That Uncertain Feeling* (1941) when Sebastian (Burgess Meredith) and Jill (Merle Oberon) flirt at the piano. The threshold response occurs when Jill leans toward Sebastian, the camera dollies up to the two, but she pulls back out of the frame and so denies us a clear view of the climax to their approach. But Lubitsch has Sebastian return to the frame almost immediately and play joyfully, suggesting the exhilarating effect of their unseen contact. That evokes our knowing laughter. Lubitsch has led us through the threshold response but let us participate in the fun of our own duping.

Lubitsch often exploits these threshold responses by leading us to believe we want to see the unseen when there is nothing to see. He deflates our false expectations, laughing at and making us laugh at our foibles. For instance, in *So This Is Paris* (1926), Lubitsch has Suzanne (Patsy Ruth Miller) and Paul Giraud (Monte Blue) look out her window and at the window across the street. There she sees the top half of Maurice Lalle (André Beranger), who appears to be naked. To disguise her sexual interest (as much from herself as from her husband), Suzanne sends Paul across the street to "demand satisfaction," her anger displacing her excitement. But Suzanne's foibles simply reflect the spectator's. In the first scene of the film, Lubitsch has shown us a luridly melodramatic battle between a turbanned man and an exotic woman on a curtained bed covered with silks and brocades and piled high with pillows. Then the camera pans casually to the left across an implied threshold to show a piano player, giving the cue to the players to relax. Suzanne's attraction to the turbanned, naked man only exemplifies our own attraction to this kind of melodramatic fiction: Lubitsch implicates us as spectators before we meet Suzanne or Paul or participate in their desires.

This threshold response can be drawn out; that is, the transition from one space to another under a different aegis can challenge our temporal as well as our spatial instincts. Our frustration rises in *Ninotchka* both because we are spatially cut off from the merrymaking and because we watch the cigarette girls cross the threshold without restraint. Our watching them mounting the stairs to the landing and then making their way (the camera pans slightly to accommodate the motion) down the hall depends upon Lubitsch's use of the fourth dimension of space, time. Similarly, in *Trouble in Paradise*, we watch Gaston Monescu, alias M. LaValle (Herbert Marshall), after his encounter with Adolf Giron (C. Aubrey Smith), which exposes his identity as a thief, running up and down the stairs and up again to meet Madame Colet (Kay Francis), who is now also aware of his identity. As the narrative accelerates, so do Gaston's transits — this staircase and the landing at the top being the spatial locus of his sexual charm from the beginning of his relationship with Madame Colet. The revelations to all concerned of what everyone knows are delayed while his activity within the spatial territory of the threshold accelerates.

When exaggerated by time, the threshold response gains more power over

In Lubitsch's *To Be or Not To Be,* the Jack Benny character in the midst of Hamlet's soliloquy watches the Robert Stack character leave his audience. The Benny character is caught behind the threshold of the stage and of the prompter (Edgar Licho); the dramatic role that normally boosts his ego ironically begins to subdue it.

us. This power intensifies our responses. Toward the end of the framed fiction of *Heaven Can Wait,* the camera returns us to the sickroom door after Henry's son, his son's wife, and the doctor move on along the landing. We are privileged to hear about Henry's erotic dream and to see Gene Tierney's Martha reincarnated in the body of the night nurse. We finally withdraw from the closed door thinking not in apocalyptic, but rather in satisfied, smug terms about Henry's death. Lubitsch's thresholds are not just restraining barriers; they define, empower, and teach.

Ironic Space

Lubitsch habitually challenges the spectator's complacency. He first creates an extremely fluid space that soothes our complacency. Then, by introducing tension or an incongruous element into this complacently felt space, he explodes our lazy enjoyment. And this little explosion or epiphany for the spectator may be wickedly ignored by Lubitsch. The basic fluidity of the space he is exploring may remain undisturbed. Lubitsch thus creates a space that is ironic.[14] Like ironic language, it depends on a basic discrepancy between our expectations and reality.[15] But, just as a wit may deliver verbal irony with straight-faced adroitness, ironic space never registers the spectator's perception of incongruity (what Koestler calls the Aha or Haha responses[16]).

It takes us a minute to register that the man debarking from the gondola at the beginning of *Trouble in Paradise* and carrying a bucket back to it is a garbage collector. Lubitsch never breaks his stride in his shooting of the scene, even when a closer high-angle shot reveals the contents of the bucket dumped onto a pile of refuse. Later, Lubitsch has the garbage collector glide by singing "O Sole Mio" as he poles through the moonlit Venetian canals. The rich ironies of the scene, the trash and the sappy song, establish the discrepancies that make "trouble in paradise" seem probable. Lubitsch cuts from this scene to the next, in which the sound of an alarm-like door buzzer dominates a shadowy scene from which we see a thief making his escape.[17]

Lubitsch often creates ironic space at the beginning of his films to establish his ironic premises, to expose the contradictions inherent in reality, or to reveal the disguised truths beneath the surface appearance of a scene. Just as he juxtaposes trash with romance in *Trouble in Paradise,* for instance, he sets capitalist luxury against socialist simplicity in *Ninotchka* when he has the three emissaries of the USSR wander into the height of Parisian luxury, the Hotel Clarence, and book a suite. Again, Lubitsch creates his irony spatially. The film begins with a long track behind the tuxedo-clad hotel manager (Rolfe Sedan) through the lobby of the hotel, until he pauses amazed by the vision of the three comrades (Felix Bressart, Alexander Granach, and Sig Rumann) consecutively surveying the lobby by riding the revolving door in and then out again. The third comrade does not even pause to inspect the scene. Lubitsch thus positions the needy wonder of the materially deprived comrades against the point of view of the sophisticated manager, whose wonder is aroused by their naiveté, and he prepares the spectator for the duplication of this tension between Greta Garbo's Ninotchka and Melvyn Douglas's Count D'Algout. But by having us first identify with the hotel manager, Lubitsch also associates our perspective with the more sophisticated observer, the one who can understand and be amused by the irony.

An elaborately choreographed sequence such as the one at the start of *The Love Parade* (1929) contains several reversals of expectations, first from thinking that the jealous woman is threatening her husband to realizing that Maurice Chevalier is her lover, and then from thinking that she has shot herself when her real husband enters to having her real husband forgive her as she is resurrected. The threesome parts amiably after playing out a variety of melodramatic roles. And with each new scenario, the irony deepens. One identifies with the ironic master in the scene, Chevalier's count (later prince), since he wraps up the dramas by placing the gun back in a drawer with ten others and fixes the lady's zipper when her husband cannot.

Sometimes Lubitsch creates ironic space by structuring space like a joke. Jokes require a wit, a straight man, and an audience.[18] Ironic space requires either Lubitsch and his writers' sensibility, as in the scene described above, or a character's sensibility substituting for it; a straight man as butt of the irony; and the film's spectators. This strategy is apparent at the start of *Design for Living* (1933), when Miriam Hopkins's Gilda is Lubitsch's surrogate and Herbert Marshall's Tom Chambers and Gary Cooper's George Curtis are the straight men. The space itself encompasses the irony, because the scene is essentially silent and because Gilda sits in the enclosed space of a train compartment with the two men opposite her and draws comic pictures of them while they sleep. The two men, when they awaken, examine Gilda as she sleeps, but the drawings have given her sensibility the edge. Later in the scene, the two men lean forward into her frame, spatially suggesting her ascendancy.

Later in *Design for Living*, the charged space of the men's apartment becomes ironic when Tom leaves for the London debut of his play and George and Gilda awkwardly confront each other and their sexual needs in this space. The camera records their entrance as a just-constituted couple into the apartment through the window, panning to the left when Gilda steps onto the balcony. We watch tensely as the two pace in opposite directions, until finally Gilda states the inevitable: "It's true we have a gentleman's agreement, but unfortunately I am no gentleman." Spatially she marks their capitulation by laying herself on the couch. Lubitsch makes this event ironic in a spatial way by paralleling her spatial surrender to her earlier arrival in the apartment when both men were present. Then, she threw herself prone on the couch and a great cloud of dust billowed from it. In that scene, she declared her love for both men and the gentleman's agreement to "forget sex" was forged. By building scene upon scene, Lubitsch invests the space itself with irony.

Lubitsch probably learned to create ironic space as a director of silent films. As simple a strategy as the sliding of a foot into a sock with a hole in the toe in *The Marriage Circle* (1924) establishes ironic space shared by a discontented couple. This may be compared to the elaborately ironic space in *So This Is Paris*, the space of the Artists' Ball.[19] Paul Giraud (Monte Blue) finds himself increasingly at a disadvantage, the butt of Lubitsch's sensibility, in this space. It is dominated by pillars in the shape of giant women's legs, with a curtain fringe above suggesting the hem of a flapper's skirt. As soon as Paul enters this space with Georgette (Lilyan Tashman), he begins to shrink in stature to match the premises of the space. And when he wakens the next day to a new set of rules at home, Lubitsch makes his diminution spatial by shrinking him to quarter-size as he follows his wife. She has just declared on a title card, "From now on I'm the Big Boss, and you'll be the short-end of this marriage." The creation of ironic space in Lubitsch's films almost always dramatizes these power shifts among characters or between Lubitsch and his spectators, as in the garbage collector/gondolier juxtaposition.

Synecdoche

Synecdoche is one kind of implied space in Lubitsch's films. As is true of the figure of speech, a part of something stands for the whole. But in its use in a visual medium, synecdoche becomes a means of depriving the spectator of the whole so that he or she might be a more active participant; instead of creating a more tactile and physical reality as the figure of speech does, synecdoche in film withholds a complete and literal view of the scene. The goal, then, of film synecdoche is to abstract the spectator from the "what" of what happens: synecdoche, like other forms of implied space, is a distancing device that makes the space acute by making it more intensely felt. And as is true of any of these iconographic strategies, synecdoche always depends on the narrative context for its effectiveness.

One of the most effective uses of synecdoche in American film occurs in Preston Sturges's *Sullivan's Travels* when Sully (Joel McCrea) is unfairly sentenced to a chain gang. He and his fellow prisoners attend the showing of a cartoon at the nearby black church, and, as they file into the pews, the camera (set on the level of the floor) frames only their legs and chains. The black congregation sings "Let My People Go." The comic equivalent of this moment might be the frenzied ball in *So This Is Paris* when Lubitsch first sections the dancers into parts — legs and midriffs. Then, he sets the superimposed images in motion so that the multiple images swirl around the frame in a clockwise motion.

In *Trouble in Paradise,* the spectator is first prepared for an ironic reality with the garbage collector poling his way through a picture-postcard Venice. But the sudden cut to a darkened room and the repeated use of synecdoche in the second scene are also disorienting. The camera pans slightly to the right to face a balcony from within a darkened room. A shadowy figure dashes into the frame and onto the balcony. Successive uses of synecdoche confirm the shadowy withholding tone of this sequence. We see part of the escaping man's shadow cast on a wall as he removes a mustache in silhouette. Cutting back to the room he has escaped, the camera dollies back from its first position and tilts down to show only the feet of a man prone on the floor. Then, after cutting to two "business associates" who are pushing the buzzer outside this space, Lubitsch cuts to a shot into the room from just off the balcony to watch the prone man slowly get up and then collapse again, knocking over the ice bucket. Lubitsch complements the two examples of synecdoche in this scene with other strategies that abstract us from a simple set of conclusions. Literally, a man has been knocked out, robbed, and denied a rendezvous with two prostitutes. But Lubitsch wants to prevent us from too hasty an arrival at the literal.

Plot per se is less intensely registered in this scene than is the atmosphere that envelops both thief and victim, conveying certain aesthetic realities that carry moral weight. The cat-like grace and speed of the shadowy figure departing by way of the balcony and the tree are more visually appealing than the prone and static feet. The mirroring camera set-ups — from behind the table looking out the balcony door at Gaston's escape and from outside the balcony doors looking in at the attempted rise of Filiba (Edward Everett Horton) — frame the victimizer and victim in an equally distanced manner, suggesting, as does the film in its entirety, that the rich are thieves who needn't make an escape. The prostitutes at the door confirm this cynical assumption. The money that would have paid for their services is instead employed in a charmingly choreographed love duet between two glamorous thieves in the next scene, when the camera cuts back and forth between their witty and graceful play and Filiba's bumbling explanations to the Italian police.

Synecdoche is later used to tell us about Gaston's intentions to steal the handbag and his brief distraction with a tilt of his iris-like binocular gaze up to Madame Colet's face. Later, it dramatizes the sexual attraction between Madame Colet and Gaston: from a two-shot of them kissing, Lubitsch cuts to the two reflected in a mirror over her bed, then to a second mirror over her vanity, and finally to their two shadows on the bed.[20] By successively reframing the two and then thoroughly abstracting them into mere shadow shapes, Lubitsch startles us into a self-conscious distance from their lovemaking. Another time, immediately after Gaston has shown Filiba out and assured him he was never in Venice, we see only Gaston's feet running up the stairs just before he sets in motion the well-oiled machinery of a thief's escape. The synecdoche here prepares us for a sudden character shift into high-speed professionalism, his languorous charm now a thing of the past. In fact, some of these uses of synecdoche presage a crucial change in the emotional register of the film. For instance, the shadow figures of Mariette Colet and Gaston on the bed prefigure her ascendance to power over him, a power Gaston does not regain until he convinces her not to call the police. When the synecdoche fragments the scene spatially, it prepares us for a new narrative turn.

In *The Shop Around the Corner,* synecdoche is used both at the emotional climax of the film, when Margaret Sullavan's Klara searches her empty mailbox for a love letter, and then comically at the point of closure when she examines the legs of Kralik (James Stewart). Each is an intense moment, though the comedy of displaying Kralik's legs with gartered socks releases the tension of his earlier confession. Klara's genuine despair is apparent in the earlier scene when the camera peers voyeuristically into the mailbox from the opposite side and watches the hopeless movement of her hand searching the small space. And if we see the two instances of synecdoche as interrelated, we might see the embarrassing moment when Kralik lifts his trousers at the end as, in fact, Klara's revenge on him for her earlier suffering.[21] Lubitsch fragments each character's body in turn.

Two instances of synecdoche in *The Marriage Circle* seem similarly interrelated. The lonely foot at the start of the film that makes its way into a sock with a hole in its toe reveals the dissatisfactions of the Stocks' marriage, in contrast with the romantic foundation of the Brauns' marriage. The Brauns' morning ritual starts with their two saucers touching and proceeds to the total abandonment of the soft-boiled egg and the coffee, as hands push them away from the side of the table, where they might be endangered by (we assume) some serious lovemaking.

Synecdoche often accompanies the early establishing of ironic space in Lubitsch's films. Both techniques make special demands on the spectator. Synecdoche requires the spectator to interpret the whole from a perception only of parts; ironic space similarly requires an interpretation of the whole from a familiarly ironic perspective. Lubitsch often blends the two techniques, as in the credit sequences of *Monte Carlo* (1930) and *Desire* (1936) (the latter film directed by Frank Borzage under Lubitsch's supervision). In *Monte Carlo,* Jeanette MacDonald's countess escapes being wedded to Duke Otto von Seibenheim (Claude Allister) in a series of fragmented shots of hands gathering in gambling earnings, hands opening a metal casket and removing two rings, banners proclaiming the wedding, a wedding dress draped over a chair, and a woman's legs running and jumping onto a train. *Desire*'s credits barely distract the viewer from a woman's deep décolletage, upon which a heavily braceleted hand plays with a string of pearls by dribbling them from one hand to the other.

Transitional Space

Lubitsch often intensifies transitions and the spaces associated with these in-between portions of the narrative rather than dramatizing spaces associated with the confrontations between characters. He thus promotes implied space. The spectator becomes a witness to the moments in which the characters are evolving. The spectator may watch with delight the play between characters within rooms in which they confront each other, but these scenes are relatively static in a psychological sense. Lubitsch instead spatially exploits those moments during which a character must adjust his role or rearrange his priorities, especially when these narrative shifts also entail a transition from one space to another.

In *Trouble in Paradise,* Gaston is often captured in these dynamic moments of metamorphosis on the circular stairs leading from the social and public world of the downstairs space of Madame Colet's house to the professional and private world of the upstairs office and bedrooms. Lubitsch endeavors to make this space acute from our first movement through it by craning up the stairs with Gaston to the landing. The drama that is played out here from multiple camera angles — a high angle on him from Madame Colet's perspective once he has descended again, and a low angle from the bottom of the stairs as he again runs up — which further familiarize us with the space. The subtext and the delivery of the dialogue are considerably more important than the dialogue itself:

Gaston: Madame Colet, do you know my first name?

Mme. Colet: (shakes her head)

Gaston: Gaston. And do you know what I would like you to do with that check?

Mme. Colet: No, what?

Gaston: Make it out to cash.

Mme. Colet: As you like.

Lubitsch counterpoints the mundane nature of the transaction with the suave, seductive urbanity of Gaston. Gaston, because he declines to be embarrassed about taking the reward and relieves Madame Colet of embarrassment, becomes the more powerful of the two. His power is demonstrated as he proceeds to follow her into what will become his office and even wanders from there into his soon-to-be bedroom. The scene ends with their now-established roles confirmed by the repartee:

Gaston: Madame Colet, if I were your father, which fortunately I am not, and you made any attempt to handle your own business affairs, I would give you a good spanking, in a business-like way of course.

Mme. Colet: What would you do if you were my secretary?

Gaston: The same thing.

Mme. Colet: You're hired.

Gaston's strategy is twofold: he makes Madame Colet feel protected and more in control of her fortune, while taking control himself. That process of taking control has been dramatized by his twice mounting the stairs and then by his appropriating the space of her office and her former secretary's bedroom (while appropriating Madame Colet's erotic interest as well).

Lubitsch's use of transitional space often overlaps, of course, with his use of the threshold response, since within transitional space one often finds a threshold between spaces with different requirements. In *To Be or Not To Be,* Carole Lombard's Maria Tura often finds herself awkwardly positioned on the threshold of Professor Siletsky's hotel suite, prevented by the guards from leaving or escorted by the guards toward the suite (which represents dangerous territory to her). More comically, Don Ameche's Henry Van Cleve's transition into hell down a staircase between giant pillars is also a moment fraught with anticipation for the spectator of *Heaven Can Wait.* And at the end of the film, his ascension by elevator into at least the annex of heaven frames the film with transitional spaces.

A use of transitional spaces in a more organic way with respect to the narrative occurs in *Cluny Brown.*[22] Here, Jennifer Jones's Cluny and Charles Boyer's Belinski typically occupy transitional spaces, especially when they find themselves alone together, whereas the rest of the cast comfortably occupies the habitual space of rooms—Mr. Wilson in his pharmacy, the Carmels in their drawing room or dining room. Lubitsch embodies the unconventionality of Cluny and Belinski in the transitional spaces they typically occupy—Cluny under sinks trying to fix the plumbing and Belinski wherever he lands as an expatriate radical cum parasite.

In Lubitsch's *Cluny Brown,* the major characters, played by Charles Boyer, Reginald Gardiner, and Jennifer Jones, are shown in one of the transitional spaces (under the sink where Cluny does her plumbing) that Lubitsch is so fond of.

Transitional spaces are often the locus of comic confusion, allowing Lubitsch to accelerate the pace of a film or to postpone and thus accentuate dramatic confrontations. The climax of *The Love Parade* depends upon transitional spaces. The Prince Consort and Queen Louise run back and forth between their separate bedrooms, Chevalier's Prince Alfred redressing his loss of power and dignity with each transition. Much of the strange but intense weighting of confrontations in *The Man I Killed* (1932), perhaps the most unexpected of all Lubitsch's films, depends upon the use of transitional spaces throughout the film.[23] These spaces are especially associated with the character Paul (Phillips Holmes), who is doing a kind of penance throughout the film for killing a German during World War I. Lubitsch depicts Paul's guilt in these transitional spaces, often picturing him moving agitatedly between places, such as the graveyard and the dead man's house, down streets as though watched by the suspicious natives, or away from the center of the action up the stairs. Gradually the dead soldier's fiancée, Elsa (Nancy Carroll), joins him in these transitional spaces and leads him to the center of the dead soldier's family, where he finds peace. But the weighting of the final scene, in which Paul and Elsa play violin and piano together while the camera holds on the parents (Lionel Barrymore and Louise Carter), depends upon the contrast between this stability and all the transitional spaces that preceded it.

Lubitsch takes more risks in comedy, and therefore seems more at home with its premises. He even experiments with using transitional spaces in his conclusions, a risky strategy when the nature of closure is considered. For instance, at the end of *Ninotchka,* the camera chooses to watch the three comrades start to leave, turn (we presume, to see Ninotchka and the count kissing), and then scuttle quickly away. We see the three comrades in transition rather than the two lovers in a stable setting; Lubitsch implies rather than creates the space through our adoption of the three comrades' approving gaze. Still more tangential is the last shot, in which one of the three comrades, Kopalski (Alexander Granach) pickets the restaurant of the other two (Felix Bressart and Sig Rumann). This last small joke, though, does not threaten to destroy the unity of the plot.[24] The small detours from the central romance at the end reinforce the overall tone of ironic distance from an ideological idealism, and they thus temper the kiss that we never see. Lubitsch and his writers (Brackett, Wilder, and Reisch) do not want to undo the comrades' ideological idealism only to plunge us into romantic idealism.

Behind Glass

Lubitsch may appear to be a lover of surfaces, of the superficial social forms and decorums that conceal intense feelings or less than admirable motives. He does construct many of his American-produced urbane comedies as comedies of manners. But, like other great comedies of manners, such as Austen's *Pride and Prejudice,* these films of Lubitsch undercut manners, exposing their artificiality, as much as they delight in them and see them as controlling human perversity. Like Jean Renoir's *The Rules of the Game* (1939), whose title tells us to examine these decorums, Lubitsch's *Trouble in Paradise* (1932) parallels two classes — an aristocracy and an equally insouciant class of thieves — and finds no notable distinctions between them, except that the latter are smarter. Both classes include thieves, though the real thieves work in a more modest way. Both groups contain snobs, who must surreptitiously dunk their doughnuts. And both classes are, at one time or another, either sexually vulnerable or sexually voracious.

Lubitsch uses several spatial techniques that complement the narratives of these comedies of manners. These techniques characteristically distance us from the action to make either the manners or the emotions they conceal more apparent. His camera in *Trouble in Paradise* is often set up behind glass. By divorcing the spectator from the content of his characters' speech, Lubitsch leads us to examine the surfaces. He sharpens our sight by divorcing us from the particulars of the chit-chat at Madame Colet's cocktail party. He makes us attentive to what we otherwise would not attend to: who thinks of whom first (Madame Colet thinks of Gaston), who solicits whom first (the same), who calls upon whom when she is confused (the same). The implicit spatial relationships between the characters are made explicit as we watch the silent drama unfold.

The behind glass technique is a correlative of both the camera's restraint, as

is apparent in the threshold response, and its fragmentation of reality in synecdoche. For example, the camera backs out of the door as Gaston shows Filiba
out and then pans to the right (still outside the door) to watch through a glass
panel to the right of the front door as Gaston divests himself of his mannerly
role and runs up the circular stairs. The servant almost immediately calls Gaston back to Filiba again at the door, they exchange a few more remarks about
harems in Constantinople and about Gaston never having been in Venice, and
then we see the synecdoche of Gaston's running feet on the stairs. Space, in
response to the narrative complications, is becoming acute.

At the end of *Cluny Brown,* Lubitsch again uses the behind glass technique,
this time to turn the film suddenly into a silent. The camera dollies past a
crowd gathered on the street to a display of a best-seller, *The Nightingale Murder!*
by Adam Belinski, in a store window. Then a reverse-angle shot from inside
the store through the glass watches as a smartly dressed couple walks by the
window — Cluny and Adam, of course. The camera dollies toward them as
Cluny strokes his lapel before the display, kisses him, and then indicates to a
surprised policeman that she is his wife and he the author of the book. We understand all this from Cluny's mime. Lubitsch enforces the silence to show us
spatially what has been the verbal subtext of much of the rest of the film: the
sexual attraction between the two and their shared lack of conventionality. The
silent scene concludes with Cluny beginning to faint and Belinski miming that
she is pregnant. And a final dolly up to a second display of books, *The Nightingale Strikes Again!,* assures us that their special fertility has persisted.

Lubitsch here embodies spatially what he was unwilling to display overtly —
either spatially or verbally — in the rest of the narrative. He seems to say to us
that spatial evidence can be trusted when verbal evidence would be suspect.
Both Cluny and Belinski have escaped the artificial world of the aristocracy,
which both had inhabited under false pretenses, and they have now established
an alternative world in which they are independent. Lubitsch's use of the behind glass technique here may also serve to distance us from the Cinderella-
like ending so that it does not threaten to become mawkish. Lubitsch creates a
coy irony by posing the intimacy of the couple against the policeman's and
crowd's shock, and he distances us, the spectators, by making us work hard at
reading the drama visually. This coy irony closely resembles the mime between
Gilda and Plunkett in *Design for Living* when they are looking at a double bed in
a window before their marriage, or the positioning of the camera outside the
prince and queen's window in the last shot of *The Love Parade* before the prince
pulls the drapes.

Indeed, the behind glass technique complements Lubitsch's barely suppressed interest in voyeurism, especially the voyeurism of his audience. Surrogates for the spectator in his films often peer unabashedly into the private
spaces of the central characters. In *The Love Parade,* tourists on a bus to Sylva-
nia indifferently read their newspapers until the tour guide announces that the
castle cost 110 million dollars. Then they jump up and peer at us through the

bus windows. This particular shot unsettles us because it feels like an accusation, but it is congruent with the rest of the film, which features government officials peering through keyholes, servants spying on their employers from trees, and the prince himself (Maurice Chevalier) watching the queen (Jeanette MacDonald) through binoculars. The ending of this film resembles the ending of *The Merry Widow,* where the priest performs the wedding of Captain Danilo (Chevalier) and the widow Sonia (MacDonald) through a small window in the jail cell, delivering their rings on a lazy Susan. But this instance of creating implied space is really an example of the threshold response, and it demonstrates the essential wholeness of Lubitsch's spatial vision. The window or glass is simply a slightly more permeable threshold.

Visual Correlatives

We might call some repeated settings in Lubitsch's films acute space, because they gain complexity as Lubitsch uses them over and over again. If the reader's return to an image in a cluster of related similes carries with it a cumulative emotional effect, so does each return to a particular setting in a Lubitsch film. When the spectator has come to know that space in intensely emotional narrative contexts and from several different spatial perspectives, these returns do not simply contribute to an increasing familiarity, although the power of familiarity should not be discounted. The circular staircase in *Trouble in Paradise,* for instance, is a visual correlative for the grace of the Herbert Marshall character in the fiction. Lubitsch often records Gaston's ascents and descents of this staircase, and his witnessed physical and psychological dexterity clearly corresponds to his ability to move between the two worlds of the film spatially present in Madame Colet's house. The style of the setting is also present in his character: both his movement and the staircase's design are smooth, clean, graceful, and elegant. Both serve similar purposes as mediators between public and private spaces.

Surprised Sight

Working in the narrative as sudden revelations and among the visual elements of the film as sudden reframings or shifts in the camera's perspective, certain events in a film might be called "surprised sight." The character and the spectator alike are surprised as Lubitsch suddenly reframes the narrative. The rapid editing of the seduction scene in *Trouble in Paradise* works somewhat in this way, ending as it does with the synecdoche of the lovers' shadows on the bed. It jolts us from our complacency. But a repeated spatial shift that better exemplifies these moments of revelation occurs as the Miriam Hopkins character reenters the narrative at the end. Twice the camera acknowledges her return with visually rhyming intensity. First, Lily confronts Gaston: as he turns on the lights and draws the shades in Madame Colet's bedroom (preparing for the seduction that will follow her return), Lily appears in the window of his bedroom across the way. Lubitsch uses a very sudden cut from a shot facing the window whose shade Gaston pulls to a reverse-angle shot (also from outside) of Lily standing in the window directly across. We identify with Gaston's shock and Lily's anger as they then meet before the safe. The shift in our perspective as spectators takes us from a simple identification with Gaston's passion to a complexly divided perception of his passion and his betrayal.

But Lubitsch doesn't stop here. Our surprised sight must be made more complex still with a second sudden shift, again set up between the two windows from the outside. In the second incident, Gaston stands in the window of his bedroom. Madame Colet has just asked him why he took the money, and has left his frame. So there is a double visual shift: first the camera moves to the outside, double-framing Gaston in the window; then a swish-pan dramatically sweeps our perspective to the window of Madame Colet's bedroom, where Lily reappears. The confrontation escalates, and Lubitsch draws Madame Colet into the revelations of crumbling social facades and raw emotion between the three.

Mechanical Witness

Henri Bergson in his study of comedy identifies the repetitive action of an automaton as crucial for the creation of comic laughter.[25] While I wouldn't choose to limit the evocation of laughter to this one technique, it is an effective one. We have only to think of the repetitive poses of Chaplin on the statue in *City Lights* or of Keaton swinging the lumber precariously about in *One Week* to remember how hilarious are these repeated actions. Lubitsch uses them as well, both in special, somewhat slapstick sequences to amuse us and in separate contexts scattered throughout the film to punctuate the film with a repeated truth and its accompanying laughter.

The clearest instance of one of these slapstick sequences occurs at the start of *Ninotchka,* as we see the three Russians repeatedly appear in or simply peer into the lobby of the fancy hotel. The repetitive element is embodied in the use of a revolving door. Each in turn makes his way around it, always entering our sight (we are stationed statically in the lobby) and always disappearing again. Their investigation gets progressively more humorous. And Lubitsch knows how to exploit the repetitive action, by first tracking through the hotel lobby behind the tuxedoed manager and then using him as a startled witness as the camera successively dollies up to the second Soviet and pauses for the third.

In *The Shop Around the Corner,* the quick exits of Pirovitch (Felix Bressart) punctuate the film at regular intervals. His cue is always the boss's declaration that he wants an employee's "honest opinion" about something. Pirovitch's escapes on this line undercut the boss's sincerity, especially since we have ample evidence that the boss, Mr. Matuschek (Frank Morgan), really wants to have his own opinion confirmed and that he resents the honesty of employees like

Alfred Kralik (James Stewart). The repetitive reminder of this increasingly more obvious hypocrisy becomes funnier each time Lubitsch uses it, because Matuschek's hypocrisy has become that much clearer.

Personified Props

Just as Lubitsch relies upon the spectator imagining space, he also sometimes imagines spatial realities for the spectator. And usually these spatial realities rely upon a prop that he has endowed with some special meaning. The props may be associated with a particular side of the character, so that simply by alluding to the prop, Lubitsch can evoke certain narrative assumptions about that character's psychology (principally his weaknesses). For instance, Dr. Paul Giraud's cane in *So This Is Paris* comes to stand for the adventurous and adulterous side of his character; it is appropriately phallic.[26] It gets passed around a good deal among the characters, for he leaves it in Georgette and Maurice's apartment. And then Maurice (André Beranger) uses it, in turn, as an excuse to meet Giraud's wife and carry on a flirtation with her. Even when the cane's physical presence has been withdrawn, in a scene where Giraud is sleeping, Lubitsch reconstitutes its image in the air above the sleeping Giraud. Like his conscience, the cane hangs over him, pokes him on the forehead and cheek and nose, and then aims itself and plunges into his open mouth. Giraud wakes up suddenly, holding his stomach.

Though not explicitly embodied in a dream sequence, the same technique appears in *Ninotchka:* here hats become images of capitalist extravagance and of having fun. To show a time transition while the Russians stay in the luxury suite before the still ideologically frigid Ninotchka arrives to straighten them out, Lubitsch dissolves from their Bolshevik peasant caps on a hat stand to their new derbies and top hats. And later the same prop, this time a fanciful Parisian hat, seduces Ninotchka herself. The camera lovingly follows her as she lifts the hat from a drawer, tries it on before a mirror, and sinks onto a stool, defeated by her capitalist needs and yet pleased.

Lubitsch's indirection in his creation of film space reminds me in some ways of Sternberg's obscurity. Neither director wants to come at a confrontation head on. What is open and overt interests them less than what is partially closed or covert. I have often wondered whether their experience as immigrants might have made both men sensitive to space as a ground of confrontation, a locus where domination and subordination are defined. Wouldn't the immigrant experience educate one as a subordinate? This need not mean that an immigrant has to be weak or passive; a subordinate's inheritance includes an ability to act and react in indirect or disguised ways.[27] And an immigrant's experience of learning a new language must at first draw on all his ability to read body language and gestural codes. The natives probably expect an immigrant to read their intentions.

Sternberg and Lubitsch both specialize in depicting figures who are not part of the dominant social group in their films and who either know those in the dominant group or learn to know them. The drama of this learning is often what is played out between Lubitsch's sophisticated observer and his more naive initiate. The first often leads or watches over the second, as Belinski does for Cluny in *Cluny Brown* or Count D'Algout does for Ninotchka. At times, Lubitsch turns the tables on the dominant group in his films: the naive initiates enter that dominant group and teach them the values of subordinates — a certain self-possession, a different sort of power (not over others but a power to implement one's own ideas), and an ability to trust another's decisions and to delegate responsibility. Among the characters who must learn from subordinates in Lubitsch's films are Madame Colet in *Trouble in Paradise,* Matuschek in *The Shop Around the Corner,* and Sonia in *The Merry Widow* (1934).

In the reviews of Lubitsch's films in the thirties and forties, his work is often referred to as "frothy" or "bubbly as champagne." We might interpret the implied lightness of his technique, his charm, and his comic energy as a subordinate's way of making a point without belaboring it. Lubitsch uses spatial techniques that approach character and situations indirectly. He thus avoids didacticism while implying a great deal about the human species. He would especially have us be aware of all those traits we make a great effort to hide — pretentiousness, ambition, lust, vanity. The characters in Lubitsch's films who see these traits both in others and in themselves are doubly blessed. First, though they possess subordinate status, that status endows them with special powers of observation. Second, though outsiders to the dominant group, they can imitate it so accurately as to gain admission whenever it suits them. A Monescu or a Belinski or a Count D'Algout so amply possesses self-confidence and manners as to transcend the need for money. Lubitsch's lightness, then, is hardly insignificant. It includes an ability to penetrate the power and pretenses of a complex social world, briefly to throw it into disarray, and to lend its inhabitants insight into themselves, into their needs and natures.

NOTES

1. Peter Bogdanovich finds this phrase useful: "The phrase does connote something light, strangely indefinable, yet nonetheless tangible, and seeing Lubitsch films — more than in almost any other director's work — one can feel this spirit; not only in the tactful and impeccably appropriate placement of camera, the subtle economy of his plotting, the oblique dialogue which had a way of saying everything through indirection, but also — and particularly — in the performance of every single player, no matter how small the role." See Bogdanovich's *Pieces of Time* (New York: Arbor House, 1973), p. 220. But other critics want to distance themselves from "the Lubitsch touch," such as Leland A. Poague in *The Cinema of Ernst Lubitsch* (South Brunswick, N.J.: A. S. Barnes, 1978), who wants to emphasize Lubitsch's "strong sense of humanity" (p. 13), or Raymond Durgnat in *The Crazy Mirror: Hollywood Comedy and the American Image* (New York: Horizon, 1970), who feels the phrase is "misleadingly named, for it is not so much a something added to a story as a method of telling a story through ellipsis and

emphasis" (p. 110). Molly Haskell, in *From Reverence to Rape: The Treatment of Women in the Movies* (New York: Holt, Rinehart and Winston, 1974), points out that Lubitsch's style was "so effervescent that genius was mistaken for mere 'touch,' " and that it is often in awkward moments that his characters are most complex.

2. Herman Weinberg, *The Lubitsch Touch: A Critical Study,* 3rd ed. (New York: Dover, 1968, 1977), p. xviii.

3. See Richard Koszarski's comment in "On *Trouble in Paradise,*" *Film Comment,* 7 (1970): 47–48.

4. Lubitsch's reflexivity, apparent in his frequent use of the theater or theatrical performances, is explored by Poague (*Cinema of Ernst Lubitsch,* p. 70); Graham Petrie in "Theater Film Life," *Film Comment* 10 (1974): 38–39; and Robin Wood in "Acting Up," *Film Comment* 12 (1976): 23–24. Weinberg points out: "the audience had to contribute to the full realization of the work, to fill in the implications, often even to supply the 'tagline,' the meaning of a quick or even a slow fadeout" (*Lubitsch Touch,* p. 72). Leo Braudy argues that Lubitsch "embraces the audience as a co-conspirator of interpretation," in "The Double Detachment of Ernst Lubitsch," *Modern Language Notes* 98 (1983): 1078.

5. Herman Weinberg makes a case for Lubitsch as farceur in "Ernst Lubitsch: A Parallel to Georges Feydeau," *Film Comment* 6 (1970): 62, and William Paul explores all facets of his comedy in *Ernst Lubitsch's American Comedy* (New York: Columbia Univ. Press, 1983).

6. Poague sees skepticism as the essence of Lubitsch's irony (*Cinema of Ernst Lubitsch,* p. 48). Gerald Mast describes the primary object of Lubitsch's irony as love, the sexual love found in unromantic film; see his *The Comic Mind: Comedy and the Movies,* 2nd ed. (Chicago: Univ. of Chicago Press, 1979), pp. 207–209.

7. For discussions of Lubitsch's portrayal of sex, see Weinberg, *Lubitsch Touch,* pp. 61–62; Andrew Sarris in "All Talking! All Singing! All Lubitsch!: Ernst Lubitsch in the Thirties — Part II," *Film Comment* 8 (1972): 21; and Nancy Schwartz, "Lubitsch's *Widow:* The Meaning of a Waltz," *Film Comment* 11 (1975): 13–17.

8. Haskell sees Lubitsch's worldliness as deceptive because his characters are more complex (*From Reverence to Rape,* p. 96), whereas Durgnat sees his "blend of amorality and generosity" as part of a "hedonistic code" shared by his heroes and heroines (*Crazy Mirror,* pp. 112–113). Poague discusses the complexity of innocence and worldliness in *Heaven Can Wait* (*Cinema of Ernst Lubitsch,* pp. 121–126).

9. William O. Huie, Jr., in "Style and Technology in *Trouble in Paradise:* Evidence of a Technicians' Lobby?" *Journal of Film and Video* 39 (1987): 37–51, uses Braudy's idea about Lubitsch's reflexive strategy to argue that Lubitsch develops "deviant narrative devices" that challenge our usual notions of classical American cinema.

10. See Bogdanovich's comment on Lubitsch's holding the camera on closed doors (*Pieces of Time,* p. 220). Also, the term threshold was probably suggested to me by the chapter "Thresholds of Feeling" in Charles Affron's *Cinema and Sentiment* (Chicago: Univ. of Chicago Press, 1982), pp. 24–52.

11. See Weinberg's anecdote in *Lubitsch Touch,* p. 52.

12. Neil D. Isaacs believes Lubitsch's use of doors to be "a weathervane of the drama/movie polarity" in his films. See his "Lubitsch and the Filmed-Play Syndrome," *Literature/Film Quarterly* 3 (1975): 300.

13. See Poague's comments on Lubitsch's harmless prurience (*Cinema of Ernst Lubitsch,* p. 132).

14. Lotte H. Eisner comments that Lubitsch's "visual double meanings which, when the time came, he was to enrich with a kaleidoscopic use of sound, were thrown into relief by skillful editing." In *The Haunted Screen: Expressionism in the German Cinema and the Influence of Max Reinhardt,* trans. Roger Greaves (London: Thames and Hudson, 1969), p. 80.

15. See Paul's interesting explanation of how Lubitsch enriches his irony with metaphor (*Ernst Lubitsch's American Comedy,* pp. 9–11).

16. Arthur Koestler, "The Three Domains of Creativity," in James F. T. Bugental, ed., *Challenges of Humanistic Psychology* (New York: McGraw-Hill, 1967), pp. 31–40.

17. See Paul's comments on "the pattern of interruption" and "the fragmenting style" of *Trouble in Paradise* (*Ernst Lubitsch's American Comedy,* pp. 21–23).

18. See Eric Bentley's discussion of Freud's insights into jokes in Robert W. Corrigan's *Comedy: Meaning and Form* (New York: Harper and Row, 1981), p. 199.

19. See Poague's description of this sequence (*Cinema of Ernst Lubitsch,* p. 99).

20. See Isaacs' description of this sequence ("Lubitsch and the Filmed-Play Syndrome," p. 304), and Koszarski's ("On *Trouble in Paradise,*" p. 48).

21. This scene is a good example of what Haskell refers to as "awkward moments" in Lubitsch's films (*From Reverence to Rape,* p. 96).

22. Poague may account for this emphasis on transitional spaces when he speculates on the film's challenging of various characters' "disinclination to accept change" (*Cinema of Ernst Lubitsch,* p. 139) and connects that challenge to Lubitsch's resemblance to Charles Boyer's Adam Belinski: "mid-European exile, with a foreign name, a foreign accent (although Boyer sounds more like Chevalier than Lubitsch), and an exile's lack of security" (p. 136).

23. *The Man I Killed* evokes mostly condemnation or apology from Lubitsch's critics. Sarris says it "emerges today as Lubitsch's least inspired and most calculated effort, all surface effect, all ritualistic piety toward a 'noble' subject," in "Lubitsch in the Thirties," *Film Comment* 7 (1971–72): 55. Weinberg, in *Lubitsch Touch,* suggests that Lubitsch needed "to purge himself" of his earlier sophistication (p. 133).

24. Isaacs points out Lubitsch's tendency to have punch-lines serve as curtain-lines: "The joke ends the scene and there is often an immediate cut or dissolve, while the real zingers are punctuated by fades to black" ("Lubitsch and the Filmed-Play Syndrome," p. 302).

25. Henri Bergson, *Laughter: An Essay on the Meaning of the Comic,* trans. Cloudesley Brereton and Fred Rothwell (New York: Macmillan, 1924), pp. 8–22.

26. See Weinberg on this technique in *Lubitsch Touch,* pp. 96–98, and Mast, *Comic Mind,* p. 215.

27. Jean Baker Miller eloquently describes the psychological play between dominants and subordinates in *Toward a New Psychology of Women* (Boston: Beacon Press, 1976), pp. 29–47.

5

Sternberg's Film Space: Obscuring Space to Stimulate Curiosity

Josef von Sternberg's vision of space is based on obscurity. This may seem paradoxical, since used vernacularly, "space" suggests openness and all the possibilities of sight. But Sternberg is really working with a sound, painterly principle — that the activity of seeing can be stimulated by concealment. One could even say that a controlled denial of sight, of the sort that Sternberg is remarkable for, stimulates a second sight or the thinking that accompanies seeing. Through indirection, he finds a means of approaching subjects with obscure or submerged natures. His spatial techniques are inseparable from his narrative, since both thrive on Sternberg's reluctance to place things in clean, well-lighted places or to attend to things that would thrive in such settings. As Sternberg explains in his autobiography, *Fun in a Chinese Laundry,* "Each light furnishes its own shadow, and where a shadow is seen there must be a light."[1] He sounds like William Blake, suggesting that art depends upon the tension created by a collision of opposites.

Sternberg has been accused of constructing narratives without plots and dramas of character that make no linear progress.[2] These narratives, it is said, were designed to promote Marlene Dietrich, and focus exclusively on the ageless contours of her face. And while there is some truth in these charges, they also reflect a basic uneasiness with the sort of narratives that Sternberg does construct, and perhaps some unrealistic expectations about what haunts his imagination.

First, are Sternberg's narratives really plotless?[3] Not really. *The Scarlet Empress* is an elaborately structured initiation story of a young girl's loss of innocence and the growth of a young woman's political and sexual awareness. This is a traditional linear narrative in the best tradition of the *Bildungsroman*. Dietrich's Catherine may not be the young man from the provinces (as he is called by Lionel Trilling), but she is as sharply delineated as a Becky Sharp or a Julien Sorel. Similar to David Copperfield, she moves from country to city (the Russian court), experiencing correspondingly new demands on her social personality.[4]

It is true that none of the other Sternberg films are so traditionally structured, but none of them are plotless either.[5] In *The Devil Is a Woman,* Sternberg handles the rivalry of two men for the same provocative woman by nestling one "past-tense" narrative of the woman's manipulation of the older man within the "present-tense" narrative of the younger man's attraction to her. Neither story is without events: meetings, captures, betrayals.[6] And both are socially dense, the men being seen as playing within the conventions of the aristocracy and the woman playing upon their social assumptions. Sternberg limits our understanding of Dietrich's femme fatale, but those limits are conventional. The final twist in Concha's decision to stay with the older man depends upon the spectator not being able to read her motives or intentions clearly.

Films such as *The Shanghai Express* depend upon the familiar seventeenth- and eighteenth-century picaresque device of the journey to structure the narrative. But the plotting is far more sophisticated than in the simple picaresque adventure, where episodically the *picaro* (rogue) meets with new characters and new disillusionments at every turn of the road. Sternberg instead combines several conventions: throwing strangers together in one place and seeing what likely and unlikely chemistry will take place between them (the English country house convention used in murder mysteries and novels of manners); the adventure of the train ride into foreign and exotic territory; involvement in the political and historical upheaval of a civil war. Together these three narrative strategies create quite complex interactions between the characters, and sufficient "events" to please the searcher after story. Holding it all together is the love story of alienated lovers rediscovering each other and being reunited, and the familiar Sternberg creation of the psychologically misunderstood femme fatale proving herself worthy of devotion through small kindnesses and considerable self-sacrifice.

We might return, though, to the charge that Sternberg's films are plotless, and try to uncover why his films may leave this impression. My contention is that Sternberg is much more interested in delving into the underlying psychological realities of his characters than he is in pursuing the contexts that surround his characters.[7] And perhaps even more revealing, Sternberg isn't especially interested in the most direct and overt psychological realities that he might explore. He is intrigued by the sideways glance through slitted eyes, by the unintentional and involuntary gestures that men and women might prefer that others not notice. As a consequence, we may watch a Sternberg film and never pay any attention to the adventure story, the train journey, or the political emergence of a queen. It is not the political or social world that Sternberg would have us be caught up in.

Aesthetically, Sternberg would dislocate spectators so that their expectations shift from the story-listening mode to an extreme state of atmospheric identification with the characters' states of mind. The latter is a static mode, and while little appears to happen in this mode, many events may in fact transpire. In other words, Sternberg's techniques draw our attention away from the explicit progress of the plot to the somewhat covert subtext.

I have always felt that on some level Sternberg's films achieve the eroticism that explicitly pornographic films aim for but rarely achieve; the indirection in his techniques almost always has the effect of excluding mundane feelings and evoking feelings that are charged, if not with sexual imagination, then with extreme reactions — fears, desires, revulsion, attraction. Like pornography, Sternberg's films explore somewhat taboo states of mind and emotion. Sternberg does so by calling upon parts of our psyches that we may be less than eager to acknowledge. Certainly, if all of us were products of an entirely enlightened view of sexuality, for instance, seeing sex as special but also as an available source of pleasure free of guilt and anxiety and never carrying the weight of our egos in its initiation or expression, we would probably be far less vulnerable to some of the indirection of Sternberg's spatial language. It might strike us as overly coy or even silly instead of being titillating.

I wonder whether his films may be curiosities to a more enlightened generation, one, for instance, that is taught everything they need to know at an early age by totally unembarrassed parents or teachers. As long as we are potentially embarrassed, shy, or anxious about the extreme emotions Sternberg explores, we will be vulnerable to his films, which take on what Susan Sontag calls "the complexities of consciousness itself."[8] What Sternberg understands about these complexities is what the makers of pornography rarely understand — that the power of pornography depends upon inhibition and ignorance. If our parents had been able to wear everyday, matter-of-fact expressions when they explained the "facts of life" to us, or if our peers had never giggled or guffawed about sex, I imagine the subject would be far less charged and mysterious. And Sternberg knows this about the emotions he depicts. He veils them so that the spectator has to search them out. His compositions contain veils and nets and leaves or tree branches that extend into the frame, preventing our clear and open sight of objects and characters.

As John Baxter explains, Sternberg sees the cinema in terms of how to animate the dead space that separates camera from subject and subject from background. His aim, Baxter says, is to give things independent life. To do this, he often gives empty space the illusion of being thickened by using filters and gauzes; white walls and aluminum paint reflect more light from walls and doors in his sets.[9] Sternberg seeks in many ways to overload the spectator with sensory impressions. As Sternberg states: "But above all, the greatest art in motion picture photography is to be able to give life to the dead space that exists between the lens and the subject before it. Smoke, rain, fog, dust, and steam can emotionalize empty space, and so can the movement of the camera."[10] This impulse means that the conceptual structures of his plots rely upon the spatial thinking in his films. This impulse also identifies his central preoccupation with the material world, an ability to endow space with atmospheric power by filling it, layering it, deepening it, and peering into it from odd angles.

Because Sternberg wants to fill space or thicken it as a medium, the frame becomes an important tool for him, setting limits for his enclosed spatial illusions. His space and his characters alike are limited. No possibility of spiritual transcendence is admissable. At best, the space within the frame is activated by diagonal stairs, as at the close of *The Scarlet Empress* when Catherine's mounted troops enter the Winter Palace and gallop up the stairs. But the use of synecdoche—only the horses' legs on the steps are visible—contains and stylizes the motion even here at Catherine's moment of triumph. Her triumph is utterly secular, her transcendence only earthly. Like all Sternberg's characters, she is humanly flawed and works within the material world.

HABITUAL SPACE

The habitual space in Sternberg's films includes returns to the familiar sets that art director Hans Dreier constructed for these dramas. In *The Scarlet Empress,* two giant beds come to mind as defining the space of both bedrooms, that of the old empress (Louise Dresser) and of Catherine (Marlene Dietrich). Punctuating this film are Swiss sculptor Peter Ballbusch's gargoyles, perched like cynical personal gods, which add a half-horrid and half-comic sight to these scenes. These statues seem to gaze down on Catherine during times of revelation—when, for instance, Alexei (John Lodge) tries to detain her in a palace corridor, or when she snuffs out the candles in the old empress's bedroom before admitting Alexei up the secret stairwell.

Sternberg exploits the autonomy he has in the making of his world; he also stays within fairly restrictive studio limitations in his use of space. Take *The Blue Angel:* the classroom, the nightclub's stage, and the back dressing room with its spiral stairs leading up to another level are nearly sufficient for encompassing the deterioration of Professor Rath (Emil Jannings). One of the consequences of our repeated returns to these spaces is a familiarity against which the professor's deterioration can be measured. But we also react to the familiarity of the characters: the ennui of the travelling show, the languid grace of Dietrich's Lola Lola in her dressing room, and the professor's horror of familiarity when he must return to his home town and be humiliated as a clown in the local nightclub.

ACUTE SPACE

Veiled Shots

Sternberg often positions his camera so that between it and the subjects of its concern is some veil or obstruction that limits the spectator's clear view.[11] In this way, he both frustrates and tantalizes the spectator, for he says in effect, "Here is something to see that I will not let you see directly." The implicit challenge in this strategy is important, because it alerts us to the need for alertness and concentration in our examination of the scene.

The specific significance of these shots varies enormously from film to film and from scene to scene, but some points about how they work might be made. For instance, they almost always deepen the effect of the shots: by drawing our attention to the foreground or mid-ground of the field and by asking us to penetrate whatever obstruction he has placed there, Sternberg draws our attention very slowly to the background of the shot. The shot itself, then, functions as a sort of educator of the spectator. Consider, for instance, the wedding veil in *The Scarlet Empress,* held up by the seamstresses before Catherine as she sits before a mirror having her hair done for the ceremony. The camera is drawn back from her over the veil, emphasizing the depth of field and our distance from the object of our attention through this slight movement of withdrawal. We must seek out that wanted view of Dietrich's Catherine through the filter of the veil.

Usually these veiled shots function metaphorically to suggest that the spectator cannot know all the facts. And the pervasiveness of these shots in most of Sternberg's major sound films suggests further that his vision of reality includes an utter skepticism about clear perception, rational deliberation, and intellectual precision.[12] His characters are not only highly flawed human beings; they are also highly irrational beings, driven by both internal and external forces toward their destinies. For instance, while Catherine in *The Scarlet Empress* may gain a certain poise and adopt a certain diffidence, the changes in her personality are all identifiable as necessary responses to the circumstances around her. She literally sinks into the arms of a soldier who mistakes her for a lady-in-waiting. That encounter precipitates her elaborate adulteries. The great celebration when she bears an heir suitably reinforces the whole chain of events.

The elaborate veil metaphor in *The Scarlet Empress* carries with it the suggestion that one human being will inevitably deceive another for his or her own self-interest. The film is an elaborately contrived means of initiating the spectator into more savvy intellectual sight, just as Catherine must gain the knowledge and poise to be an effective empress. In other Sternberg films, the veil functions similarly, though without the specific allusions to wedding veils and sexual initiations. Usually the erotic element remains, but the veil is not specifically a barrier between innocence or ignorance and experience. Only in *The Blue Angel* do veils function almost precisely as they do in *The Scarlet Empress,* where Professor Rath becomes the dupe of Dietrich's diffident femme fatale. In the final, climactic scene, the professor clumsily weaves his way toward his humiliation as a clown before his home-town audience. He seems to get netted in the layers of gauzy curtain and to struggle to free himself. Where Catherine accepts the reality she is initiated into, the professor cannot. And the straightjacket in which he is confined is like that net curtain drawn tight.

In both *Blonde Venus* and *The Devil Is a Woman,* veiled shots serve as a means by which the femme fatale figures deceive the male characters. In this way, they reiterate the visual drama in *The Blue Angel.* But in both *Blonde Venus* and *The Devil,* the Dietrich character deceives partly in order to minister to others. Though she is still suspiciously cipher-like (to stimulate a sense of her as unattainable and thus desirable), Sternberg allows the Dietrich character to have a heart of gold. Concha in *The Devil* proves to be a political power as well as a personal one, for she frees her young admirer, Antonio (Cesar Romero), from jail. It is his innocence that commands the veiled shots here, as he stands behind an iron gate searching out Concha's lost image in the depth of a garden and in a villa behind. He is veiled and confused by the confetti and streamers in the Mardi Gras crowd, which he struggles to penetrate.

Later, as Pasqual (Lionel Atwill), Antonio's older friend, confides in Antonio, telling him about his experiences with Concha, Sternberg positions both men in front of a geometrical screen (not unlike the earlier iron gate and the later jail cell) with palm fronds descending in the middle of the two-shot. The men, of course, deceive each other as well as being deceived by Concha, Antonio swearing to Pasqual that he will never go near Concha and then meeting her that evening. She is viewed behind entangled bare branches in her white carriage with white horses. A reverse-angle shot captures Antonio behind these branches from the other direction. The duel between Antonio and Pasqual takes place in rain, in a forest of drooping willows. The two men are as obscured as their confused loyalties and passions are confused.

Sternberg's blonde venuses are redeemed by the fact that they do love deeply. Helen in *Blonde Venus* loves her son first, her husband second, and the playboy Nick (Cary Grant) as well. But she, like Concha, acts politically, inverting her own hierarchy and sacrificing her feelings for her husband's physical well-being. Here the veiled shots delineate Helen's shame and her passionate retention of her son when Herbert Marshall's Ned wins legal custody. When Ned is gone for his treatment overseas, Helen is framed by a booth selling fabrics and ribbons, which hang down into the frame as she gets into Nick's limousine. After Helen joins Nick on vacation, Helen and Nick recline on two crooked trees with the branches hanging down in front of Helen, who imminently expects Ned's return. Then after Ned has discovered Helen's adultery, Helen escapes with her son Johnny (Dickie Moore), who sleeps behind a dark mesh curtain. Helen's makeshift career as they criss-cross the country often shows her singing framed by palm fronds. These veiled shots, suggesting her sense of shame, end with Helen behind bare hanging branches and frondlike tree leaves in the station where she turns Johnny over to Ned. Finally, behind hanging ropes in a flophouse for women, she drunkenly gives away Ned's money to a destitute woman.

The veiled shots in *Blonde Venus* cease abruptly during the ensuing sequence when Helen is reunited with Nick in her meteoric rise to fame again in the nightclub circuit. She is called an iceberg in the script, is dressed in masculine attire — a white sequined tuxedo — and adopts certain masculine mannerisms, to suggest she is suppressing her maternal love and marital devotion. Only at the very end of the film, when Helen and Ned are brought together ministering to Johnny, is there again a veiling effect, this time by the bars of Johnny's crib beside which Helen kneels.

In each of these films the veiled shots work metaphorically and richly in internally consistent ways, but from film to film there is no single metaphoric signification. And within each film, this technique is versatile, evolving within its narrative context. For instance, in that final scene of *Blonde Venus* described above, the crib bars and Ned's arm around Helen's shoulders represent a closing in of the frame, but enclosure and shadows here are a healthy antidote to the sterile openness and glitter of her nightclub act. Just as her maternal role was preserved and represented by the veiled shots earlier, she regains her son and husband here, but without the despair and cynicism inherent in her flight from Ned.[13]

Sometimes Sternberg combines these veiled shots with movement, either the movement of character through a labyrinthine space or the movement of the camera through the obstruction. The former can be seen in the professor's emergence from behind the gauzy curtains for his final humiliation in *The Blue Angel*. The latter can be seen in *The Saga of Anatahan*, Sternberg's 1953 film about Japanese soldiers who are stranded on an island inhabited by only one woman and one man. Though World War II has ended without their knowledge, the central drama of the film is the competition between the men for Kaito (Akemi Negishi), the one woman—a familiar Sternberg theme. One particular shot of relevance is the chasing of Kaito's "husband" (Suganuma) through the jungle by one of the soldiers. The camera's movement becomes quite sinuous as it moves through the dense vegetation, past vines, around and under branches and moss. Or consider the sequence in which the soldiers first explore the island: the camera adopts something like a point-of-view shot, as it tracks ahead of them through threatening spiky plants just before they come upon the hut of Kaito and her husband. In a sense, this shot's assertive movement predicts the trouble that will inevitably result from this discovery of Kaito, for it carries with it a certain aggressiveness that portends the aggressiveness that will also emerge from the characters.

The two sequences that I have described here simulate passion spatially by creating a look and feel to the film that alerts the spectator. A repeated pan over a labyrinthine gambling pit, but behind the "veil" of the central chandelier, is a similar way of alerting the spectator in *Shanghai Gesture* to a background mob that cannot be simplified spatially. Its complexity of design is a visual clue to the complexly manipulated passions of the gamblers, with Madame Gin Sling (Ona Munson) at their center.

The Grotesque

Sternberg often incorporates what I would call the grotesque in his films; his intention is to create worlds that dislocate both the characters in his films and

The smoke of fireworks exploding on Chinese New Year punctuates Sternberg's *Shanghai Gesture* and increases our wish to penetrate the partial obscurity.

his spectators. These particular effects produce a startled reaction in his spectators by confronting us with implicit violence, madness, or oddity. Often Sternberg will juxtapose the sacred and the profane, and often he will use the grotesque to satirize a character's behavior or expectations.

The Russian court in *The Scarlet Empress* comes under fire for its barbarity, and the grotesque statues by Peter Ballbusch often set off the relative innocence and beauty of Catherine. Of course, none of these gargoyles is as bad as the grotesque images of torture and cruelty that stock Catherine's imagination when, as a child, she is read Russian horror stories. Sternberg's camera depicts the "mindscreen" of Catherine's imagination as her mind pictures the events being read to her.[14] Like the pages of a book, the screen images seem to curl back, capturing writhing bodies, iron maidens, whippings, men stretched on wheels and racks, women burned at the stake, and men turned into bell clappers.

These images dissolve into the flouncy white image of Catherine swinging in her parents' garden. Sternberg juxtaposes light and dark, innocence and brutality, and he ironically suggests that Catherine has hardly been traumatized by these tales. The "Tsarina of all the Russias" (as she is called in an introductory text following the opening credits) is inherent in this child's capacity to absorb and, no doubt, be entertained by the grotesque. Later it seems perfectly fitting for the odd-appearing actor Sam Jaffe, playing the grotesque Peter, Catherine's intended, to pull her down to sit before a cluster of oddly distorted figures to show her one of his toy soldiers. Then he leaves, whispering, "I'm in a hurry. I must witness an execution." All is in keeping with Catherine's earliest fantasies about Russia.

The wedding supper is a masterpiece of the grotesque, where Sternberg brings the inanimate gargoyles to life: a retainer bites into a pig's snout, and the empress herself grabs a drumstick, mistaking it for her sceptre. For Sternberg, the grotesque always borders on the absurd and the ludicrous. Slight shock, as when Peter's giant screw comes through the eye of a religious icon (he wants to spy on his wife), gives way to ironic laughter.

The grotesque also works in a very traditional way in Sternberg. Like grotesques that ornament cathedrals, his conception of the grotesque blends human and animal characteristics. Liturgical craftsmen would have us contemplate our beastly as well as our divine natures; Sternberg asks the same, though with a different end in mind. His grotesque always distorts human visages and bodies. It may be a simple distortion, such as the figures made mechanical who emerge from the town clock in *The Blue Angel*. (Sternberg is working with designers Otto Hunte and Emil Hasler here.) But more often this distortion is slightly terrifying, like the old and bent or gnarled and gnome-like sculptures by Ballbusch in *The Scarlet Empress*. The giant puppet heads that dance above the crowd in *The Devil Is a Woman* give us a clue to the terror that Sternberg and designer Hans Dreier may wish to inspire.

These semihuman figures remind us of our mortality. They are bent over and puffed up like excruciatingly present reminders of our imperfections. And they accomplish this moral task by being positioned always above the mass. The clock figures, connected as they are with the medium of time itself, are almost always seen from below as though we are looking up at them or being watched by them. The grotesque puppet heads in the carnival are reduced to heads alone, bouncing above the crowd and seeming to examine its human foolishness. They punctuate that scene in which Antonio is first enraptured by the sight of Concha, suggesting his intoxication. Similarly, Walter Huston's Sir Guy Charteris is surrounded by the undulating dragon of a Chinese New Year and a dancing mob when he loses his daughter Victoria/Poppy (Gene Tierney) in *Shanghai Gesture*. He is trying unsuccessfully to escape the complexities of his own past, and the grotesque dragon seems to embody those complexities. The sculptures in *The Scarlet Empress* seem to confine the characters who sit on benches or in chairs above which they hover. That these grotesques are seers of human frailty is mockingly played upon also by Peter's screw coming through the icon's eye and by their presence over each candle in the empress's bedroom, witnesses of her affairs.

The startling effect that the grotesque can produce is especially apparent in *The Shanghai Express* when a balanced composition in front of the train turns suddenly bizarre: a camel's head rises into the frame, surprising and also frustrating the spectator's expectations.

Receding Space

Though Sternberg uses camera movement sparingly, as one would expect of a director dependent on his studio in budgetary matters, he occasionally uses a forward track along a receding line into deep field to great advantage. These tracks into receding space are always leisurely and sometimes quite emotionally effective, since these movements seem to indulge the spectator's curiosity. These shots may also have some special power, since they exploit the three-dimensionality and the Renaissance illusion of three-point perspective. Is there some metaphoric illusion in these shots that the camera is penetrating the mere surface and two-dimensionality of space? Perhaps.

In *The Saga of Anatahan,* Sternberg, acting as his own cinematographer, uses this track as cleverly as Renoir and his cinematographer Christian Matras do in *The Grand Illusion* when the prisoners of war are startled into attention at the appearance of a man dressed as a woman. This shot (half-pan, half-track) successively capturing their faces conveys the utter pathos of their isolation from every woman — mother, lover, child — and the depth of their usually suppressed needs. In *Anatahan,* Sternberg, as one would expect, deals only with the lust and physical vulnerability of his isolated soldiers, but the effect is much the same. First a point-of-view shot from a low angle shows the plantation foreman emerging from the elevated hut. Then Kaito, the one woman on the island and the foreman's apparent possession (Sternberg calls her the Queen Bee in the credits), emerges behind him. What follows is a slow track down a line of staring men, awed as if by a vision, and definitely diminished and made drone-like before this vision. As in Renoir's shot, Sternberg's camera captures a fixed moment with spatial movement, which through its activity seems to stretch out the timeless suspension in which these men are caught. The camera's movement also emphasizes their frozen vulnerability; they are immobilized while the camera examines them in a self-possessed manner.

These techniques (really a cluster that we might call receding space, since they exploit that look of the frame and field) endow the camera with an autonomy that startles the spectator out of a certain complacency. The adoption of receding space resembles a shift in register for a singer; the camera shifts from a relatively passive and reserved mode to an active one in which its own presence is suddenly disclosed. These techniques simultaneously introduce a certain participatory mode for the spectator. For example, in the postwedding sequence in *The Scarlet Empress,* the camera suddenly glides down the supper table in an elaborate crane from a high angle past the bloated and unmannerly gluttons at the table. Such an omniscience is both somewhat disturbing and absolutely appropriate for Sternberg's satiric purposes here.

Sternberg's vision of flawed humanity requires this detachment at intervals. And what he achieves in relation to the spectator is twofold: we participate in his satirical omniscience, but also identify with the characters' vulnerability. The latter is apparent in the composition of a sequence in *The Scarlet Empress* in which Catherine reviews her officers—though her review resembles a seduction. Alexei (John Lodge) follows her down the line of uniformed, tall men, each staring stoically and (one feels) with difficulty straight before him. Catherine makes her selection with agonizing slowness, looking each man up and down admiringly. The point of view of Alexei, condemned within the scene to witness her selection and wish himself selected, is implicitly present in the slow track, and his discomfort is readily apparent in his somewhat abrupt but compliant gestures.

A certain wickedness on both Catherine's and Sternberg's part toward the subjects of this scrutiny colors the sequence with a delicious eroticism, which is both self-conscious and playful. With Alexei's presence, Sternberg achieves a doubling of the subordinate's discomfort in the presence of a certain voracious female self-confidence. And, unlike the crane over the postnuptial supper, Sternberg aligns the spectator with those who feel subordinated rather than with the camera's omniscience. Catherine is beginning to turn her personal power into political currency. Reinforcing that theme in this particular scene is the chosen lieutenant's gift of jewels to her and her pocketing of the proceeds. (After all, even an empress has expenses!)

The slight high angles from which Sternberg captures these receding space shots tentatively associate them with other high-angle choices that Sternberg makes. These instances of observation from above the scene are scattered throughout Sternberg's films. In themselves, they refreshingly vary the angle of vision during narrative lulls or transitions, as in *The Scarlet Empress* when the camera peers down through tree branches into a courtyard into which the Russian troops gallop, accompanying Catherine/Sophia on her way to the Russian court. The odd, distanced observation down onto this scene vitalizes the wintery bleakness of the journey. Similarly, in *Shanghai Express,* Sternberg poises the camera above a train, snatching a detail of a cow and calf on the tracks, blocking the train's progress, and in *Shanghai Gesture* the camera hovers over the deeply receding gambling pit below. A similar shot from high above the carnival crowd in *The Devil Is a Woman,* as if from the balconies surrounding the square, records a child being carried up by helium balloons; then its perspective tilts down to view the confetti-blanketed crowds in the street.

All of these shots, set early in the film, establish a certain omniscience and independent prerogative for the camera. They are a little too odd, and they call a little too much attention to themselves, to be viewed simply as establishing shots. Though they do not premise the same degree of autonomy in the camera as do certain shots in Hitchcock or Welles films, they do relate spectators to the space of the scene somewhat self-consciously, alerting us to the acute resonance of that space. Of course, almost any variation from the ordinary might accomplish this goal, but Sternberg's techniques have a peculiar unity. Not only are they repeated from film to film, they also interact with each other and become sometimes only artificially separable, like the veiled shot from a point of observation above the Russian troops in *The Scarlet Empress.* Stern-

This high-angle shot under the chandelier and down into the gambling pit in Sternberg's *Shanghai Gesture* shows a familiar spatial strategy used by Sternberg and his
cameramen. The baroque detail of railings and chandelier gives the scene a complexity that matches the characters' interaction. Characters here are played by Ona Munson, Victor Mature, and Marcel Dalio.

berg's impulse is to balk our ordinary expectations of space — to give space
plenitude and to animate its volumes in such a way that it exudes atmosphere.

Concealed Sight

Closely related to what I have called veiled shots are a cluster of techniques
that seek similarly to reveal only by concealing. The spectator's view of a subject is consequently a shadowy one, hampered in some way by constricting
barriers or by a carefully composed distribution of shadow and light. Doors
may be closed before the camera's eye, or the edges of the frame may seem to
close in on a point deep in the field seen by a camera poised between narrow
walls. Sternberg often composes his shots so that the foreground (and sometimes the side as well) is darkened by shadow, and the mid-ground or background of the field is illuminated. The effect of a solid barrier or darkened
frame is similar: it directs the action into the background, consequently away
from the spectator's clear view of detail. It suggests a certain preordained des-
tiny for the figures within such a composed frame, but it also maintains a cer-

tain sense of the unpredictable, because the overall obscurity conveyed by these shots promises no clarity of sight.

I've named these techniques concealed sight because a certain paradox is inherent in them: they do, indeed, provide us with sight, though limited, and with insight, though it is sometimes conveyed in a negative way by the absence of an expected quality. For instance, Sternberg positions the camera behind and above the back of the bed against which Peter (Sam Jaffe) is murdered in *The Scarlet Empress,* thus concealing Peter's suffering from us and preventing our identification with him. That he is backed against a cross, though, suggests that his slaying has a sacrificial, almost ritualistic function, like the annual slaying of the king to mark the winter's sterility and the creation of a new king to insure the goddess's and the land's fertility.

While it may seem confused on Sternberg's part to position Peter like a Christ against a cross, what is unseen is more significant here than what is seen. The spectator's wish is for Peter's death, but also for an absolution from any ensuing guilt. By staging the death in this concealed way, Sternberg allows the suggestion of ritual fitness to predominate over the particularity of the allusion. Concealment, then, abstracts spectators from both the violence of the scene and our own somewhat guilty pleasure in that violence.

Unlike Lubitsch's threshold response, which works similarly with barriers to clear vision, Sternberg's instances of concealed sight do not invite us to imagine what is not present. Sternberg, for one thing, seldom conceals what would be altogether pleasurable to see, and so his withholding of the possibility of sight in part grants our wish that he do so. Sternberg seems to tread on potentially traumatic ground, although the same thing might be seen by Lubitsch in a joyfully lusty or romping way.

Consider, for example, Catherine tending the old empress (Louise Dresser) by blowing out the candles in her bedroom and then admitting her lover through a secret staircase. Since this is an initiatory and disillusioning event for Catherine, Sternberg treats it with somberness. He half reveals and half conceals Catherine's dawning horror of two things: that Alexei who flirts outrageously with her is the empress's lover, and that the empress (a mother surrogate) is having an illicit affair with a much younger man. Catherine progresses around the room blowing out the candles one by one, protective grotesques hovering over each. Then she descends the secret staircase, the walls on either side seeming to close in on the narrow margin between. But the combination of enclosing walls and the use of streaky shadows occurs when she sees Alexei run up the stairs and she follows. That she listens at the top of the stairs to the lovemaking of the empress and Alexei is only implied by the superimposition of her bewildered face on the barrier of the closed door; that her face in closeup bears a certain resemblance to the grotesques above the candles earlier, that Catherine is often reduced to silhouette, and that her face as she again descends should be lighted eerily from below, all suggest Sternberg's vision of her inner anguish and sense of betrayal.

The same highly erotic situation in Lubitsch — a sexual encounter taking place behind a closed door — would coyly ask us to imagine it in lieu of its concealment, and to enjoy our imaginative powers as we assume the couple is enjoying the liaison. The narrative clearly creates our spatial expectations as much perhaps as the spatial techniques imply what is omitted in the narrative.

As with the narrow walls of that secret staircase in *The Scarlet Empress,* Sternberg lights his sets to draw us away from the foreground and deeper into the field. These instances of concealed sight are apparent in Sternberg's films as early as *Underworld* (1927) and *The Last Command* (1928). Even certain scenes in a film like Sternberg's *Crime and Punishment* (1935 version produced at Paramount) can boast of acute space, a space permeated by a psychological intensity that the otherwise tedious narrative in the film can't sustain. Though overplayed, the two confessional meetings of Raskolnikov (Peter Lorre) with Sonia (Marian Marsh), first at her rooms and then on the bridge, position him in the dark foreground with a lighted but unoccupied space behind. Sternberg's driven, at best morally ambiguous characters often remain shadowed in this way. In *Blonde Venus,* when Helen leaves Ned and Johnny for the first time

In Sternberg's *Blonde Venus,* the character played by Marlene Dietrich tries to prevent her husband from gaining custody of their son. The tension of her life on the run is apparent in the mottled lighting and in the spatial barriers that she must penetrate as she and the maid (Hattie McDaniel) check the boy.

to go to work in the nightclub, the two follow her down the stairs from their apartment until they are half-silhouetted in the darker foreground.

At other times, the spectator feels detached from the characters because they exist on the other side of this shadowy foreground. And sometimes Sternberg uses veiled shots as well to create barriers between our sight and the characters in deep field. This is true of both Catherine in the wedding scene in *The Scarlet Empress*, and of the professor as he weaves his way through narrow alleys toward the nightclub where Lola Lola works in *The Blue Angel*. In the former, the camera cranes down from the old empress high in a pulpit, past monks holding banners and candles, past and behind candles and incense (now silhouetted in the dark foreground) to peer through a veiled canopy, behind which the well-lit ceremony is occurring. As is true of Catherine behind a veiled curtain after her first child is born, the camera seems to have no access to her. Both the lighting and the veil remove her into a space separate from our own spectators' space.

Face Space

A large part of Sternberg's creation of acute space is centered in the way he directs Marlene Dietrich (and, of course, the way in which she acts). His concentration on her face and gestures is both positive and direct, unlike his treatment of other kinds of space. But, in a sense, this exception proves the rule. All of Sternberg's indirection serves what he handles with directness, and all of his concealment serves to reveal her in the films. And, perhaps, were it not for this exceptional center around which all of his stylistic evasiveness circles, his stylistic evasiveness would feel gratuitous. Certainly this important spatial dialectic (concealment/revelation, indirection/directness) is missing from his silent films, such as *Underworld* (1927), *The Last Command* (1928), and *The Salvation Hunters* (1925), though his attitudes toward concealment are visible in embryonic form.

But perhaps more telling is the flatness of *Thunderbolt* (1929), *Crime and Punishment* (1935), *Jet Pilot* (1957), and even *The Saga of Anatahan* (1953), though in the last of these Sternberg uses Akemi Negishi spatially very much as he uses Dietrich. The result resembles a parody of Sternberg's best direction. Aesthetically *Anatahan* fits into Sternberg's career as *The Old Man and the Sea* fits into Hemingway's and *A Fable* fits into Faulkner's. It is a pared-down version of the story that obsessed him throughout his career, but it is so simplified as to become an allegory. It is skeletal Sternberg, taking his career nearly full circle back to *The Salvation Hunters*, in which the cast is listed as "the boy, the girl, the child, the man, the woman, the brute, and the gentleman."

Sternberg treats the face as a familiar landscape; every contour is lighted or shaded with precision, though in treating Dietrich's physiognomy he is largely an impressionist. The close-ups use a diffused light, made soft by filters over the camera lens. In the "Hot Voodoo" number in *Blonde Venus*, Dietrich's face is sculpted by shadow and light, dark shadows beneath her cheeks stylizing her look and creating a visual equivalent for her smoky voice. Later, when Dietrich's Helen loses her son and husband and returns to the nightclub circuit, her face looks much the same—itself stylized so that the cheek bones seem to protrude sharply—and her costume further stylizes her appearance. She is dressed in a white tuxedo with sequinned lapels and is smoking a cigarette in a long black holder.

But most of the drama of Dietrich's face in *Blonde Venus* is the drama of its withdrawal from us. When Ned (Herbert Marshall) confronts Nick and Helen in Nick's apartment after he has returned from his treatment in Europe, Sternberg withholds Helen's face from us by positioning it behind an elaborate fur collar. Ned's face likewise is shadowed beneath his hat. Then later when Helen voluntarily gives up their son Johnny to Ned at the train station, both sit on a bench facing to the right, their faces shadowed by hats. Whereas we see her surprised eyes in the first of these two scenes, they are lost to us in the second until the crucial moment of Ned and Johnny boarding the train. Because Sternberg has withheld it from us, he can achieve the impact of then revealing this despair as Helen watches them board, eyes wide with terror.

Dietrich's face in this film either recedes from or projects what the narrative demands. And Herbert Marshall's face seconds hers, doubling the hurt and defensiveness between them in mid-film and venting some of this defensiveness on Nick at the end, when Nick tries to buy ten minutes for Helen with Johnny at 1,000 dollars a minute. Ned retorts, "I suppose you feel pretty good the way you can throw money around; 10,000 dollars for ten minutes doesn't mean very much to you. Well, it doesn't mean anything to me. I can throw money around the same as you can. Let her come in, for nothing." During this exchange, Nick (Cary Grant) has withdrawn under his hat, his face shadowed, unlike the situation when he controlled Helen earlier. The withdrawal of his face is an elaborate, almost ritualistic gesture that forecasts a plot reversal, though the dialogue doesn't effect this until Ned joins Helen in Johnny's going-to-sleep routine later in the sequence.

During the final angry exchange between Ned and Nick, it is as though Nick absorbs Ned's righteous anger, drawing it from him and then leaving the scene. Faces in the film are the repositories for the extreme emotions felt by the characters, but are often withheld from the spectator under some cover—either a literal cover like a hat or an aesthetic cover like the costumed, stylized world of the nightclub show. In the second nightclub sequence in *Blonde Venus,* one observer says of Helen, "They say she's as cold as the proverbial icicle." Indeed, the rigidity of her face and the stylized sensuality of a woman's body poured into masculine attire convey a mask as readily as do the mask-like shields in the "Hot Voodoo" dance.

An important part of the way Sternberg defines the space of faces is in his use of double frames. A similar relation exists in his films between stylized gestural language of the whole body and the double framing of doors. The first close-up, for instance, of Dietrich's face in *Shanghai Express* frames it in a train window on the left. Sternberg reserves this sort of portraiture for crucial moments like this one in which Dietrich's Shanghai Lily is again meeting Captain Harvey (Clive Brook), after having known him in the past, one assumes intimately. Or in *The Scarlet Empress,* Catherine as a young girl sits in a chair, which frames her, and the spirals of the gilt frame on the back of the chair also seem to double the coils of her hair. The bodice of her dress completes the frame of her smooth face.

Sternberg and Dietrich call on physiology to develop a very stylized facial language that can convey a variety of messages about love, hatred, and most of what lies in between and to either side. By stylized I mean that, even in a close-up, Sternberg requires a certain exaggerated timing in his capturing of these emotions on the face. In real life, if these fleeting messages were caught by a glance, they would be less blatant, more accidental, and less observable. Sternberg exaggerates time to make them more visible and so forces the spectator into a state of slightly uncomfortable self-consciousness, for these moments are somewhat taboo, and here is a director making them unavoidable.

One of these uncomfortable moments occurs when Shanghai Lily shifts her eyes in a half-curve from side to side to indicate to Captain Harvey that she is sexually interested in him. His slow descent to kiss her is equally excruciating, since it is interrupted. Certainly, most of us have been guilty of the indirection of seduction, the glance from the side of the eye that is meant to be caught only by the object of the glance. But Sternberg takes an intimate, momentary, almost involuntary, and certainly unplanned impulse and creates a facial drama. The double shift of her eyes from side to side occurs again in the film when the lovers are reconciled. The gesture oddly combines innocence — a seeming inability to focus directly on the doctor due, one supposes, to embarrassment — with experience; Lily wishes both to be seen as vulnerable and to be known to be desirous.

It has always struck me about Sternberg that he is far more intrigued by the invitation to desire than he is by the satisfaction of desire. In *Shanghai Express,* the final kiss of Lily/Madeleine by Captain Harvey is obscured by a superimposition over their kiss of a shot of passengers swarming through a gate. Whereas invitations can be direct and clearly seen, facial expressions must be indirect and obscured. As long as Poppy (Gene Tierney) in *Shanghai Gesture* remains mysterious and resists the gambling addiction that later overtakes her, Sternberg treats her face as he does Dietrich's, but her face loses its definition as she succumbs, becoming blurry as have the boundaries of her personality.

In the extreme close-up of Catherine during the wedding ceremony in *The Scarlet Empress* (1934), Dietrich's face seems to be qualified by the positioning of a candle before it. And the direction of her glance distracts our attention first toward Alexei, with whom she exchanges glances, and then toward Jaffe's Peter and his mad, bulging, shifting eyes. Later, Sternberg modifies the close-ups of Catherine blowing out the candles in the empress's bedroom by positioning her face, again, next to a source of light, and next to the odd sculptures that grace each candleholder. Such small, dark, gnarled figures would seem only to set off Dietrich's extreme beauty. But like the glances exchanged with Alexei during the wedding, this juxtaposition within the frame also suggests a mirroring between Catherine and these shadow figures. Space may typically be thought of as a mere void offering nothing more or less than freedom of movement. But Sternberg's aim opposes these assumptions. He defines space by its limits and his characters by their flaws or their learned disillusionment. Space is clearly an extension of character in these techniques.

Gestural Posture

Sternberg does not just use the face to create and modify the space within the frame. He also uses the potential of the whole body for conveying gestural messages and for activating the space of the frame, a strategy that I call gestural posture. This strategy is nonverbal and emphasizes the whole body in space, the body's upright or slouching posture rather than particular gestures by the hands or shoulders.

The Scarlet Empress is a film of particular note in this regard, since Catherine's growing up is recorded, like Citizen Kane's decline into old age, in the changing rhythms of her body in space. No one scene marks a sudden transition from her childhood to her adulthood, although the climactic, shadowy disillusionment after she admits Alexei to the old empress's bedroom and her subsequent sexual awakening in the wintery garden with a lucky common soldier are turning points. The younger Catherine's relation to space is to bounce within it. Her body occupies space in great curves. For instance, she romps down a curving staircase to meet the envoy from the Russian court, and our first view of her as a young adult is her ascent toward the camera in a great arching swing so that her petticoats fill the frame flower-like. Even after Catherine's marriage to Peter, Sternberg often captures her on the run. A promising relief from this flurry occurs with Alexei's attempted seduction of her in the stables, for Catherine actually holds still, though she sways seductively in a curve from a descending rope. Sternberg uses some languid music on the sound track. But a comic and startling horse's whinny launches her into action again: she jumps up, twirls, and runs.

Real stillness, and a new recognition of political ironies, seem to follow her sense of having been betrayed by Alexei and the ironic celebration of her for having borne an heir (not Peter's child but a common soldier's) to the throne. Spatially the latter of these events may be the more important. After picturing the old empress, triumphant though ill in her bed, Sternberg shows Catherine also in her bed. But the vulgarity of the old empress contrasts with Catherine's nearly complete stillness. Only her hand moves languidly, twirling a jewel sent to her by the old empress. Sternberg's camera remains behind the net curtain surrounding the bed, nearly abstracting Catherine's body into a still pattern of black and white dots.

From this point forward in the film, Catherine's physical movements in space are only politically motivated. As Sternberg has distanced Catherine from the camera and stilled her projection of movement from within, Catherine becomes psychologically self-contained. Her movements within the frame begin to reflect her intellectual reactions to events around her rather than her feelings about them. Also, Catherine is seen veiled only twice more — once when she, in fact, controls the veil to separate herself from Alexei, and later when she emerges from behind it to claim total political power. This change in the nature of veiled shots suggests that Catherine's posture and face now function not as expressive agents but as reflecting ones. Rather than being made to seem subordinate to external veils and obstructions in the space of the frame, Catherine usurps that spatial prerogative. What has been earlier controlled spatially by those veils and obstructions is now displaced by her gestural posture, and the veils that remain are under her control.

Gestural posture exerts control in space by its grace, slowness, or deliberation. The last is probably the most important. For instance, Catherine pulls the bell rope at the end of the film, pealing her own ascension to the throne. This act's deliberation contrasts with her listening passively as a child (played by Maria Sieber) to the Russian tales of terror, ending with a hanged man used as the clapper of a giant bell. Similarly, she is carried into the cathedral by the same route the camera had used to approach her during her involuntary wedding earlier in the film. The slowness of her movements is apparent when she seduces the army and teaches Alexei a lesson. Her deliberate slowness forces those around her to adopt her pace and to rivet their attention on her.

Sternberg further emphasizes the grace and slowness of her movements by double-framing her body, as he also does to highlight her face in a spatial way. When Catherine is reviewing the troops, she positions herself between two bunk beds, drawing a straw from one of the mattresses into her mouth. This use of an inner screen is a much more pervasive technique than just in the work of Sternberg, of course. Perhaps more than with any other director, I associate this double-framing with John Ford. Who can forget Martha (Dorothy Jordan) standing first in the door and then double-framed between the porch supports as Ethan (John Wayne) arrives from a distance in *The Searchers*? Compared to Sternberg's use of double-framing, however, Ford's is highly self-conscious, as can be seen in the closing shots of *The Searchers* when Ford reverses the angle through that door and has Ethan framed outside the house when he turns from it.

Sternberg certainly has his self-conscious moments, framing Lily in *Shanghai Express,* for instance, in a door right before she offers to go away with Chang (Warner Oland) in return for Captain Harvey's life. And Concha in *The Devil Is a Woman* poses provocatively in the governor's doorway when she is trying to finesse Antonio out of prison. Like Ford's use of the door frame in *The Searchers,* these self-conscious moments remind us that we are watchers, as well as alert us to the acute spatial significance of a narrative moment. The purpose of that reminder is to distance us from Lily's or Concha's overt action, the seduction of a powerful bureaucrat, and to alert us more sympathetically to the underlying personal sacrifice. In *Blonde Venus,* Ned's double-framing in the doorway of Nick's apartment, when he surprises Nick and Helen with his early return from Europe, similarly sets him apart morally from the other two.

Silhouettes and Superimpositions

These two techniques have nothing intrinsically to do with each other, but they both are related to Sternberg's spatial attitudes in similar ways. Both maintain and reinforce the frame as an absolute boundary of vision. The silhouette does this by reiterating the frame within the frame, inserting an otherwise three-dimensional, detailed figure in a flat dark space that reinforces the power of the larger dark frame outside the focal space. The silhouette also confirms Sternberg's attitude that what can only be seen with difficulty may be more stimulating to the spectator than a clear, sharply focused picture. Like his veiled shot, the darkness in a silhouette obstructs the spectators' vision and potentially alerts us to the acute need for vision in a less literal sense.

Superimpositions function spatially in the same ways for Sternberg; that is, they call our attention to the frame by having it frame and contain two or more shots at once, and they make the spectators' task more difficult by asking us to see more than one scene at once. Superimposition always convinces me of Bruce Kawin's idea of the screen acting as a "mindscreen," a sort of self-conscious medium that tries to convey the content of a mind, often the director's or the narrative's (if we want to be more formalist). The resemblance of superimposition to what we call "free association" has always amused me. It is as though the director packs more than one image on the screen, sits back with a certain glee, and challenges his spectator to read the metaphor that results from tenor and vehicle, juxtaposed in this way. Not unlike Eisenstein's theories of editing, but going another step by positioning one image on top of the other, the technique does indeed require some simple dialectical thinking.

Perhaps the most startling use of silhouette occurs in the intensely shadowy scenes in Sternberg's *Blonde Venus.* Unlike the silhouetted action, for instance, of the changeover of troops in *Shanghai Express,* the use of the silhouette in *Blonde Venus* cannot be wholly attributed to budgetary considerations; the elegance is too deliberate. As Helen departs for her first night at the club, she moves down the stairs and into shadow, and then out of the frame. Ned and Johnny are partially silhouetted as they move down the stairs to see her off. The light falls behind them in a pool by the apartment door. Shadow envelops them, especially Johnny, who retreats farther and farther from that light source. Both Johnny and Ned become featureless. This movement reflects what will also occur in the narrative: Helen will be lost to them both, and the two consequently will be plunged into emotional darkness. Johnny will lose most, since Helen, after all, makes Ned's cure possible.

Later in *Blonde Venus,* two similar shots gain narrative resonance when compared to one another. The first is a low-angle shot through the silhouette of some chairs in the foreground, as Helen stoops in the doorway to collect the mail accumulated in Ned's absence. She herself is not silhouetted, although she wears a black dress that associates her with the obstruction through which the shot is taken. Later, Ned arrives home earlier than expected, picks up the accumulated mail including his telegram telling about his own arrival, and opens the shades. Sinking into a chair facing the windows, his back to the camera, he reads the telegram and shades into a silhouette as he drops it. These echoing shots establish the necessary complication in the plot.

But there are also important contrasts between the two scenes. Although Helen is having an affair, she is maintaining contact with Ned, always assuming that she will return to the ordinary life they had lived together. Ned, on the other hand, is both a pessimist and an absolutist (the latter quality, a form of self-righteousness, is probably what makes him less sympathetic to Sternberg). Helen simply absorbs the tension between the two men's worlds. Ned, put in a defensive position, turns aggressively against Nick's world and in so doing feels obliged to reject Helen with it.

Sternberg uses light and shadow metaphorically. He sees all humans as existing within a shadowy world, which they themselves help to create. But some characters sink into shadow, as Ned does, and others like Helen move in and out of shadow, resisting it when it is possible.

Sternberg doesn't admire the depressives in his films. That may in part account for the young Dietrich's unexpected dominance of *The Blue Angel,* even though Emil Jannings had top billing as a big star and respected veteran actor. Sternberg does admire resilience. And, while he is not particularly interested in spelling out Dietrich's motives in the various films, her actions are archetypically realized in the film's space.

Sternberg uses superimposition in a very conventional way in *The Scarlet Empress* to construct transitional montages that usually mark the passage of time or make a simple thematic point, though there is the exceptional moment when Catherine listens at the top of the stairs to the empress and Alexei's lovemaking. Here it clearly makes a psychological point, since it seems to lift her face out of one frame and place it in another, thus suggesting her alienation from her former innocent self.

Sternberg also uses superimposition for psychological purposes in *Shanghai Express* and *Crime and Punishment.* In the latter film, it conveys the obsessive quality of Raskolnikov's mind. Here Sternberg and editor Richard Cahoon displace his memories and fears into the space surrounding him — usually the enclosed confines of a room. This seems to suggest that Raskolnikov is driven to commit the murder by a certain paranoia, for as he prepares to go to the pawnbroker's he imagines slights that have occurred to him. These superimpositions, though, are more ghostly pictorializations in the space of the closed room than spatializations of a state of mind. Sternberg identifies what he is thinking about rather than showing us how he is thinking.

The latter is more the case with his use of a superimposition in *Shanghai Express*. In this instance, Lily prays for Captain Harvey's life. We see only her hands pressed in prayer in the light superimposed over the steam from the train. Then a clock emerges from the shot. Though the last touch is a bit too literal a way to show that time has passed, the agony of waiting, the associations of emotional arrivals and departures, reunions and separations that the steam carries are highly successful ways of conveying Lily's prayer and the fears that motivate it. Sternberg also cuts the sentimentality of the lighted hands with the superimposed billowing steam, and he contrasts the motion of the train and Lily's vagabond life with the stillness of her prayer. The dialectic within the shot is, as a consequence, a dialectic within Lily, between her contradictory impulses. Her settling, loving impulse toward the captain conflicts with her image in others' eyes, the image she will in fact exploit in the next sequence when she trades her sexual favors for the captain's life.

Independent Camera

Sternberg uses the independent movement of the camera rather sparingly compared to Hitchcock's slightly eccentric and slightly wicked granting of autonomy to the camera. Nor is Sternberg's use of the camera as relentless as is Welles's once an opportunity arises. Instead, Sternberg tends to limit these highly expressive moments to the crucial narrative demands of the beginnings, middles, and endings of films. *The Blue Angel* is a good example. The middle and the ending of the film both rely upon the same retreating movement of the independent camera away from the professor and slowly back over the desks in the classroom before him. This repetition of the shot, in retrospect, suggests a certain inevitability in the professor's fate after he is forced to resign and the camera first retreats in this way. The camera seems to disavow any involvement, though, since the retreating movement broadens the scope of the frame and abandons the professor to a larger context.

Hitchcock's use of a retreating camera in *Frenzy* is considerably more wicked. It stops abruptly at the necktie killer's apartment door after tracking behind him and his next victim up the stairs. But there it stops and reverses itself, travelling backwards down the stairs, out the door, and even across traffic with a dissolve. Hitchcock's retreating camera implicates the spectator in a way Sternberg's does not. We clearly don't want to see this murder and don't want to get involved, so that Hitchcock's fulfillment of our wishes is also something like an accusation.[15] Sternberg's characters are so much more a part of a benighted world that we feel relieved of guilt when the camera retreats from them. The camera's act is self-conscious, but its retreat allows us contemplative distance rather than accusing us of escape.

Like Lubitsch, Sternberg wishes to reveal what is hidden; but he does not use comedy to delve into the human psyche. Lubitsch deflates the pomposity and peels back the masks of his characters with a certain mischievous glee. Sternberg, on the other hand, creates a dark, shadowy image of his characters' psyches. It is as though Sternberg identifies the labyrinthine moral state of his characters and then projects it onto their spatial contexts. He endows the seemingly inanimate objects on his screen with a kind of psychological tension — what we expect to find only in an actor's performance. In this way, Sternberg charges his film space with the intensity that locales can possess in dreams or nightmares.

Sternberg's film space is often most acute when he exploits the paradox that what is hidden may most stimulate our curiosity to look and find. And Sternberg understands another side of this principle — that what is most examined and revealed (such as Dietrich's face) may be most mysterious, if the character's motives remain undefined. Sternberg seems to get into trouble with critics because he wants to maintain mystery and complexity rather than resolve it. When directors withhold characters' motives, they force their spectators to remain active; Sternberg also maintains a certain bleakness in his narrative world, which can frustrate spectators who want happier endings and simple moral dualism.

Sternberg's films, as I see them, might well be used to illustrate the more complex moral stages identified by Perry and then by Belenky, Clinchy, Goldberger, and Tarule in their studies of young adults.[16] The more complex thinkers have given up the wrong-versus-right, either-or dualistic thought patterns of their adolescence. They come to know the world as Sternberg knows it, as full of multiple perspectives. Still, Sternberg's plots do not create an entirely relativistic world, since his characters do make choices based on a sort of contextual ethics. Perry or Belenky would place him in their most reflective and self-conscious category.

While recognizing the multiplicity of points of view and their relativity, Sternberg's central characters choose one creative option from among many. In addition, they rarely choose stereotypically. Sternberg often explodes the conventions of romantic narrative — by having Concha choose the older man in *The Devil,* by having Catherine choose no man in *Scarlet Empress,* by having Poppy killed in *Shanghai Gesture,* by having Professor Rath die in *Blue Angel,* by having a series of murders in *Anatahan.* Even the somewhat conventional reconciliation of Helen and Ned in *Blonde Venus* is a patched-together job, representing compromise, not idealization. Perhaps only the closure used in *Shanghai Express* offers a facile solution for a morally ambiguous set of problems, Lily having earned Captain Harvey's forgiveness.

Of the four directors in this study, Sternberg strikes me as the most attentive to all aspects of film space — volumes, props, camera movement, actors, and optical techniques — while also creating the most spatially consistent body of films. In part, his spatial consistency depends upon the marginal worlds that he features — a gambling den, a travelling nightclub troupe, worlds in political upheaval, and places where characters are unnaturally isolated or in stress. Sternberg captures his spectators' ambivalence, in part, by his arrangement of film space — its murkiness correlating with our reluctance to enter these spaces.

A second area of reluctance for his spectators is to acknowledge an intriguing gender-neutrality. It is not that Sternberg doesn't acknowledge all of the sexual forms of play between men and women, but rather that he doesn't assign to each sex any gender-specific roles. As a consequence, his women characters can be as sexually aggressive as his male characters — and often are even more so. His male characters, such as the jilted Antonio in *The Devil,* can be merely passive. Sternberg invests his actors with an unpredictability that complements the labyrinthine qualities of his film space.

NOTES

1. Josef von Sternberg, *Fun in a Chinese Laundry* (London: Secker and Warburg, 1966), p. 311.

2. Andrew Sarris, for instance, says, "Although there is much violence and death in Sternberg's world, there is relatively little action"; see *The Films of Josef von Sternberg* (New York: Museum of Modern Art, 1966), p. 8. Peter Baxter includes some of B. G. Braver-Mann's complaints in 1934 about Sternberg's "pictorialism for its own sake" and "directorial incoherence" in his collection, *Sternberg* (London: British Film Institute, 1980), pp. 28–34.

3. John Baxter says that Sternberg's visual sense dominates any narrative impulse: "True art, whether painting, sculpture or film, had, he sensed, little to do with story"; see *The Cinema of Josef von Sternberg* (New York: A. S. Barnes, 1971), p. 10. Florence Jacobowitz sees Sternberg's aestheticism as distancing the viewer "by drawing attention to its artifice," in "Power and the Masquerade: *The Devil Is a Woman,*" *CineAction!* 8 (1987): 33. But she sees these techniques as serving a complex plot in *The Devil* that "counters the male narrating point of view" (p. 41).

4. Lionel Trilling, *The Liberal Imagination: Essays on Literature and Society* (London: Secker and Warburg, 1951), pp. 61–65.

5. John Baxter points out that "most of his films leap years in the telling, charting an emotional relationship or moral decline without respect for chronology" (*Cinema of Josef von Sternberg,* p. 16).

6. Sarris emphasizes the hopeless quality of these events: "His characters generally make their first entrance at a moment in their lives when there is no tomorrow. Knowingly or unknowingly, they have reached the end or the bottom, but they will struggle a short time longer, about 90 minutes of screen time, to discover the truth about themselves and those they love" (*Films of Josef von Sternberg,* p. 8).

7. Sarris sees Sternberg's films as egocentric: "Sternberg's exoticism is then less a pretense than a pretext for objectifying personal fantasies" (*Films of Josef von Sternberg,* p. 8). The feminist debate over Sternberg's work is waged in Jacobowitz, "Power and the Masquerade"; Robin Wood, "Venus de Marlene," *Film Comment* 14 (1978): 58–63; Bill Nichols, "*Blonde Venus:* Playing with Performance," in Nichols, *Ideology and the Image* (Bloomington: Indiana Univ. Press, 1981), pp. 104–132; and E. Ann Kaplan, "Fetishism and the Repression of Motherhood in Von Sternberg's *Blonde Venus* (1932)," in

Kaplan, *Women and Film: Both Sides of the Camera* (New York: Methuen, 1983), pp. 49–59. Peter Baxter examines the psychoanalytic dimensions of the mother-child relationship in *"Blonde Venus:* Memory, Legend, and Desire," *CineAction!* 8 (1987): 42–50; and Gaylyn Studlar sees the Sternberg/Dietrich texts as exemplifying a "masochistic aesthetic," *In the Realm of Pleasure* (Urbana: Univ. of Illinois Press, 1988), p. 4. Barry Salt meticulously studies the relatively greater number of close-ups in the films that feature Dietrich in his essay, "Sternberg's Heart Beats in Black and White"; see Peter Baxter, *Sternberg,* pp. 103–118.

8. Susan Sontag convincingly explores some of these complexities in her essay, "The Pornographic Imagination," in *Styles of Radical Will* (New York: Farrar, Straus and Giroux, 1969), p. 41.

9. John Baxter, *Cinema of Josef von Sternberg,* p. 20.

10. Sternberg, *Fun in a Chinese Laundry,* p. 325.

11. Both Sarris (*Films of Josef von Sternberg,* p. 11) and John Baxter (*Cinema of Josef von Sternberg,* pp. 20, 29–30, 71) discuss the use of veils and other obstructions to sight. Jacobowitz believes that these veils and masks dramatize the reversals of gender roles in *The Devil Is a Woman* ("Power and the Masquerade," p. 36).

12. Robin Wood discusses "Sternberg's strange personal fusion of anguish and cynicism" in the *Scarlet Empress* in his article, "Sternberg's *Empress:* The Play of Light and Shade," *Film Comment* 11 (1975): 7.

13. Lea Jacobs argues for perceiving *Blonde Venus,* and especially its final ending, as a subversive text in her study of its censorship history, "The Censorship of *Blonde Venus:* Textual Analysis and Historical Method," *Cinema Journal* 27 (1988): 21–31.

14. Bruce Kawin coins this term in *Mindscreen: Bergman, Godard, and First-Person Film* (Princeton, N.J.: Princeton Univ. Press, 1978), pp. 3–22.

15. I am indebted in this discussion to Joseph W. Miller's ideas as presented in his Hitchcock course at the University of Maryland, 1975.

16. William Graves Perry, *Forms of Intellectual and Ethical Development in the College Years: A Scheme* (New York: Holt, Rinehart and Winston, 1970); Mary Field Belenky, Blythe McVicker Clinchy, Nancy Rule Goldberger, and Jill Mattuck Tarule, *Women's Ways of Knowing: The Development of Self, Voice, and Mind* (New York: Basic Books, 1986).

6

WYLER'S FILM SPACE: ARRANGING CONFRONTATION TO INTENSIFY UNDERSTANDING

William Wyler's example helps us to distinguish between auteur directors and those directors who promote a consistent spatial look in a number of films. The two are not the same. As Michael Anderegg points out in his study of Wyler, Wyler would have been the first to admit that his corpus lacks the consistent themes, character types, or recurrent visual configurations that mark an auteur director.[1] And though Anderegg in part refutes this position by locating recurrent concerns and themes in the films, I think most of us would admit, especially in relation to a director like Frank Capra, that Wyler took on projects of much greater variety. Capra or, to take another example, Hitchcock, seemed able to create genres. Perhaps they had the freedom to foster this creativity. But something recognizably "Wyleresque" did flourish for a time in his career within the relatively strict bounds set by producer, script, and studio.[2]

I will not deal here with the reasons for the impressive peak in Wyler's corpus. (Warren French Smith theorizes that his later decline coincided with his disillusionment during the McCarthy era, along with a loss of perhaps necessary bounds, due to the breakdown of the studio system.)[3] I want to examine more simply the "look" of Wyler's peak films. What, for instance, does Wyler's vision of space consist of? How can it be identified? Why is it more appropriate for some fictions and less successful for others?

Wyler's peak, as I see it, comes midcareer, following a thorough apprenticeship in both silent and sound film and followed by a number of well-crafted but unmoving films in his later years. I don't mean this as an absolute statement. Faulkner wrote *Requiem for a Nun* even after *The Town* and *Intruder in the Dust;* it seems to escape the tendency that he had to parody himself. Wyler made *The Collector* late in his career, but I will argue that it succeeds differently than those films for which Wyler is most justly remembered—for those films that cohere in a body. His midcareer films work because Wyler imposes a certain view of space upon their narratives.

Where does this vision of space most obviously occur? In *Dodsworth* (1936), *The Letter* (1940), *The Little Foxes* (1946), and *The Best Years of Our Lives* (1946). I see similar effects even in other films that are not quite as impressive, such as *The Good Fairy* (1935), *Jezebel* (1938), and *Wuthering Heights* (1939), and in a later film like *The Heiress* (1949). Wyler's vision of space is least apparent in *Detective Story* (1951), *Carrie* (1952), and *Roman Holiday* (1953). Their spatial acuity seems lax, for reasons I will try to explain.

Wyler's view of space emerges most dramatically in circumstances where, by occupying certain spatial configurations, a character can define his own relationship to space. These spatial configurations, especially triangular structures and deep-focus or double-framed space, allow characters to define themselves within space by reorienting themselves in relation to a new set of possibilities. This sort of narrative action complements Wyler's point of view, which eschews explicit expressions of the characters' inner states in favor of an implicit delineation of their feelings and the tensions between them in the screen's space.[4]

Wyler and his cinematographer on many films, Gregg Toland, have a number of means by which they achieve this. Wyler tends, for instance, to have characters confront each other in space, two or three characters among whom the spectator senses emotional vectors that charge the space they occupy. When Wyler achieves this charged space, he further exploits it by reusing it, charged still with entities now absent but whose memory continues to intensify the space. Another characteristic means by which Wyler emotionalizes space (or spatializes emotion) is by focusing and tightening space itself. When Gregg Toland shoots down a hallway or between barriers, the effect is to narrow and, by contrast, to deepen the space within which characters act out the fictions. By contracting space, Wyler narrows his characters' choices and creates a sense of inevitability by constricting their movement. Wyler is most interested, though, in characters confronted with concrete dilemmas, especially in how they learn to encounter others in objectified situations, in which one character cannot project his inner assumptions upon space due to the presence of others. Wyler's three-person configurations minimize this sort of projection, which he regards as socially negative.

ACUTE SPACE

The Character Triangle

With a character at each point of the triangle, Wyler produces a spatial configuration that acts as an equivalent for the emotion between them. Likewise, he uses Toland's already developed deep focus to convey powerful emotions. Both these techniques result in the embodiment of emotion in space. Wyler's strategy opposes that of a director like Ingmar Bergman, for whom all emotion seems to reside in the face, and who as a consequence relies upon close-ups and superimpositions or the close proximity of face to face. Emotion for Wyler is a social reality; it is always seen in the context of a community, though that community may be simply a three-way confrontation. We do not necessarily see Wyler's perspective as social rather than psychological, or as public rather than private. But we recognize that Wyler is utterly intrigued by the emotionalized vectors that bind characters to one another.

In some ways, *The Best Years of Our Lives* can be seen as a film in which Wyler closes the distances between characters. The film's initial layering of the returning soldiers in the plexiglass nose of the airplane sets an initial standard of health in this spatial closeness, but it is a health that serves a simpler, all-male society. The film as a whole must reachieve this closeness, but between men and women. Triangular configurations can also lead to redefinitions of relationships, as in *Dodsworth*.

Consider, for instance, the very social way in which Wyler composes Al's homecoming and reunion with Milly in *Best Years*. Al (Fredric March) meets

Characters are often arranged in triangular configurations in Wyler's films, as is true here in *The Best Years of Our Lives*. The character played by Fredric March is welcomed home from the war by his children (Michael Hall and Teresa Wright) as his wife (Myrna Loy) watches from deeper in the field.

Milly (Myrna Loy), double-framed by the hallway in their apartment, which funnels each toward the other. But Wyler does not give them privacy. Their two children watch from either side of the frame, stabilizing it with their approving gazes directed at their embracing parents in the apex of the triangle; but the children's gaze also (as we soon learn) qualifies the romance and purity of the reunion. In the same sequence, Al realizes that the household has become disturbingly independent of him. His children have grown up in his absence and developed points of view not his own. Even though the framing of his reunion with Milly is not fraught with anxiety, it prefigures anxiety that Al cannot yet sense. The structure suggests Wyler's larger structures in the film. Although Fred (Dana Andrews) and Homer (Harold Russell) have the more difficult problems of readjustment after being released from the service, Al's readjustment remains the most incomplete and unresolved at the end of the film.

Character triangles can also demonstrate the impossibility of healing in a relationship. Three of the films that Wyler made at the peak of his career, *Dodsworth, The Letter,* and *The Little Foxes,* all use these configurations as much as a means for the spectator to assess the characters as for the characters to do so. In *Dodsworth,* the confrontation between Fran (Ruth Chatterton), Sam (Walter Huston), and Arnold Iselin (Paul Lukas), the man with whom Fran has her first affair, portends the triangle's absence in Fran's seduction of Kurt (Gregory Gaye) and even the awkward presence of a triangle when Fran confronts Kurt and his mother (Maria Ouspenskaya). Sam's strong presence in the first triangle is missed in the second, and his sensibility seems to be represented in the third by the mother, though in harsher terms. Wyler's triangular structures, in other words, define personal realities that may be later structurally absent or that implicitly compare similar situations. We are thus able to sense the tensions in these spatial arrangements and to understand a scene by its relation to another.

When Fran and Sam meet after her affair with Iselin, she is unaware that Sam has invited Iselin to meet them as well. First, Wyler frames the threesome with Fran's dark back to the camera sitting in the foreground, Sam standing in control on the left deeper in the field, and Iselin framed in the door and entering on Sam's plane to the right. Fran stands up into the frame. Sam even calls their meeting "the old triangle stuff" as Wyler reframes the triangle with Sam in the center back and Fran and Iselin to either side in the foreground. Sam's move into the center of the frame gives him an ascendancy over the figures of Fran and Iselin, who are alike in the way they are framed and who will both insinuate themselves out of Sam's control. In a later scene when Fran and Kurt sit on the couch in the sitting room, Sam's lighted bedroom door is behind them, reminding us of his absence, though Fran and Kurt have forgotten it. It also reminds us of his earlier control of the triangle when Iselin played Kurt's part.

In *The Little Foxes,* character triangles are rife, defining the tensions among the brothers and sister, Ben (Charles Dingle), Oscar (Carl Benton Reid), and Regina (Bette Davis), and among the brothers and Leo (Dan Duryea), Oscar's son, when they scheme to have Leo steal Horace's bonds.

Deep-Focus Emotion

Some directors and cinematographers, among them Wyler and Toland, can use depth in the frame, not to distance us, but to convey the emotion felt by two characters in the space between them.[5] One option is to close this space so that the emotion culminates in an embrace. Across the distance, the spectator's emotion depends upon the characters' eye contact among themselves.[6] Wyler creates emotional vectors with these confrontations across space, because our gazes match a character's gaze in a particular shot.

As early as *The Storm* (1930), Wyler spatially prefigures some of the best sexual confrontations in *Dodsworth* years later. Burr (William Boyd) tries to prevent Dave (Paul Cavanagh) from raping Manette (Lupe Velez) in the confines of a small cabin during a winter blizzard that severely limits their space. In one beautifully realized scene, the camera follows Dave from the loft, where he looks down at Manette's door across the space of the room, thus defining his intention. Then tilting down with Dave as he descends the ladder, the camera remains behind the ladder as he crosses the space between the ladder and Manette's door with Burr asleep to the right. Wyler and cinematographer Alvin Wyckoff contrast Dave's impetuosity with Burr's greater sense of responsibility by dramatically charging the space between them and creating an effective territoriality within the cabin; we feel the violation of this territoriality because of the camera's restraint in remaining behind. Wyler and Wyckoff invest this deep space with emotion (ours and the characters').

These tensions are even more apparent in as atmospheric a film as *The Letter*, where many of the central confrontations are between two characters. When Leslie Crosbie (Bette Davis) asks Howard Joyce (James Stephenson) to get her letter back, his first action is to retreat into deep field from her in the foreground left. Wyler exploits the full impact of this depth and distance by then panning to the left to a close-up of her face turning toward us. The meeting between Leslie and Mrs. Hammond (Gale Sondergaard), the wife of the man Leslie has murdered, similarly uses this deep-focus emotion, as does Leslie's final confrontation with her husband (Herbert Marshall) when she confesses that she still loves the man she murdered. Of course, Wyler has other ways to reinforce the unfolding horrors of Leslie's obsession, as Charles Affron points out in *Star Acting*.[7] Wyler complements his use of space with an almost Sternberg-like partial obscuring of that space, so that the spectator must visually struggle through that space. Wyler's camera is unusually animated in this shadowy space, tracking and panning through the lush foliage of the set at the beginning and end of the film.

Somewhat paradoxically, open space and high-key lighting signify an unexpressive, artificial demeanor in Wyler's characters, whereas closed spaces and deep shadows correspond to the honest expression of the problematic qualities of existence. In *Wuthering Heights,* for instance, Heathcliff (Laurence Olivier) returns and confronts the now-married Cathy (Merle Oberon) and Edgar (David Niven) in their own deep, well-lit space. The shot is Wyler at his most controlled and (paradoxically) extravagant. Heathcliff walks from deep, deep field across the broad expanse of the Linton drawing room to the three Lintons in the foreground. Heathcliff is dressed severely and formally in black, and in his speech he has adopted the indirection of the aristocracy: "It occurs to me that I have not congratulated you on your marriage. I have often thought of it." What he has thought of it, or whether he is now congratulating them, is left in doubt.

The contrast of spaces in the film is also the contrast of the two households. Cathy thinks that by decamping spatially she can free herself of complex social dilemmas, but Wyler's camera belies this. The camera, for instance, seeks out the social drama in the expansive spaces of Thrushcross Grange by tracking through deep space at the Lintons' ball; it finds Heathcliff staring at Cathy. Open space becomes a mask in the film and an emblem of hypocrisy. The closer spaces of the household at Wuthering Heights encourage confrontation, though Wyler's camera independently seeks out the less apparent confrontations in the supposedly more civilized household.

Wyler's creation of acute space thrives on certain limitations, yet Wyler does not care to retreat still further into the intimate and isolated psyches of his characters. Ingmar Bergman would follow a character's nightmare inside his unconscious, projecting that psychological reality onto what Bruce Kawin calls a "mindscreen."[8] Wyler's choice is to identify more directly with action than with static states of mind, and more with the social implications of inner drives than with the pain of the drives themselves. Neither director's choice is simple, but the complexity of Bergman is in showing a convoluted inner realm, as in *Hour of the Wolf,* whereas the complexity of Wyler is in capturing the "in-between" of characters' psychologies. Gestalt psychologists are especially sensitive to what Wyler spatializes so well — interaction and character in context, seldom treated in isolation. But I think most of us are trained (at least before reading Lacan and Irigaray) to think of the self as somewhat firm and impermeable — myself, itself, yourself — rather than as constantly in flux. Like Wyler, we see the self as seeking a healthy set of relations with objects and others.

In the scene depicting Fred's nightmare in *Best Years,* Wyler spatializes, not Fred's suffering, but the social context in which his nightmare takes place. Wyler cuts from Fred's contorted face to the living room where Peggy (Teresa Wright) is sleeping on the couch. He pans slightly from Peggy awakening to the door to show the distance she must traverse, and then cuts back to the bedroom to follow her movement from the door in deep field to Fred struggling in her bed. The broadening out of the nightmare into the space of these rooms does not displace our concern for Fred, but all sorts of multiple messages complement that personal drama. We see, for instance, that Peggy has given up her bed to Fred, though her mother suggested that Fred sleep on the couch; we see Peggy's typically girlish bed festooned with canopy and skirt; we see the special kind of alertness in Peggy's response to Fred's moans, which connotes the light sleep of mothers with infants.

What strikes me about the scene is the starkness of a masculine nightmare originating in an unseen but thoroughly masculine war (someone named Gadorsky has not escaped a burning plane) being imaged in an identifiably feminine space.[9] In contrast to Robert Warshow's view of the women characters in *Best Years* as castrating,[10] I see their influence as analogous to Wyler's point of view in the film: a healing social perspective. The emotion in this nightmare sequence is deep-focus emotion, not close-up emotion. Fred's war trauma becomes the basis of trust between him and Peggy as he thanks her offhandedly for not having mentioned the nightmare at breakfast. (Later in the film, Wyler contrasts that trust with Fred's wife's scorn for his nightmares.)

In *Dodsworth,* deep-focus space is primarily the healthy space of characters maintaining their own identities while also gently attending to each other. Sam

The depth of the shot can intensify the film space. In this scene from *Dodsworth,* Walter Huston's character discusses his retirement with the new manager played by Charles Halton, while his secretary (Margaret Fielding) looks on. Wyler and cameraman Rudolf Mate give the Huston character's decision to retire ominous dimensions by extending the space well beyond the large framing window.

and Edith (Mary Astor) reencounter one another in this sort of space, an American Express office; her flat offers the same sort of space, a space still free of long-term commitments but fraught with the good-humored potential that each invites the other to explore. This space only becomes threatening when Fran symbolically enters it by reaching Sam on the telephone. Then the distance between Sam in the foreground on the telephone to Fran and Edith double-framed by the door behind is ominous.

Double-Framed Reality

If a director creates a second frame within the film's outer frame, he may be adding a reflexive element to the film. That is, he may be drawing our attention to the fact that we are watching a visually framed fiction, just as D. H. Lawrence has his characters discuss various artworks in the novel *Women in Love* or Conrad's Marlow comments on the structuring of a tale in *Heart of Darkness*. Reflexivity is a familiar element in modern art. Wyler uses double-framing to incorporate the spectator within the film rather than to make us overly self-conscious. He makes some of his characters become spectators like us. And then they and we together watch the fictional and highly emotional drama within the second frame. We as spectators consequently become part of the assumed community in the film.

Part of the reason that Wyler is so attracted to staircases is that they often provide the means to double-frame his figures. As early as *Jezebel,* he uses the stair railings to define the space in the frame. After Pres (Henry Fonda) has been diagnosed as having yellow fever, Amy (Margaret Lindsay) and Dr. Livingstone (Donald Crisp) are on the stairs, while Julie (Bette Davis) is in deep field to the right below them in the living room. When the doctor leaves, the ascending stairs form a diagonal linking the two women, both of whom love Pres. Amy's back is partly toward us in shadow and Julie is double-framed under the arch of a door with drapery behind her.[11] The composition of the shot is dramatic and charged enough to support the pleading speech that Julie delivers: "I am asking for the chance to prove I can be brave and strong and unselfish. Help me, Amy. Help me make myself clean again as you're clean. Let me prove myself worthy of the love I bear him." The double-framing around Julie makes her claim and her strength more credible. And though Amy is elevated on the stairs, her silence and shadowy volume make her wish to accompany Pres to Lazarit Island (where the fever victims are quarantined) seem foolhardy. But her elevation above Julie also acts as a kind of grace that oddly does purify Julie and make us forget her earlier manipulative exploits. Similarly, when Pres's diseased body is removed in the last sequence in the house, both his body and Julie are double-framed by the front door, with its large "Y" painted on it to the left of the exit. The levels from the earlier scene are replicated here with Pres's brother and Julie's aunt and uncle looking down on the departure from a second-floor landing.

A certain stasis in Wyler's framing of scenes often carries an admonition to his audience to be calmer than his characters are: the lessons of the space seem to apply to us more than to them. In *The Heiress,* Wyler is interested in the ironies of the narrative, especially the way in which Dr. Sloper (Ralph Richardson) brings about precisely what he has abjured. Ironic also is the way in which Catherine (Olivia de Havilland), though she hates her emotionally repressed and cynical father, becomes very much like him in the end. Wyler's earliest shot of Dr. Sloper tells us about his stiff disapproval of Catherine, as, expressionless, he watches through a window of his study as she departs. Their separation in space — her distance from him — is reiterated when they meet, spatially double-framed by a shaded, brick entrance to the yard. Sloper has nothing but admonitions for her, suggesting his wish to reshape her. Shortly afterwards he explains to her aunt (Miriam Hopkins), "The result is what you see, an entirely mediocre and defenseless creature without a shred of poise."

An interesting clue to the audience in this film is that Wyler frames Morris Townsend (Montgomery Clift) just as severely as he does Dr. Sloper, inviting a comparison between them. As Catherine leaves the party where she has met Morris, he kisses her hand in the darkness of a doorway, not unlike her and her father's meeting under the arch earlier. And throughout the film, Morris draws parallels between his own and Dr. Sloper's good taste in drink and cigars. He might add that they treat Catherine with equal cruelty and teach her to return it in kind. While we expect the meetings between lovers in arched doorways to signify the private passion of their romance, Wyler prepares us for something quite different. The lovers' last kiss is in the same brick passageway where Catherine first passed her father. Her petitions seem fated to be received with as much coldness as her father evinces toward her.

In *Best Years,* Wyler uses double-framing to alert us to the tensions while also giving us some emotional distance from them. Many of the extensively double-framed sequences in the film establish Wyler's views about the difficulties facing the returning soldiers and their families. The double-framing of Al and Milly's reunion embrace, both by the hallway and by the framing gazes of their children, is one example. But even earlier in the film, the framing window of the taxi distances us as spectators and divides our identification so that we share Al and Fred's anxiety and pity for Homer. Spatially we remain with Al and Fred within the waiting taxi, and we feel that we are deserting Homer as the taxi pulls away. Fred's belated reunion with his wife is similarly framed by the car window through which Peggy watches as he awkwardly tries to gain entrance to his wife's apartment house. In both these instances, the reunion is qualified by the warmth and trust between the departing figure and the figures remaining in the cars, so that the double-framing of the car window makes us anxious for Peggy and for Al and Fred inside the cars and also for the isolated figures outside the cars who must face the "unframed" world.

Wyler often double-frames fearful realities, ones that both the characters and the spectators might wish to control. The effect of this use of space is to increase the element of stasis in a highly emotional context and to make us more alert. In *Wuthering Heights,* the overly gothic dolly up to Lockwood (Miles Mander) in bed, followed by a reverse-angle shot in close-up of Lockwood from outside the window, is a failed instance of Wyler wishing to capture our attention. It contrasts with the young Cathy's approach to the Lintons' window to watch the dancing within. The dolly up to the window from without (followed by the somewhat fanatic look on Cathy's face as the camera cuts to a shot of her face peering over the sill) conveys her feelings of pleasure and fear as she and Heathcliff spy on the Lintons.

Very traditionally, double-framing can signify restriction or imprisonment in Wyler's films, though usually these static contexts occur, as one would expect, at moments of closure. Both *The Little Foxes* and *The Letter* condemn the Bette Davis characters to this sort of self-imposed finality: Regina moves away from the camera and is double-framed through the rails of the staircase associated with many of her ruthless acts; Leslie is pointedly framed first in silhouette in the door to the veranda and then between two pillars as she steps into the garden from the relative safety of the house.[12] The camera seems to draw her forth because it is positioned at some distance from the house in the shadowy bushes where her murderers wait. This double-framing at the film's close seems to echo her imprisonment behind shadowy, bar-like shades throughout the film and within the obsessive love that she still feels for the man she murdered.

Absent Presence and Eidetic Memory

Directors may use a certain space repetitively because it carries into subsequent scenes the emotions or meaning attached to it in earlier scenes. Manipulated well, this sort of carryover can occur in the same sequence. The emotions felt in an earlier scene or shot of Wyler's films are often attached to our memory of an entity, normally a character who was present but is now absent. Because Wyler defines the context of the space around a character's presence, we might say that that presence is then later implied by the spatial context. So while the entity or character is actually absent later, his presence is still implied. I've called this technique "absent presence" for those reasons. The character continues to intensify the space and to help define a later confrontation within that space.

Wyler's use of absent presence, then, relies upon spectators' eidetic memory, that is, our ability to reproduce the basic volumes and compositions of a visual image from earlier in the film. "Eidetic" also denotes a special accuracy in reproducing visual images. This phenomenon is probably most familiar to us in our daily lives when we grieve for a friend or family member or when we return to a place in which we spent many hours at some time in the past. A place may be permeated by memories of a person no longer living or by memories of our younger selves. We encounter some places painfully because we have invested them with so many ghostly presences. Wyler, by investing some of his film spaces with ghostly presences, compels the spectator to understand these charged emotional contexts.

As early as *The Good Fairy*, Wyler is exploiting this technique. Luisa (Margaret Sullavan) and Max (Herbert Marshall) meet in Max's office, which had been the setting for the meeting between the younger Max and Luisa's would-be seducer, the older Konrad (Frank Morgan). When these three characters and the waiter (Reginald Owen) straighten out their interrelationships at the end and variously propose to Luisa, that space carries some of the tensions that the earlier misreadings produced. Max, framed by his law books and his desk displaying "a pencil sharpener with a holder and different sized holes," represents the orderliness that inevitably breaks down, as the chaotic and semihysterical other three characters invade this domain and shatter his assumptions. As Max complains, "Honesty is the shortcut to success, the standard of ethics, long may it wave, integrity brings its reward: Mr. Konrad coveted my wife — that was my reward." Wyler plays the orderliness of the space against the charming chaos introduced into the space and Max's life by Luisa, but the space always carries with it the humorous primness of Max's life in pre-Luisa times. He resembles the husband in Gustav Machaty's film *Ecstasy*, who straightens rug fringes and arranges the contents of his pockets geometrically on the nightstand before undressing for the first night of their honeymoon. But Wyler's fastidious younger man, Max, is capable of change, as the dialectic between the space of his office and those who occupy it gradually draws him from his premature primness.

There is nothing particularly remarkable about reusing space; every stage drama does this out of necessity. But in his *Mrs. Miniver*, Wyler combines gesture and space as only film can do with great subtlety. Here space does not simply function as location. It does not simply provide a stage. Instead, it becomes an intimate carrier of the thematic implications of the scene, not just by controlling the movement of the characters, but by implying their presence even in their absence. A number of crises in the film converge in the space of the front hall, from which the stairs lead upstairs and from which the dining room can be seen in deep field. Throughout the film, the gesture of Clem Miniver (Walter Pidgeon) correcting the clock on the stair landing punctuates the ongoing historical drama with the sort of irrelevant pause that causes the spectator to look at the space. When Vin (Richard Hey), the Minivers' oldest son, is called back to combat duty, the Minivers and Carol (Teresa Wright) watch from the dining room in deep focus; Vin has just proposed and been accepted in this space. Later, when the Minivers return to the house after a night in their bomb shelter, they step into this space to see that a bomb has ripped through the dining room ceiling. Still later, Carol dies in this space.

The severe control of feeling in this space, especially when Carol dies, informs all of the returns to it. The camera is stationed at the bottom of the stairs, and the scene is deeply shadowed. Clem Miniver descends the stairs slowly. A slight acknowledging gesture, a turn of his head, alerts the spectator to Mrs. Miniver (Greer Garson) sitting in the shadow of the stairs' turning. Then a reverse angle from behind her toward the dining room completes the space as he goes away from her to pull back the curtain from a window. This entire scene is preparatory to Vin's return, when they stand and watch him ascend the stairs to Carol's body.

It is difficult to identify the techniques that together create the sense of desolation conveyed by this sequence. Perhaps much of it works on this principle of absent presence, which Wyler perfects in later films. Carol's absence is felt in the blocking out of sight — Clem's and our belated discovery of Mrs. Miniver in the scene reminds us of Carol's absence since Carol cannot reappear. The camera remaining at the bottom of the stairs restrains the spectator from seeing Carol's body upstairs, and this restraint is matched by the Minivers restraining their looks even from one another. The absence of Clem's familiar gesture of correcting the slow clock on his way down the stairs suggests that the quality of time and space has been altered. Time has become irrelevant, and the familiar is too painful to resume or acknowledge.

At his best, Wyler spatializes characters' feelings and motivations. Wyler's point of view works best when it does not coerce his spectator. Yet to invest the space of the screen with his characters' inner feelings and motivations demands that the spectator actively participate in "reading" these inner states. At his best, Wyler doesn't need to have his characters divulge how they feel or why they do something. Wyler makes all that information spatially felt.

In *The Good Fairy* and *Mrs. Miniver,* Wyler projects human feelings onto his space. In *The Good Fairy,* Max's office reflects the uninitiated (Luisa-less) Max. In *Mrs. Miniver,* the front hall takes on the composite courage of all the family members who pass through it and occupy it. It has a sort of communal character. But in his more sophisticated films, such as *Dodsworth* and *Best Years,* Wyler uses this dialectical relation of space to character more in the service of the narrative to create greater complexity among characters present and absent. This greater complexity positions spectators more creatively in relation to the film, inviting us to make connections beyond what is merely present on the screen.

When characters walk out of a framed triangle in *Best Years,* they are not absent; their presence is still implied, intensifying the space. Wyler relies upon his audience's eidetic memory of that spatial relationship. He does not demand the reproduction of the original image, but rather a more general, emotionalized sense of the original image's spatial design. Wyler may trigger his audience's eidetic memory of an earlier configuration by reconstituting it only in part. By allowing the audience only a partial secondary image, Wyler may thus evoke our wish for the more satisfying completeness of the original image.

March's Al and Loy's Milly talk in *Best Years* after Peggy and Rob leave the frame; Milly jokes, "I tried to stop them from growing, to keep them just the way they were when you left. But they got away from me." Then Al paces around her, making no eye contact and agitating the space that Peggy and Rob earlier occupied. Milly tries to orient him to the children, who are absent but whose presence continues to move Al, physically and emotionally. The emphasis is both on Al's psychological adjustment and on the complex social implications of his children having grown up in his absence, having surpassed him in some ways. Rather than centering the spectator on Al's inner state as he might do with a series of close-up portraits or a flashback to the war itself, Wyler chooses to locate Al's inner state in his movement through space, already intensified by the problematic adult presence of his children.

The implied presence of an absent third character privileges the spectator by involving him. In *Best Years,* the theme of absence is all-important; as Charles Affron points out, Homer's hooks are a startling reminder of how problematic and incomplete are the arrivals of the soldiers.[13] The hooks are a configuration of a partial body. But the absence of Homer's hands also implies an earlier Homer presence, the one in the photographs that Homer gazes at in his bedroom as other characters tend to gaze at themselves in mirrors or in old pictures. Homer and Wilma's confrontations imply this haunting, unspoken presence of an absent third, the earlier Homer who had hands, because Homer imagines that Wilma (Cathy O'Donnell) is speaking to and loving that figure. The presence of this absent self keeps him from listening to her until she can finally acknowledge her love for him in his bedroom, where the absent third is imaged on the wall.

The absent presence of Fred (Dana Andrews) occurs in the confrontation between Peggy (Teresa Wright) and Marie (Virginia Mayo) in the ladies' lounge. Privileged already by knowing Peggy's motive for creating this evening and by seeing her plan then being undermined by Marie's crass sensibility, we are further privileged by seeing Fred's ghostly presence in Peggy's thoughts. He is present in the ladies' lounge, not because he was ever present in that sacrosanct place (heaven forbid!), but because he is evoked by the self-consciousness of Wyler and Toland's play with surfaces in the scene. The camera looks paradoxically more deeply than their reflected surfaces and thus into Peggy's thoughts. Though she is trying to make Fred absent from her deepest emotions, his presence is even more potent than if she had accepted his presence in her life.

Straight vectors between characters are often strained in Wyler's compositions. When Al confronts Fred with his own feelings about the growing intimacy between Fred and Peggy, they meet in a booth at Butch's bar, where Peggy and Fred met and were earlier framed sitting next to each other. In Al and Fred's meeting, however, the space occupied by Fred and Peggy earlier is empty. Al and Fred sit on opposite sides of the table, each precariously on the edge of the frame, with the empty space that Fred and Peggy had earlier occupied between them. This space is charged with the couple's absence. Al and Fred are both angry; their loyalties have shifted from the drunken and irresponsible familiarity between military men when they first met at Butch's to a shared wish to protect Peggy and the family. What Peggy's presence stands for, the more future-oriented goals of a peacetime society, has intervened between them. Al declares, "I don't like the idea of seeing you sneaking around corners to see Peggy, taking her love on a bootleg basis." Fred too is angry, but at himself. The horizontal vector between them shifts to a deep-focus diagonal, Fred diminished in a phone booth calling Peggy in deep field left, while Al looks on from right front field. Al divides his glance between Fred on the telephone and Butch (Hoagy Carmichael) and Homer sitting below him at the piano playing chopsticks. The coziness of the low-angle shot of them playing with Al at the end of the piano contrasts with the impression of hollow space between Al and Fred in deep field. The spectator follows Al's glance to Fred, but Fred is withdrawn and brooding, ignoring or unaware of Homer's call to him on his way out the door.

This one-directional diagonal vector is repeated but reversed in the next sequence in the film as Peggy returns to the kitchen after speaking to Fred. Milly stands at the stove in deep field left, while Peggy shells peas in the right foreground. Peggy is withdrawn and brooding as Milly watches her. The pairing in these two shots implies a father/son relationship between Al and Fred. And the brooding withdrawal of the "son" and daughter reflects the watching parents' values. Peggy confesses, "I guess you and Dad don't have to worry about me anymore. That's the end of my career as a home-wrecker." But Fred's acceptance of Al as father initiates the same values in him. After he has defended Homer at the soda fountain, he counsels Homer as a father, telling him to get married — to take his prewar fiancée Wilma in his arms, stroke her hair, and propose. Temporally in the film, this healing of the distance between Homer and Wilma finally leads to the healing of the distance between Fred and Peggy at Homer and Wilma's wedding.

In *Dodsworth* too, absent presence is at work helping to define the moral standards and deficiencies of the characters. It is not that the empty space comes to symbolize the absent character or the character's values, but the space evokes the spectator's memory of that character so that the spectator feels the full moral complexity of the choices being made. Fred's choice in the situation described above is difficult and wrenching for him. But Wyler uses absent presence in *Dodsworth* to alert the spectator to the shallow choices being made by Fran. When Fran and Kurt return to the suite where Fran and Sam are staying after a night of dancing, they gradually move toward a declaration of their passion for each other. They move through the space of the living room. The space is dimly lit, but the space of deep field near Sam's bedroom door is more brightly lit, implying his absent presence. Sam, in other words, remains present to us even though Fran is denying any responsibility to him. Both she and Kurt occupy a space that Wyler makes illusory with mirrors.

Constricted Space

Often in combination with deep-focus photography, a director may choose to constrict his characters' movements. In Wyler, this constriction often makes exterior shots look like interior shots. Wyler uses constricted space at the beginning of *Best Years* to establish a lack of tension between the returning soldiers. They are more layered than spaced as they travel in the bomber's plexiglass turret. Wyler uses the constricted space here to provide a contrast with the distances that must be traversed in the relations between men and women. When Wyler isolates a single character in a constricted space, as he does when he has Fred climb into the bombardier's seat in one of dozens of surplus airplanes, the space becomes charged with the character's anxiety.[14]

Isolated moments for characters in Wyler's films are generally threatening, and Wyler recognizes that isolation may occur in the midst of company. This is true for Catherine Sloper (de Havilland) in *The Heiress*. Both her father and her lover constrict the space that she occupies. For instance, before Morris (Clift) has proposed to Catherine, he and Dr. Sloper (Richardson) drink sherry together, Morris filling the screen black-coated to the left and Dr. Sloper filling the screen in his dark coat to the right. Wedged between their dark images, Catherine sits lower in a chair looking up at them in hopeful awe. The camera dollies forward until she is wedged only between their arms before the shot dissolves. Double-framed throughout the film by arches, furniture, stairs, pillars and draperies, and even her own embroidery frame, Catherine experiences the shrinking of space as her view of herself shrinks. She gradually acquiesces in this slow constriction until the static quality of her needlepoint depicting their house (in the film's credits) matches the static reality of Catherine's life.

More anxiety-laden is the constricted space that Wyler creates between the parked cars with an oil tank looming behind in *Best Years*. Fred and Peggy snatch their first illicit kiss in this setting. It is an exterior space, but it really resembles an interior space. By isolating and enclosing themselves, the couple try to block out the implied presence of Marie, Fred's wife. They seek out space that will serve as a hiding place.

Wyler is interested in the way that characters exert will and intelligence, especially on one another. This concern with conscious decision and deed results in a vision of social reality largely divorced from natural reality. The latter simply doesn't seem to interest Wyler. Even in *Wuthering Heights,* Wyler's exteriors often look like interiors, and Brontë's psychological drama becomes a less mystical and more social drama in Wyler's hands. The uncontrollable forces within Brontë's romantic characters, echoed by animistic atmospheric effects, become confrontations of will between Laurence Olivier's Heathcliff, Merle Oberon's Cathy, and David Niven's Edgar Linton.

Much of this film creates a contrast between the shadowy spaces of the house called Wuthering Heights and the open, well-lighted spaces of the Lintons' house. When Heathcliff happens upon the conversation between Cathy and Nellie Dean (Flora Robson) and hears only the part in which Cathy says she is ashamed of him (but does not hear her declare, "He's more myself than I am"), the spaces are dramatically contrasted. Cathy and Nellie stand in the well-lit kitchen, light being a signifier of civilization and artifice in the film, and

Heathcliff stealthily stands in shadow in the foreground in a dark, tight, closet-like space. Thus, the lighting and the handling of constricted versus open spaces confirm Heathcliff's suspicions and not Cathy's denial of having gone over to the Lintons in her loyalties. The constricted space associated with Wuthering Heights matches the dark and somewhat incestuous bond between Heathcliff and Cathy, a bond that flourishes only in isolation from other social realities.

Wyler often isolates morally ambiguous characters by constricting space. Space, in fact, only becomes acute in *Carrie* after Carrie (Jennifer Jones) decides to leave George Hurstwood (Laurence Olivier). One shot of the backstage space of the theater where Carrie goes to apply for work as a dancer explores the space from behind some skeletal stairs. Similarly, Wyler often isolates Bette Davis's Leslie in *The Letter* by constricting the space she occupies. When the lawyer, Howard Joyce (James Stephenson), confronts Leslie with the implications of the letter she has sent to the man she has killed, Leslie, bathed in shadow, leans back against a wall, and Howard in the right foreground constricts the space that she occupies. Throughout the film, the shadows of window slats and a lace mantilla worn by Leslie partly hide her.[15] The dead man's wife recognizes that Leslie is deceiving everyone and demands that she remove the mantilla; she thus strips away Leslie's disguise.

Surface Doubling

Wyler often uses mirrors and photographs to double a character's image. He employs these very sparingly, but effectively, at moments when individuals are questioning themselves or making crucial decisions.[16] A reflexive element is at work: yet another image is being projected onto the screen's two-dimensional surface. Neither image is actually three-dimensional, but the screen possesses an illusionary three-dimensionality. In Wyler's doubling shots, that illusion is partly challenged by the flatter second image. And perhaps it is this challenge that stimulates a self-consciousness in both the spectator and the characters in the fiction. The latter inevitably become conscious of some flaw or motive in themselves when confronted by mirrors or photographs.

Wyler trains his spectator's eidetic memory by using mirrors and photographs. The spectator becomes aware of the camera's presence as a third but unseen fulcrum, comparing the doubled figures before it. The mirror scene in the ladies' lounge between Peggy and Marie in *Best Years* teases the spectator into a special attentiveness to the play between two- and three-dimensionality in the double images of Marie and Peggy. The photographs in the film also demand a special attentiveness from Wyler's audience. But here the play is between two temporal schemes. The photograph retrieves the past so that the camera might compare it to the present.

The ladies' lounge scene in *Best Years* might be thought of as one of Wyler's familiar triangular compositions if we were to think of ourselves, the specta-

Wyler and cameraman Gregg Toland alert us to the fact of our witnessing by doubling the characters' images. Mirror images and photographs punctuate films like *The Best Years of Our Lives,* here intensifying a confrontation among characters played by Fredric March, Myrna Loy, and Teresa Wright.

tors, as a third point of the triangle. Wyler gives us special privileges. He admits us to his play with surface and depth in the scene. Marie (Mayo) is surface; she glows and is animated by this confrontation with herself in the mirror. She leans toward the mirror and seems to be intimate with it. The image of Peggy (Wright) is still and opaque; her inner division and hesitation gives her depth and keeps her from relating to the medium of the reflecting mirror. Marie, on the other hand, is in her natural element, applying a surface, her makeup, and admiring a surface, her own looks, while she discusses Fred, Peggy's date, and Peggy in the superficial terms that she understands. Wyler positions Peggy's reflected image as distant from her inner self. This distance suggests her divided reaction to Marie; Peggy's conscience confronts and complicates her instinctive reactions.

Wyler challenges our assumptions about space with this doubling. Sometimes, as in the scene described above, Wyler is deliberately disorienting. In the ladies' lounge, cameraman Gregg Toland's lens shows the two in the mirror, pans to reveal their backs in another set of reflections, and then pans to show Peggy's profile and her reflection. When the camera again shows their double mirror image and pans to yet another angle in another mirror to capture their departure, we should be thoroughly alerted to Wyler's ironically reflexive strategies. He is not playing an expressionistic Wellesian game of mirrors as in *The Lady from Shanghai,* but Wyler's purpose is analogous. The mirrors are a way that Wyler can play with issues of depth — not literal depth but depth as a measure of the character's values.

Surface doubling also allows Wyler to alert the spectator to concerns that are external to the fiction's premises. Wyler gently mocks the spectator apt to rely on a star's persona when Al (Fredric March, aged 49 in 1946) stands with a bad hangover in front of a mirror on his first morning back, comparing his decrepit morning-after visage with a glamorous picture taken a decade earlier — the thirty-something matinee idol Fredric March. Wyler is disavowing a flatness of space that might encourage the spectator to rely on the star's persona. March's photograph, the snapshot of the two couples in the nightclub, and the snapshot of Fred and Marie taken during their courtship before the war — all mask essential truths.

Both Bette Davis's Regina in *The Little Foxes* and Fredric March's Al in *Best Years* confront a younger self in a photograph and compare that younger self to their present mirror reflections. Regina does this right after her brother has suggested that her daughter, Alexandra, is old enough to be married, and Al does it after facing his now grown-up and sophisticated children upon returning home. The alternation between these double-framed images is yet another way that Wyler draws the spectator's attention to the way in which space impinges on and defines the characters. These are special moments when the characters feel especially vulnerable and constricted by time and circumstances. Neither character feels in control, and the spatial reduction of each to a more two-dimensional and a more contained image impresses them, and us, with their mortality and limitedness.

Wyler associates mirrors with the flawed wives in his films. Marie in *Best Years,* Fran in *Dodsworth,* Regina in *The Little Foxes,* and Leslie in *The Letter* all sit before mirrors; mirrors suggest deception and self-deception in these films. When Fran is flirting with Kurt in *Dodsworth,* she is seen in the mirror tiptoeing to Sam's door while Kurt stands next to the mirror. And at the moment of her betrayal of Sam (when she asks Kurt, "What if I were free?"), she stands reflected in the mirror; Kurt then leaves the real frame and reenters it by joining Fran in the reflected space of the mirror. Wyler does not assign Fran to real space, because she is living in illusions, which the space of the mirror represents. Fran is double-framed and distanced by the mirror. The spectator certainly feels more spatially distant from her because Wyler keeps constricting the earlier-seen spaciousness of the room for Fran, imprisoning her and Kurt either in mirrors or in the frames of doors. In contrast, when Sam awakens following this betrayal scene, Wyler makes the spaciousness of the room again apparent. Sam walks into and out of the sitting room as Wyler follows him to his wife's bedroom door.

The narrative pattern for Fran's affairs is that Fran insinuates herself into the man's notice, draws him to commit himself, pursues the affair, and finally turns back to Sam when it fails. Fran sits before a vanity table right after she has withdrawn from her first flirtation with Clyde (David Niven) on the boat. When she says to Sam, "You've got to take care of me," Fran looks at herself in the mirror. Sam too is seen in the mirror after he turns around and looks at her back, intuitively sensing Fran's fear of her own needs. Later, her face smeared with cold cream before another vanity, Fran refuses to return to the States with Sam when their first grandchild is born. Fran is unable to acknowledge any event that implies her age. Used as a motif in *Dodsworth,* the mirror comes to function like a screen, but an ambiguous one; the character immediately before it sees inaccurately, while from behind the character the spectator intuits more deeply and accurately. The characters before the mirrors see what they expect to see, whereas we and our surrogate witnesses see more acutely.

Witnessing

Sometimes characters within the frame become witnesses, and their seeing in effect doubles our seeing. There is an analogy between witnessing and double-framing since both techniques circumscribe the space of the primary action with a secondary element that draws our attention to that action. Both tell us to look and to see, but witnessing tells us to look by surrounding the central action with surrogate watchers. Hitchcock will sometimes turn the spectator into a voyeur, for example having us become as much a Peeping Tom as James Stewart's character in *Rear Window.* Often Hitchcock's means of making us aware of our complicity as watchers is through the use of an independent camera, one that moves so dramatically through space as to make us aware of our ambiguous wishes both to see and not to see what Hitchcock promises.[17] Wyler's strategy of making us aware of our own activity as watchers is more sociable. He gives us access not to the bizarre and cruel, but to the self-conscious positions of watching and being watched.

In *Best Years,* many characters watch the returning soldiers, with a variety of motives. Some of their watching is perfectly benign, though perhaps laced with a modicum of curiosity. All the entrances that the soldiers make are witnessed by other characters: Homer's through the taxicab window by Fred and Al; Al's reunion with Milly in the hallway by Peggy and Rob; Fred's entrance to his wife's apartment house by Peggy. These witnesses are all friendly. But an element of aggression also pervades witnessing. The soldiers all feel vulnerable and would choose more invisibility if they could. For example, Fred thanks Peggy for not bringing up his nightmare, which she has witnessed. And the self-conscious sense of being on exhibit plagues Homer when he faces the curious, sorrowful, or doubtful gazes of his family and neighbors looking at the hooks that have replaced his hands.

The soldiers feel less vulnerable among themselves or among other males in the society to which they return: Homer relaxes at Butch's bar, for instance. The tension of being witnessed arises from being in mixed company or having women as the watchers. Robert Warshow has extrapolated from this tension that the women in *Best Years* are castrators of the men; this leap isn't necessary, but it does identify one of the spatial tenets that Wyler employs and perhaps one of the irrational subtexts available for the male characters. Wyler lets us feel such irrationality, though, without allowing us to accept it or argue with it. Most startling is the over-the-shoulder shot when Homer smashes his metal hooks through the garage window, through which his little sister and her friends have been watching him and from which she is backing away. Homer's anguish and his sister's horror are both felt deeply as irreconcilable positions; the dark space of the garage in the foreground contrasts starkly with the brightly lit driveway where the children stand.

Wyler's acute space, of course, often embodies the irrational but justified feelings that the characters can't express. Homer's vulnerability in this scene is apparent in his attempt at being invulnerable by shooting his rifle, an action witnessed by his girlfriend Wilma, whose point of view is closest to the spectator's during the climactic breaking of the glass. Homer is trying to cope with his anger about being handicapped and his anger toward those around him for continually reminding him of his handicap. His sister's witnessing is simply the last straw.

All the characters are on view in *The Little Foxes,* as the Hubbards pit themselves against Horace Giddens and then against each other. Witnessing in this film often functions as a way in which Wyler describes the patterns of dominance and submission among the characters. Early in the film, Regina is often the powerful one being watched from an extremely low angle by her brother(s) at the bottom of the stairs. Similarly, the brother Oscar and his son Leo witness Horace and Alexandra's arrival from a high angle in a second-story window. Their intention to dominate Horace is made obvious.

In a few instances, Wyler creates a sense of the spectator's witnessing by employing an "independent camera" similar to Hitchcock's in *Frenzy* or to Welles's at the beginning of *Touch of Evil.* The opening to *The Letter* creates the kind of suspense that we associate with a camera that is actively searching out its subject and also making our gaze very active. Tilting down a rubber tree to its tap, dollying back, panning to the right, and tracking past native workers playing cards and sleeping in hammocks, tilting up and travelling over a roof: the camera draws us inexorably into the fiction. A match dissolve into a second long track to the right in front of the house and up to the murder taking place extends the initial searching motion of the camera still further. Wyler seems to be making us conscious of depth in the scene, as when he captures the marching ushers issuing down a staircase from an extremely high angle in *The Good Fairy.*

That perception of depth, and the implication of complexity that accompanies it, allow Wyler to invest the space with tension before an important action arrives to fill it. In *Jezebel,* the camera travels through space to set the dramatic tone of the scene that we know is coming. Julie (Bette Davis) has framed Pres (Henry Fonda) into taking her to a ball despite her wearing a red dress (tradition insists that unmarried women wear only white). The camera seems suddenly to acquire a life of its own as it cranes away in a long sweeping withdrawal from the court, over the orchestra and then over the dancers, just under a hanging chandelier. Next, Wyler cuts to a long pan behind the orchestra toward the dangerous point of entry into this now dynamic space. The restraint of the camera as it tracks behind the guests seated in boxes along the edge suggests our reluctance to see what we know they will see. The camera draws us reluctantly through this space. Our reluctance to some extent corresponds to Julie's once she understands the import of her willfulness, the price that Pres and then she must pay for challenging the whole community.

In some of these instances, as in the witnessing of the murder and Julie's entrance at the ball, other witnesses are present in the scene, but the camera makes the spectators superior to them by alerting us to the complexity of the situation and to the imminence of a climactic moment. This separation of our witnessing from the witnessing of minor characters is especially apparent in *Jezebel* when Pres collapses from the yellow fever in the St. Louis Hotel's bar. Here a high-angle long shot captures Dr. Livingstone (Donald Crisp) as he exhorts the men withdrawn in a semicircle around him to help him carry Pres out. The high angle differentiates our perspective from that of the other witnesses.

Stairs: Ascent and Descent

Wyler's vision of space informs *The Heiress* effectively because the narrative, with its strained and often repressed emotions, is so congruent with his talents. This narrative also grants Wyler a house, a staircase, arches, and doors separating self-contained spaces in the house. These are the stuff of his spatial vision. Stairs especially dominate some of his narratives, for they tend to layer an action, making characters more or less dominant as seen from a perspective above or below them. Stairs are not passageways from one sort of space to another sort, because for Wyler they do not lead anywhere in particular. Instead, they are important places in themselves where emotional recognition or confrontation takes place. In *The Little Foxes,* major confrontations take place between the levels of the first floor and second floor. They justify the extreme angles that Wyler needs to delineate his characters. An extreme angle like the more purely expressionistic ones in Welles's *Citizen Kane* are rare in Wyler's films. Instead, he builds his angles into the structural premises of the scenes. Stairs also provide him with an image of constriction. Like the embroidery frame, the pillars, and the draperies in *The Heiress,* stairs shut Catherine into spaces that funnel her attention and movement, just as the characters around her constrict and depress her temperament.

Wyler structures *The Heiress* architectonically. In the first sequence, Catherine descends the stairs toward the camera below her. The first part of her descent we see reflected in a mirror on the landing, where she meets the maid bringing her a dress for the party at which she will meet Morris Townsend. At the end of the film, the camera records from a high angle her climbing those stairs in the dark house as Morris is pounding on the front door to be admitted. A cheerful, smiling Catherine in the early scene has given way to a hard, vengefully pleased look in the last.

Other moments punctuate the spatial centrality of these stairs in the progress of the film. After Morris has proposed to her, Catherine waits up for her father, and Wyler records her subsequent ascent of the stairs. Followed by Dr. Sloper sinking into a chair and Wyler dollying toward him and framing him off-center, these two shots ominously foreshadow Catherine's disappointment and Sloper's reluctant cruelty. After Sloper's meeting with Townsend the next day, the two men leave the front room as Catherine watches from a high angle; she is positioned on the stair landing. Then her horror, when she understands what has transpired, is seen in a low-angle shot from below her on the stairs. In the interview that follows, Wyler aligns her and Townsend by framing them between two pillars, and divides Sloper from them.

Finally there is a high-angle shot when Catherine climbs the stairs after a futile night of waiting for Townsend after they plan to elope. Here the camera prolongs the movement of her climbing by backing before her, following her progress and tilting up at the landing. These stairs, sadly, are Catherine's territory in the film; she occupies space that would normally be transitional space in the household. This connection indicates her subordinate position, though by the end of the film she has come to occupy the front room as a practical matter, due to her father's death. Still, Wyler associates her with the stairs to the very end, suggesting that she will never escape her subordinate status. The puzzling look of beatitude, of a sort of redemption in achieving her revenge, that characterizes her expression in the last frames, is one of those nearly inexplicable moments in film. And its occurrence once more on those stairs, which have punctuated her naiveté and misjudgments, lends a certain horror to the conclusion.

In *The Little Foxes,* stairs are the arena within which characters broker power, jousting between separate levels in the struggle to grasp real and illusionary power; most of the narrative, in fact, is devoted to this struggle. Teresa Wright's Alexandra is the character being initiated both into her father's gentle but firm ethics and into a clear grasp of the disguised cruelty in her mother and her mother's family. Characteristically, Bette Davis's Regina (as one might expect from the name) occupies the high point on the stairs, looking down from the upper hall over other characters below the stair railing. Often her brothers and nephew (Charles Dingle, Carl Benton Reid, Dan Duryea) occupy the subordinate position. But at the end of the film, with Alexandra standing below her on the stairs, Regina's power seems to evaporate. Regina, realizing that Alexandra now sees through her, hesitantly mounts the stairs toward her husband's dead body on the second floor. Alexandra sneers at her,

"Why Mama, are you afraid?" after Regina has invited her to sleep in Regina's room. Wyler's camera captures the threat to Regina by rearranging the space of the stairs: we watch Regina walk away from the camera through the bars of the upper level's railing. This retreat complements the shot early in the film in which she walks up to that railing and thus into the low-angle shot where she faces her brothers at the bottom of the stairs. She walks into their frame and into a dominating position above them, while at the end she retreats powerlessly from the frame, which is imprisoning her image.

In *Jezebel,* Wyler uses stairs to dramatize conflict again and again. Pres ascends them with a stick to beat Julie into obedience. Julie descends them in her red dress. Julie mounts them toward the camera, which is watching her from an ominous high angle, after the ball. Julie misses the ascent of Aunt Belle (Fay Bainter) and Amy, Pres's new wife (Margaret Lindsay), before she descends the stairs, and so is unprepared for the news that Pres has married. But as with Wyler's other successful uses of space, the staircase and the balcony leading from it along the second floor are not fully used to match the narrative action until nearly the last scene. Julie and Amy confront each other between the stairs and the deep space leading down from the last curving stairs into the space of the living room. Also, Wyler dramatizes Julie and Pres's departure to the quarantine island by separating them from the family on these levels, the family standing on the upper level while Julie is isolated below. A ghostly image of a draped chandelier seen in the high-angle shot down at Julie makes the family's gratitude to her more credible, for it suggests that the family is already in mourning for the two, Pres and Julie, isolated below.

HABITUAL SPACE

Wyler's spatialization of his narratives in the first third of his career, as in *The Good Fairy* and *Mrs. Miniver,* includes the creation of habitual space and the complementary use of repetitive gestures by the characters. Max in *The Good Fairy* repeatedly swipes at his beard with a comb and shakes a pointed finger. In *Mrs. Miniver,* the daughter Judy (Clare Sandars) habitually wipes off adult kisses with the back of her hand, and Mrs. Miniver listens for Vin's plane. Spaces like Max's office and the Minivers' hallway become habitual spaces for the spectator.

Jezebel is an interesting transitional film in Wyler's career, better realized spatially than any other up to this point, but itself a turgid Southern drama, which film buffs seem to love despite a great deal of drippingly melodramatic dialogue. I maintain that the film also works spatially because Wyler creates beautifully realized moments, for the most part in the pauses and the absence of the heavy or hysterical dialogue. Perhaps this welcome silence functions in the film to make us actually look at the screen and its composition; Wyler also paces these set-ups so that they precede the entrances of Bette Davis's southern belle.

Wyler is most at home with characters who are intelligent agents struggling to control the natural world and themselves. His Sam Dodsworth is such a character. Dodsworth exploits his world, frames and reframes it to accomplish what he can. The social tension in *Dodsworth* is a gradually deepening one that causes the spectator to side with Sam against Fran, as it becomes increasingly clear that Fran's impulses are uncontrolled and thoughtless. Like the men in *Best Years,* Sam leaves a milieu of great activity (compare his industrial success to the war in *Best Years*) at the beginning of the film, enters an enervating new milieu to which he must reorient himself, and finally redefines that milieu, accepting its changed character, in order to affirm his own potential for action once again at the film's end. An outer sense of space in Wyler's major films reflects the inner states of characters, framing them in the way that they frame their worlds.

The Best Years of Our Lives is probably William Wyler's best film, because Wyler works with a cast of characters who never undercut his subtle spatializing of emotion. Wyler likes to work with a character's reticence — Walter Huston's Dodsworth is an example. In contrast, Ruth Chatterton's Fran or Bette Davis's characters project a barely restrained hysteria. In *Best Years,* Wyler follows the three central male characters, whose readjustments are all problematic. But none of the men has a shrill or inherently dramatic personality. The central women characters are similar to the men, accepting their need to be stoical and to adapt gradually to the new culture. Wyler sees neither the men's stoicism nor the women's acceptance as easy or simple. Wyler leaves Al's drinking and his ambivalence toward the bank hierarchy unresolved. And he depicts with complexity and humanity Milly's tense acceptance of these problems.

Wyler does not sacrifice our understanding of character motivation. But perhaps he and writer Robert E. Sherwood are somewhat conservative in their adaptation of narrative events from MacKinlay Kantor's *Glory for Me.* He does not choose to focus the narrative on the psychological struggles of the returning soldiers understood from within (as he does, for instance, focus later on the psychological anguish of Kirk Douglas's McLeod in *Detective Story*). We see no flashbacks to war scenes, for example. Instead, Wyler focuses his narrative on the social pressures that the returning soldiers confront. We see their anguish from outside. The film narrative is a series of concrete dilemmas. Through his characters, Wyler argues against too deep a probing into the characters' inner selves by the spectator. As the three soldiers fly low over the landscape of rural America, Al confides to Fred, "The thing that scares me most is that everybody's gonna try to rehabilitate me."

This is Wyler's reticence — that we are shown truths spatially. Wyler does not eschew psychological truths or an understanding of his characters' innermost selves. But context and confrontation within space delineate inner realities. We have only to think of Bergman's very different strategies in *Persona* — close-up dissolving into close-up, white space setting up portraiture as an isolated and insular reality — to perceive those strategies' absence from Wyler's space. The one moment in *Best Years* that seems to contradict this is Fred's reliving of his nightmare in the abandoned plane. But the reticence of Wyler's spatialization of this moment is still apparent in the way in which the sound track and the camera position and the stained plexiglass carry the impact of Dana Andrews's acting. The moment quickly gives way to a social encounter and Fred's first chance at challenging employment.

The decline in Wyler's ability to spatialize his point of view occurs quite suddenly. The recognizable Wyler, a presence that isn't a presence in the same sense as a Hitchcock or a Ford presence, is still missed. Wyler seems to lose his ability to spatialize the tensions of his narratives, to embody his characters' inner selves in outward configurations of volume and space. Part of what the spectator feels in this loss, oddly enough, is the absence of Wyler's humility. To give himself over to the spatial mode of his medium, rather than guiding the spectator through it (as Ford does) or manipulating the spectator (as Hitchcock does), is Wyler's method. This absence of self in the space of the screen creates a coolness, a control, and a certain lack of self-consciousness on the director's part. I, for one, revel in the subliminal rightness of Wyler's space.

In *Detective Story*, all of what Wyler would seem to require to assert his presence is available. The drama is enclosed, mostly in the central space of a police station, but diverted now and then into closets, small rooms, or a roof. All these spaces could suggest the psychological claustrophobia of McLeod (Kirk Douglas) as he inexorably progresses toward this discovery: "I've built my whole life on hating my father. All the time he was inside of me laughing. Maybe he was crying." But despite the ingredients, the brew does not blend. Wyler's view of space is missing.

Wyler does not exploit the narrative's spatial limitations and aesthetic possibilities. Instead, the weight of the drama's tensions is carried in the dialogue, which is generously laden with the baggage of psychoanalysis. The fiction becomes a mere illustration of a set of verbal confrontations, with good and bad performances but little credibility lent, as it must be, by the context.

As I watched this film, I kept imagining how the Wyler of *Best Years* would have handled the psychological discoveries of McLeod. How much more subtle and spatially accomplished it would have been! Wyler at his peak could have had the spectator sympathizing with McLeod even while abhorring McLeod's lack of humanity, but in *Detective Story* the spectator finds McLeod's brutality distasteful from the start. Think of the subtlety of Wyler's psychological "analysis" of Homer in *Best Years*. The association of Homer with phallic symbols, like the rifle he shoots in the garage and a sword mounted on his wall,[18] alternates with his frustration, when he drives his hooks through the glass panes on the garage door, or his nostalgia, when he examines the photographs of his high school basketball career where his hands are present and all his confidence is intact. Wyler delicately portrays Homer's fears that he cannot support and protect Wilma, that he is in fact castrated. Wyler realizes these fears spatially — they never need to be explained. We feel them and identify with them even if we do not register these fears as "castration anxiety."

Detective Story may be successfully filmed theater. (Philip Yordan and Robert

Wyler adapted Sidney Kingsley's stage play.) But spatially, Wyler's reticence and holding back, which make certain demands on the spectator, are missing.[19] Nor has a new vision of space emerged to displace the old — not yet anyway.

Warren French Smith's speculations about the effect of the McCarthy era on Wyler are intriguing in relation to the drama that Wyler develops so compulsively in *Detective Story.*[20] Kirk Douglas's McLeod is a McCarthy figure — self-righteous, cynical, modelling himself on a vengeful God who single-handedly will rid the precinct of evil. What the dialogue gradually reveals is that while McLeod thinks he is righting the evil done to his mother by his father, he is really perpetuating it by allowing no compassion in his enforcement of the law and by becoming brutal when his false ideals are sullied. The whole weight of his discovery that his wife (Eleanor Parker) had had an affair and an abortion before he married her and his subsequent compulsive inability to forgive her is carried by the dialogue, almost as though Wyler were talking to himself. Camera positions are noteworthy only because they deny significance in the most cynical way. In the next to last sequence, following McLeod's murder/suicide, his body slumps over and falls into a fetal curl. But the positioning of his lumpish, lifeless body seems perfectly arbitrary in the middle of the office where most of the action has taken place.

Carrie also seems badly realized spatially: the characters merely circulate within the space of the frame and field, instead of revealing their relations. The tensions between them are spoken and explicitly labelled rather than being spatially embodied. For instance, David Raksin's musical score roars up to alert us to the drama of Hurstwood's run from his home to take a cab to Carrie's, and again at the moment she decides not to leave him and to return to Drouet (Eddie Albert). Only the sequences built around Carrie (Jennifer Jones) leaving Hurstwood (Laurence Olivier) are visually interesting. A high-angle tracking shot, for instance, follows him past the bars at the foot of the bedstead and across the room to the opening of a drawer, which he finds empty except for the key. Hurstwood is seen here only as a fragmented person, a shadowy torso.

Wyler's talent surfaces in *Carrie* to record a lack of emotion between characters, whereas in his earlier films he would concentrate on the subtle spatial embodiment of this emotion. His reticence has ceased to intensify our identification with the characters. The distancing of the camera here merely reflects, rather than counterpoints, the alienation of character from self (George's lack of emotion) and of character from character (Carrie from Hurstwood). One must ask, with Warren French Smith, whether Wyler's vision of space in the post-McCarthy era has cynically altered to portray most readily a barren, disillusioned landscape.

In *Roman Holiday,* where the gently comic premise needs to be delicately played against the seriously thwarted love affair between the princess (Audrey

Hepburn) and Joe Bradley (Gregory Peck), Wyler's vision of space is altogether absent. The space of the film just sprawls in a travelog sort of laxness as the couple wanders through it.

CLAUSTROPHOBIC SPACE

After so many films late in Wyler's career that seem to have no acute space, and whose spatial look often seems arbitrary, *The Collector* comes as a surprise. For here, Wyler once again inscribes his narrative in space. But his techniques are not those he used at the peak of his career. The vision of space in *The Collector* inverts the assumptions about acute space that Wyler demonstrated earlier. In his middle films, space is a social medium within which social and personal health develops and thrives, whereas space in *The Collector* is threateningly enclosed, and its enclosure portends the grave. Enclosure comes to signify the mortality of the characters who move within it, the ultimate limits of their movement.

Wyler's new vision of space gives credence to Warren French Smith's theory that Wyler's talent was paralyzed by his cynical response to the McCarthy period, for this new vision is a paranoid one. Wyler has to a large degree projected the obsession of the butterfly collector (Terence Stamp) onto the space that this character controls: he collects beautiful, vital objects, kills them, and mounts them statically in a vacuum-like, sterile space. Like McLeod in *Detective Story*, he is isolated from other points of view, and in his morbid, death-attracted way he embodies the ugly, psychologically skewed world that liberals felt themselves to be occupying during the McCarthy era.

The collector kidnaps Miranda Grey (Samantha Eggar) and confines her to the world that his obsession has created. And, in a sense, the film is narrated from his first-person point of view. Certainly the only voice-over narration is his. But more significantly, the camera conveys Miranda Grey's fear, a fear we come to understand is also his (though his is paranoia). There is no hope for social health in this film, for neither character can ever hope to draw the other into his or her spatial or ethical assumptions. When Miranda attacks his collection, saying "Is that what you love? death?" he complains, "You didn't even try to understand my collection."

Whereas in Wyler's earlier films will and conscious intention were dignified and viable faculties in the characters, in *The Collector* they have been muted and overpowered by inner drives no longer controlled by conscious decision-making. Miranda calculates her moves to choreograph her escape, but her inner drive to be free causes her to strike out in mad, uncontrolled flutterings. The collector assures Miranda that he has no sexual desire for her, but his inner sexual drives make him both dangerous and cringingly prudish. After sensually stroking her hair, for example, he says, "I forgot myself. I can't explain."

This new spatial world of Wyler's contains only two people at a time, never the three often present in earlier films. And between the two there is no meeting. Each is an object for the other, an object of curiosity and idealization for the collector, of horror for Miranda. But neither can empathize with the other, except in pretense.

Rotating Camera

Space in *The Collector* is hollow and unresonating. Wyler creates it deliberately, using camera movements and framing techniques foreign to his other films. Embodying the film's atmosphere of claustrophobia is a rotating camera. The camera's motion is not so simple as to be called a pan. It moves deliberately around in space, testing the limits of that space and determining its capacity to hold or release its prisoner. The camera's action is indicative of claustrophobia in the sense that it seems to assess the limits of space and, despite its sweep, to discover only the barriers of enclosing walls.

The first use of the technique is when the collector discovers the house with its attached underground storeroom. The camera rotates around the perimeter of the room, examining its confines, after he pulls down cobwebs that block his entrance. His voice-over thought explains why the space attracts him: "I suppose it was the loneliness." Later, when he has brought Miranda to the room and arranged her chloroformed body on the bed, the camera rotates from her legs, as he pulls down her skirt, to the head of the bed, as he covers her and turns out the light. In both these instances the camera rotates as the collector's point of view might, assessing the potential of a place and then of his own acquisition. There is an impersonal quality in the assessment, as of a piece of property.

In the next instance when this technique is used, this diffidence becomes the director's: the camera revolves from behind the collector's back as Miranda in a robe comes down the stairs in the main house. She has just made a desperate attempt to escape by turning on the taps in the tub when a neighbor has come to the door. Here the rotating camera duplicates first the collector's and then her point of view as he circles her to chloroform her into submission. Later, the camera independently rotates around the end of the bed and goes to the other side after he enters her room to find her dead. The rotation of the camera, which began as a way of representing his terror of and alienation from the world, becomes associated with her terror and is finally an attribute of the space itself. Terror of the outer world and an insular shyness breed the attitude of a simultaneous terror of the world and desire to appropriate it. After recording his discovery of her death, the camera rotates back around to watch him climb the stairs and sit thoughtfully on the top step. He rationalizes her death from exposure and starvation and plans his next acquisition: "I ought to have gotten someone ordinary, someone I could teach."

Enclosed Space

A complementary technique to the rotating camera is the use of the Romanesque arch of the cellar room, which, along with the windows of the collector's van, Wyler and cameramen Robert Surtees and Robert Krasker use to frame and enclose the spaces of the film. Like the rotating camera when it takes on a certain independence, this framing also connotes the voyeurism that is first the collector's, but which gradually comes to pervade the "objective" space of the film. When Miranda tries to exploit the collector's voyeurism, she succeeds only in making him so conscious of his perversion that she angers him and belittles herself in his eyes.

The tight framing in the film is somewhat reminiscent of the equally tight frames around the returning soldiers in *Best Years* when they ride to Homer's house in a cab from the airport. But in *Best Years,* the tight frame of the cab window and of the rear-view mirror open up as the soldiers gradually confront their fears and insecurities. In *The Collector,* the last frames of the film capture the collector's next victim through the blinds covering the van's rear window. And throughout the film, the depressing cynicism of Wyler's view of human nature and of space is always present as the Romanesque arch in the cellar frames the two characters: from a low angle as he dictates a letter to her mother; from a high angle on her and a low angle on him as they argue about Picasso's worth; of him just under the arch from a low angle as he says, "You could fall in love with me if you tried." The sense that space is limited also conveys the apprehension that time and life are limited. Miranda realizes what Wyler implies from the start through his spatialization when she asks, "I'm never getting out of here alive, am I?" It's a rhetorical question. And it speaks vividly to Wyler's late-career view of space, a view fully realized but one inverting the principles behind his earlier creation of acute space.

Wyler may be unique as a director, since he creates two wholly different spatial visions in his career. I have called one acute space and the other claustrophobic space, but both possess the intensity of acute space. Of the directors I have examined in this volume, only the two dramatic shifts in Capra's career in sound films seem analogous. What amazes me about Wyler's development as a spatial artist is that he was able to exploit his own disillusionment; with the help of cameramen Surtees and Krasker, and designers John Stoll and Frank Tuttle, he finds a vehicle for doing so in *The Collector.* But perhaps that should not be so surprising, since Wyler often developed his most acute film space from literary sources.

NOTES

1. Michael A. Anderegg, *William Wyler* (Boston: Twayne, 1979), Preface.
2. John Baxter seems to display this ambivalent attitude when he says, "Diligent

search among the films of William Wyler for anything approaching a personal style has not revealed a great deal which might be called either individual or fresh, yet his films are among the most likeable, entertaining, and deeply felt that the cinema has produced"; see *Hollywood in the Thirties* (New York: A. S. Barnes, 1968), p. 115. Axel Madsen discusses Wyler's "styleless style" in *William Wyler: The Authorized Biography* (New York: Thomas Y. Crowell, 1973), p. 94.

3. Warren French Smith, "Editor's Foreword" in Anderegg's *William Wyler*.

4. Andrew Sarris says of Wyler, "It would seem that Wyler's admirers have long mistaken a lack of feeling for emotional restraint," in *The American Cinema* (New York: E. P. Dutton, 1968), p. 168.

5. See what Wyler says about his collaboration with Gregg Toland in Richard Koszarski's *Hollywood Directors, 1941–1976* (New York: Oxford Univ. Press, 1977), p. 112. Also, Charles Affron explores Wyler's use of closed sets to create depth in *Cinema and Sentiment* (Chicago: Univ. of Chicago Press, 1982), pp. 79–82.

6. André Bazin discusses spectators' "more active mental attitude" and their "more positive contribution . . . to the action in progress" in *What Is Cinema?*, vol. 1, trans. Hugh Gray (Berkeley: Univ. of California Press, 1967), pp. 35–36.

7. Charles Affron, *Star Acting: Gish, Garbo, Davis* (New York: E. P. Dutton, 1977), pp. 237–241.

8. Bruce Kawin, *Mindscreen: Bergman, Godard, and First-Person Film* (Princeton, N.J.: Princeton Univ. Press, 1978), pp. 3–22.

9. I owe this observation to Edward Benson's unpublished essay, "The Screen of History and the Construction of the Middle Class in *The Best Years of Our Lives*."

10. Robert Warshow, "The Anatomy of Falsehood," in his *The Immediate Experience: Movies, Comics, Theatre and Other Aspects of Popular Culture* (Garden City, N.Y.: Doubleday, 1962), pp. 155–161.

11. Gary Carey mentions this scene and the dramatic staging — "The scene is staged on a staircase and Wyler always goes into high gear whenever there are a few steps to whet his imagination" — in the context of exploring why Wyler is Davis's best director, in "The Lady and the Director: Bette Davis and William Wyler," *Film Comment* 6 (1970): 19. Affron also considers the use of staircases in Wyler's films with Davis, especially *The Little Foxes*, in *Star Acting*, pp. 230, 254–255.

12. Bazin discusses the collaboration between Wyler and Toland, and specifically mentions *The Little Foxes*, in *What Is Cinema?*: "Between them, director and cameraman have converted the screen into a dramatic checkerboard, planned down to the last detail. The clearest if not the most original examples of this are to be found in *The Little Foxes* where the mise-en-scène takes on the severity of a working drawing" (1: 34).

13. Affron, *Cinema and Sentiment*, pp. 88–89, and his paper on the same subject presented at a conference at the Center for Twentieth Century Studies, Milwaukee, Wisconsin, March, 1980.

14. See Edward Branigan's intriguing discussion of point of view in this scene in *Point of View in the Cinema: A Theory of Narration and Subjectivity in Classical Film* (Berlin: Mouton, 1984), pp. 135–137.

15. See Affron's discussion in *Star Acting* of the lighting effects, pp. 239–241.

16. Kenneth Geist makes this point when he comments, "Wyler has a notion of using mirror images of his principals to suggest fleeting and fragmented awareness," in "Carrie," *Film Comment* 6 (1970): 27. Affron examines the use of mirrors and photographs in *Best Years*; see *Cinema and Sentiment*, pp. 83–85.

17. These ideas about Hitchcock's use of the camera were pointed out by Joseph W. Miller, as expressed in his Hitchcock course, which I sat in on, at the University of Maryland, 1975.

18. Benson's "The Screen of History" discusses the oedipal themes in *Best Years* in relation to the returning soldiers' sexual anxieties.

19. Carey perceptively points out: "Too many of his later films become pompously inflated as they rise higher and higher in their quest for purposefulness" ("The Lady and the Director," p. 19).

20. See Smith's "Editor's Foreword" in Anderegg, *William Wyler.*

7

CONCLUSION: HABITUAL AND ACUTE FILM SPACE

Certain directors—I think immediately of Preston Sturges—are masters at creating habitual space in their films. The spectator feels at home in this space, because the director returns to certain sets over and over again. Other directors—such as Ford, Hitchcock, and Welles—create films so visually intense that the mix of habitual and acute space in them is heavily weighted toward acute moments. I've dealt in this book with directors between these two extremes, hoping in doing so to distinguish among their achievements and to describe the film spectator's experience.

The term acute is often used to describe a disease, and may strike some of us as hardly a desirable term. And some of us, for one reason or another, may choose not to seek out the intensity of acute space in films. We may prefer the neutral or habitual space of a film by John Farrow to the excruciating painfulness of a Hitchcock film or the coy playfulness of a Lubitsch film. The self-consciousness that tends to accompany acute film space can be wearing. Perhaps it also strikes some actors in this way. Should we be surprised that Garbo usually worked with Clarence Brown?

The spatial patterns that I have described in these films are ones dependent on some dialectical contrast, what structuralists would call an opposition. Capra creates intense vortex-like space, which I have called hallucinatory space, to dramatize the psychological hell that a protagonist occupies—yet we tend to think of Capra's films as cheerful and celebratory. Lubitsch frustrates us by halting at a threshold so that we imagine a scene more vividly than we might see it. Sternberg cloaks figures and objects, making them only semi-visible, in order to enhance our interest in seeing them. Wyler makes us recall an absent figure to create an ironic link between two scenes. These four directors, with their cameramen, master space in certain films because they go against the grain of their spectators' expectations. This talent might be seen as deliberately subversive.

I also have noticed that these master directors thrive despite fairly severe spatial limitations on their creativity. One has only to think of the spatial expansiveness of films made in the last 20 years (I think of the landscapes of *Barry Lyndon* or the cityscapes of *Atlantic City,* for example) to put the inventiveness of these master directors in context. I have come to the conclusion that these spatial limitations became a tool for their visual and sometimes aural imaginations, just as a painter's canvas accommodates some designs and not others. In fact, all four directors used spatial limitations to suggest psychological limitations in their characters or to focus their spectators' attention.

Capra's standing-men frame first subdues his protagonists, but later challenges them to confront false authorities. Wyler creates constricted space to demonstrate the sometimes self-imposed oppression that characters feel. Lubitsch's use of synecdoche implies that a part of something may be far more eloquent than the whole. Sternberg silhouettes his morally ambiguous characters, but he does so lovingly, seeming to prefer their complex limitations (and the spatial limitations he imposes on them) to the well-lighted arrogance of more self-righteous characters.

The techniques of these four master directors and their colleagues alert us to some universal uses of space among directors, especially the way in which they involve spectators. The recurrence of witnessing—by figures in the frame acting as our surrogates or by the camera implying the act of our looking—and the use of techniques to frustrate (and so stimulate) our sight suggest the intimacy that these directors strive for with their spectators. Lubitsch's behind glass technique resembles Sternberg's concealed sight. Wyler's witnessing resembles Capra's self-conscious space.

Some of these directors demonstrate an ability to create the human body or a portion of it in space, giving it remarkable qualities—mystery, intense emotion, or humor. Sternberg creates what I have called face space, and Capra appropriates faces in a recognizable way. Lubitsch fragments the human body with synecdoche in order to allow spectators a certain laughing distance from his characters. We attend to the attitudes conveyed by the entire body in space when Sternberg exploits gestural posture, when Capra depicts a devoted heroine's posture, or when Wyler has three characters confront each other in a character triangle.

Finally, all of these directors teach their spectators how to see. Wyler directs our gaze into the depth of the screen's field, or layers our vision by using stairs or the illusionary layers of mirrors. Capra creates linear space to show us where to look and what to see intensely. Sternberg's receding space forces us to follow and seek out what is elusive. Lubitsch, on the other hand, teaches us to see imaginatively by stopping us at thresholds and daring us to imagine what lies beyond. All four directors teach us also about their unique visions, as in Sternberg's portrayal of the grotesque, Lubitsch's odd personified props, Capra's intense exploration of his protagonists' hallucinatory space, or Wyler's late-career creation of claustrophobic space.

I have been intrigued by the mysteries of creativity in some of these directors' careers — why styles shift and why creative peaks occur. But does anyone ever answer these questions satisfactorily? For one thing, we would all have to agree on what constitutes a peak or a shift in their careers. Detailed historiography will unravel particular decisions on particular films, I have no doubt. But I yearn for a psychological map of the creative process. Sternberg's and Capra's autobiographies give us important clues, and the films themselves provide a sort of developmental map that we can work at deciphering.

Appendix: Career Survey of Capra, Lubitsch, Sternberg, and Wyler

Steven P. Hill

Information for this survey was gathered from numerous recently published and older sources, which frequently do not agree among themselves. I have tried to synthesize the data and to correct as many apparent errors as possible. The result is presented in a highly abbreviated format, which, although surely not flawless, may be a bit less inaccurate than some of the past publications on these filmmakers and their films. Here and there one may even find a bit of data, particularly linguistic, not previously published. One small illustration of the problems encountered by the researcher is the inconsistent spelling of Russian names in *Scarlet Empress:* the names of historical figures Ivan Shuvalov and Archbishop Todorsky are misspelled in several sources as Ivon Shuvolov and as Tevedovsky. Equally inconsistent credits belong to Columbia's art director, Stephen Goosson (1889–1973), whose names have been spelled in various publications as Stephan and Steven, and as Goosen, Gooson, Goossen, and Goossens, in addition to correct renditions.

The filmographies are arranged in vertical columns to display significant contributions (by designers, cameramen, writers, or studios) in a format easily scanned, unlike many other filmographies. Arbitrary decisions had to be made about criteria for inclusion of films and other credits. Much more extensive detail, of course, can be found in studies of individual filmmakers. (See Bibliography.) In limiting each director's credits to those films directed by each, I omitted their other credits, as producers, writers, assistants, actors, and so on. Further, I restricted the titles to features, defined strictly in terms of length: at least 60 minutes and either 5,400 feet or 1,630 meters. (To convert measured celluloid to minutes, I use this formula, usually applied to sound films: feet divided by 90; meters divided by 27.17.) My definition of feature-length, contrary to the American Film Institute (AFI) definition (4,000 feet, four reels), necessarily excludes all semifeatures, such as Wyler's five-reel Westerns and most of Capra's World War II and TV documentaries.

Script credits were an even tougher call. I tried to be generous in culling writing credits from many different, often contradictory sources, accepting not only "screenplay," but also "dialogue," "comedy construction," "(inter-)titles" (of silents), even "adaptation" in some instances. But I chose to omit the source stories or other literary source materials for screenplays; in Wyler's case, especially, such an omission may be questionable. In the script column and generally, I used parentheses to indicate uncertain credits, such as one cited in one or few sources, or where a writer's work may have been on a "treatment" rather than on a final screenplay. An idea of the chaos in script credits may be gotten from just one of Wyler's early sound films, *The Storm*. I checked nine sources, from AFI to *Variety*, among which there was virtually no agreement. In fact, the only two clusters of total agreement between themselves were the AFI catalog and Anderegg, on the one hand, and on the other, Shibuk and Madsen (see Bibliography). Among the nine total sources, some sort of script credit was given to scenarist Wells Root by eight, to Clarence Logue by seven, to Tom Reed by three, and to Anthony Brown by only one source.

For assistance with my research, I am grateful to Robert Carringer, Maurice Friedberg, Bodo Fritzen, Jan Herman, Leith Johnson, Henry Kahane, Joseph Laurenti, Clifford Librach, Ruth Lorbe, James Marchand, Diane Musumeci, Meri von Sternberg, Charles Wolfe, Catherine Wyler, to the California Institute of Technology, and especially to Frank Capra and Josef von Sternberg, both of whom I had the good fortune to meet personally in earlier years.

Abbreviations. YR = year of release (28 = 1928); * = film was co-directed or finished by another director; # = completed, but never released. PRO = studio, or country other than the United States, where the film was produced, specifically: AA = Allied Artists, COL = Columbia, FN = First National (Warners), FOX = Twentieth-Century Fox, FR = France, GB = Great Britain, GER = Germany, GLD = Goldwyn, ITA = Italy, JPN = Japan, MGM = Metro-Goldwyn-Mayer, PAR = Paramount, RKO = Radio-Keith-Orpheum, UA = United Artists, UNV = Universal, US = U.S. government, and WB = Warner Brothers.

CAPRA BIOGRAPHY

The most Americanized of film directors, known in the United States as Frank Russell Capra, was born in 1897 and lived his first six years on the island of Sicily, where his baptismal name probably was Francesco Rosario Capra (KAH-pruh; nicknames: "Cecco," "Chico," "Franco"). His home town, Bisacquino (population 8,000; misspelled in most sources), is just a few miles from the towns of Corleone and Prizzi—perhaps Capra's later recollections of contacts with Sicilian-American gangsters are not so farfetched? Capra's illiterate, starvation-poor parents, Salvatore "Turiddu" Capra (1855–1917) and Rosaria "Sara" (Nicolosi) Capra (1859–1941), had fourteen children, seven of whom died young. The survivors eventually made their way to the United States, settling first, like many of their fellow countrymen, in Los Angeles's Sicilian slum. Workaholic young Frank emerged as the family's highest achiever, holding after-school jobs while still earning top grades that got him a scholarship to California Institute of Technology, where he completed a B.S. in chemistry (1918).

After a mysterious few years burdened by illness, unemployment, and underemployment (some probably illegal), Capra fell into a succession of odd jobs in San Francisco and Los Angeles film companies. Ironically for someone with his dismal background, he wound up specializing in comedy, mainly as a gag-writer for the *Our Gang* series, for Mack Sennett, and especially for the popular new screen comic, Harry Langdon. Langdon eventually hired the 29-year-old writer Capra to direct features for the first time, and the result was two highly successful slapstick silents.

After further setbacks, Capra found a long-term home at Harry Cohn's little Columbia Studio, where Capra was to direct 25 features during the next 12 years, 1928 to 1939. Having proved his ability to direct purely visual silents, Capra quickly took to the new sound medium: his 25 Columbia features included two part-talkies and 17 all-talkies. The now versatile Capra broadened his range beyond comedy to action-adventure, melodrama, drama, romance, even an exposé of religious charlatans in *Miracle Woman* and a Sternberg imitation in *Bitter Tea*.

Frank R. Capra became one of a tiny group of film directors with a reputation big enough to sell tickets. Many consider that Capra almost alone elevated Columbia from Poverty Row to the ranks of Hollywood's major studios. His gag-devising skills from the silents were in the 1930's blended with a high-speed, dynamic editing style and very effective use of voice, effects, and music on the sound track. On the story side, Capra and his writers added a new element in the 30's: sociopolitical themes usually revolving around media hype and the evils of Big Business versus the saintly innocence of common people. He created countless unforgettable personifications of Americana, embodied in his "little people" and played by character actors like Irving Bacon, Charles Lane (Levison), and, most prominently, Regis Toomey and Ann Doran — to whom Capra and his writers often gave their best sermon-like speeches about Faith, Hope, Charity, and the American Way.

In his career, mainly at Columbia, Capra worked most often with cameraman Joseph Walker (1892–1985), who photographed 20 Capra features, and with art directors Stephen Goosson (approximately 10 features) and Harrison Wiley (about 8). Perhaps even more important were Capra's writers, Jo Swerling (6 features), Dorothy Howell (7), and particularly Robert Riskin (9), who wrote punchy dialogue and memorable characterizations.

Finally leaving Columbia after 1939, Capra remained fully active in the next dozen years, directing nine more features at various other studios and in the military (1942–1945; the *Why We Fight* series). After 1951, however, now in his mid-fifties, Capra became increasingly alienated from Hollywood: in the next fifteen semiactive years before retirement, he had more shorts and unfinished feature projects than he did finished features (two).

In addition to appearing on the cover of *Time* (1938) and winning three Oscars for Best Director (in 1934 for *It Happened,* 1936 for *Deeds,* and 1938 for *You Can't*), Capra was honored by the D. W. Griffith Award from the Screen Directors Guild (1959) and the AFI Lifetime Achievement Award (1982). Preaching in his films the obligation to work within the system for social and economic change, Capra practiced the same philosophy in the outside world: he served three very active terms as president of the Screen Directors Guild, and four as president of the Academy of Motion Picture Arts and Sciences. Capra served on the board of directors of Cal Tech, to which he later donated his ranch. He received an honorary Ph.D. (1981) from Wesleyan University, where his archives are located.

Capra's first marriage in 1923 to Helen Howell ended in divorce (1928) and was childless. His second marriage, in 1932 to secretary Lucille (Warner) Reyburn, lasted until her death in 1984. In addition to three children, Frank, Jr. (1934–   ), Lucille

"Lulu" (1937–   ), and Thomas (1941–   ), they suffered the loss of a stillborn child in 1933 and of three-year-old John in 1938. Frank Capra, Sr., died quietly in his sleep at 94 on September 3, 1991.

CAPRA, THE DIRECTOR (39 FEATURES)

YR	PRO	FILM TITLE	SCRIPT, TITLES	CAMERA	DESIGN
26	FN	*Strong Man*	Ripley, Eddy, Conklin, (Hennecke)	Lessley, Kershner	(uncredited)
27	FN	*Long Pants*	Ripley, Eddy, (Hennecke)	Lessley, Kershner	(uncredited)
27	FN	*For the Love of Mike*	Miller, (Hayward)	Haller	(uncredited)
28	COL	*That Certain Thing*	Harris, Boasberg	Walker	Lee
28	COL	*So This Is Love*	Harris, Taylor	June	Lee
28	COL	*Matinee Idol*	Harris, Milne	Tannura	Lee
28	COL	*Way of the Strong*	Milne, (Counselman)	Reynolds	(uncredited)
28	COL	*Say It with Sables*	D. Howell, (Milne, Capra)	Walker	Wiley
28	COL	*Submarine*	D. Howell, (Dunn)	Walker	Wiley
28	COL	*Power of the Press*	Levien, (Thompson)	Lyons, (Tetzlaff)	Wiley
29	COL	*Younger Generation*	Levien, Green	Tetzlaff, (Reynolds)	Wiley
29	COL	*Donovan Affair*	D. Howell, Green	Tetzlaff	Wiley
29	COL	*Flight*	Green, Capra	Walker, (Novak, Dyer)	Wiley
30	COL	*Ladies of Leisure*	Swerling	Walker	Wiley
30	COL	*Rain or Shine*	Swerling, D. Howell	Walker	Wiley
31	COL	*Dirigible*	Swerling, (D. Howell)	Walker, (Dyer)	(uncredited)
31	COL	*Miracle Woman*	Swerling, (D. Howell)	Walker	Parker
31	COL	*Platinum Blonde*	Swerling, Riskin, (D. Howell)	Walker	Goosson
32	COL	*Forbidden*	Swerling	Walker	(uncredited)

YR	PRO	FILM TITLE	SCRIPT, TITLES	CAMERA	DESIGN
32	COL	*American Madness*	Riskin	Walker	Goosson
33	COL	*Bitter Tea of General Yen*	Paramore	Walker	(Goosson?)
33	COL	*Lady for a Day*	Riskin	Walker	Goosson
34	COL	*It Happened One Night*	Riskin	Walker	Goosson
34	COL	*Broadway Bill*	Riskin	Walker	(Goosson)
36	COL	*Mr. Deeds Goes to Town*	Riskin	Walker	Goosson
37	COL	*Lost Horizon*	Riskin	Walker, Dyer	Goosson, Johnstone, (Murphy)
38	COL	*You Can't Take It with You*	Riskin	Walker	Goosson, Banks
39	COL	*Mr. Smith Goes to Washington*	Buchman	Walker	Banks
41	WB	*Meet John Doe*	Riskin	Barnes	Goosson, (Menzies)
44	WB	*Arsenic and Old Lace*	J. & P. Epstein	Polito	Parker
44	US	**Battle of China*	Veiller, Heller, (Knight)	(uncredited)	(uncredited)
44	US	**Tunisian Victory*	Hodson, Veiller	(uncredited)	(uncredited)
45	US	**Know Your Enemy: Japan*	Wallace, Peterson, Foreman, Hackett, Goodrich, Duff, Ivens	(uncredited)	(uncredited)
46	RKO	*It's a Wonderful Life*	Hackett, Goodrich, Capra, (Swerling)	Walker, Biroc	Okey, Kuri
48	MGM	*State of the Union*	Veiller, Connolly	Folsey	Gibbons, McCleary, Kuri, Willis
50	PAR	*Riding High*	Riskin, Shavelson, Rose	Barnes, Laszlo	Dreier, Tyler, Kuri, Comer
51	PAR	*Here Comes the Groom*	Van Upp, O'Brien, Connolly	Barnes	Pereira, Hedrick, Kuri
59	UA	*Hole in the Head*	Schulman	Daniels	Imazu, MacLean
61	UA	*Pocketful of Miracles*	Kanter, Tugend, (Cannon)	Bronner	Pereira, Anderson, Comer, Moyer

LUBITSCH BIOGRAPHY

Ernst Lubitsch was born on January 29, 1892, in Berlin, the son of Ssimcha ("Simon") Lubitsch (1852–1924) and Anna (Lindenstaedt) Lubitsch (1850–1914). Judging by the surnames, Lubitsch's Jewish ancestors on both sides may have migrated north from the Balkans. Anna Lindenstaedt was born in Wriezen near Berlin, but her ancestors may have come from present-day Austria, since Lindenstadt (or Lindenstedt, now renamed Leibnitz) is a small town in southeast Austria, a few miles from the borders of both Yugoslavia and Hungary. On his father's side, the ancestral home might be present-day Yugoslavia, since Lubitsch appears to be Germanized from Serbo-Croatian *Ljubić* (i.e., "Ljuba's son" or "love's child"). But since Ssimcha Lubitsch himself was born in Grodno province, an equally likely theory is that his ancestry goes back to the northwestern (Belorussian) part of what used to be the USSR. The surname Lubitsch may be simplified from the place name Liubavichi (Lubavitch), a Belorussian market town, which was also the home of a major Jewish Hasidic sect.

The youngest of four children, Ernst finished school at 16 (Sophia Preparatory School), and worked in his father's tailor-clothing shop until he began a stage-acting career in 1911. Two years later, young Lubitsch switched over to the German screen, appearing in many short films as the comic heroes "Meyer" and "Moritz." Eventually he began directing shorts (mainly comedies), then moved up to the direction of features, including some of the most successful, popular, and sophisticated German features just after World War I.

Lubitsch moved to the United States and directed his first American film in 1923, spending the rest of his career in Hollywood; he lost his German citizenship and became a U.S. citizen in the mid-1930's. A number of his one-time German collaborators also came to Hollywood in the 1920's and early 1930's: scenarist Hans Kraly, performers Pola Negri and Emil Jannings, cameramen Theodore Sparkuhl and Karl Freund, producer Heinz (Henry) Blanke, director Paul Stein, and costume designer Ali Hubert.

In directing his 39 feature films — 12 of them in Germany and 11 in the United States at Paramount — Lubitsch often worked with scenarists Kraly (20 features), Samson Raphaelson (9), and Ernest Vajda (5); cameramen Sparkuhl (9), Victor Milner (6), and Charles Van Enger (5); and art directors Hans Dreier (11) and Kurt Richter (9). Lubitsch's phenomenal directing success at Paramount even led to his appointment as head of production for the entire studio (1935–1936), but he soon returned to directing.

Some of Lubitsch's American pictures, particularly *Trouble in Paradise* and *Ninotchka*, are ranked by experts among the greatest comedies in film history. In 1947, the director was awarded a special, honorary Oscar by the Academy of Motion Picture Arts and Sciences. In 1958, the Ernst Lubitsch Prize, an annual award for best acting in a comic film, was created in West Berlin.

Lubitsch's two marriages each preceded or coincided with major career advances. In 1922, just before coming to the United States, he married the widowed Helene (Leni, not Irni) Kraus and acquired an instant family of two boys, Ernst (1913–) and Edmund ("Edi," 1916–). This marriage ended in divorce in 1930; the boys remained with their mother. In 1935, around the time of his promotion to studio chief, he married Sania Bezencenet ("Vivian Gaye"), and they had one child, a daughter Nicola (1938–), before divorcing in 1943, with custody awarded to the mother. Lubitsch died of a heart attack in Los Angeles on November 30, 1947.

LUBITSCH, THE DIRECTOR (39 FEATURES)

YR	PRO	FILM TITLE	SCRIPT, TITLES	CAMERA	DESIGN
18	GER	*Eyes of the Mummy Ma*	Kraly, Rameau	Hansen	Richter
18	GER	*Carmen*	Kraly, Falk	Hansen	Machus, Richter
19	GER	*Oyster Princess*	Kraly, Lubitsch	Sparkuhl	Richter
19	GER	*Intoxication*	Kraly	Freund	Gliese
19	GER	*Madame Dubarry*	Orbig, Kraly	Sparkuhl	Machus, Richter
19	GER	*The Doll*	Kraly, Lubitsch	Sparkuhl	Richter
20	GER	*Kohlhiesel's Daughters*	Kraly, Lubitsch	Sparkuhl	Winter
20	GER	*Sumurun*	Kraly, Lubitsch	Sparkuhl	Richter, Metzner
20	GER	*Anne Boleyn*	Orbig, Kraly	Sparkuhl	Richter, Poelzig
21	GER	*Mountain Cat*	Kraly, Lubitsch	Sparkuhl	Stern
22	GER	*Wife of the Pharaoh*	Falk, Kraly	Sparkuhl, Hansen	Metzner, Stern, Richter
23	GER	*The Flame*	Kraly, Kurtz	Sparkuhl, Hansen	Stern, Richter
23	UA	*Rosita*	Knoblock, Kraly	Rosher	Gade
24	WB	*Marriage Circle*	Bern	Van Enger	Gade
24	WB	*Three Women*	Kraly	Van Enger	Gade
24	PAR	*Forbidden Paradise*	Kraly, Johnston	Van Enger	Dreier
25	WB	*Kiss Me Again*	Kraly	Van Enger	(uncredited)
25	WB	*Lady Windermere's Fan*	Josephson	Van Enger	Grieve
26	WB	*So This Is Paris*	Kraly	Mescall	Grieve
27	MGM	*Student Prince*	Kraly, Ainslee, Cummings	Mescall	Gibbons, Day
28	PAR	*The Patriot*	Kraly, Johnson	Glennon	Dreier
29	UA	*Eternal Love*	Kraly, Hilliker, Caldwell	Marsh	Reimann
29	PAR	*Love Parade*	Vajda, Bolton	Milner	Dreier

YR	PRO	FILM TITLE	SCRIPT, TITLES	CAMERA	DESIGN
30	PAR	*Monte Carlo*	Vajda, Lawrence	Milner	Dreier
31	PAR	*Smiling Lieutenant*	Vajda, Raphaelson, Lubitsch	Folsey	Dreier
32	PAR	*Man I Killed*	Raphaelson, Vajda	Milner	Dreier
32	PAR	**One Hour with You*	Raphaelson	Milner	Dreier
32	PAR	*Trouble in Paradise*	Raphaelson	Milner	Dreier
33	PAR	*Design for Living*	Hecht	Milner	Dreier
34	MGM	*Merry Widow*	Vajda, Raphaelson	Marsh	Gibbons, Scognamillo, Hope, Willis
37	PAR	*Angel*	Raphaelson	Lang	Dreier, Usher, Freudman
38	PAR	*Bluebeard's Eighth Wife*	Brackett, Wilder	Tover	Dreier, Usher, Freudman
39	MGM	*Ninotchka* +	Brackett, Wilder, Reisch	Daniels	Gibbons, Duell, Willis
40	MGM	*Shop Around the Corner*	Raphaelson	Daniels	Gibbons, Rubottom, Willis
41	UA	*That Uncertain Feeling*	Stewart	Barnes	Golitzen
42	UA	*To Be or Not To Be*	Mayer	Mate	Korda, Heron
43	FOX	*Heaven Can Wait*	Raphaelson	Cronjager	Basevi, Fuller, Little, Scott
46	FOX	*Cluny Brown*	Hoffenstein, Reinhardt	LaShelle	Wheeler, Spencer, Little, Fox
48	FOX	**That Lady in Ermine*	Raphaelson	Shamroy	Wheeler, Spencer, Little, Scott

+ Properly stressed, in Russian, on the first syllable, and thus pronounced NEE-nuch-kuh.

STERNBERG BIOGRAPHY

Sternberg was born "Jonas Sternberg" (civil birth certificate) or "Yona ben Moyshe Shternberg" (phonetic spelling of religious appellation) in Vienna on May 29, 1894. He was the oldest of five children of Moses ("Moische," "Moyshe," later "Maurice") and Serafin (Singer) Sternberg, an Orthodox Jewish couple. The highly intelligent father had completed an advanced degree in mathematics (with dissertation), but failed to rise above the level of a talented tinkerer and carnival gypsy, migrating from place to place and job to job (including amusement parks). Sternberg's mother likewise had performed in a circus as a child. Perhaps their peripatetic existence was affected by the waves of official and unofficial anti-Semitism that swept through Vienna from 1897 to 1910.

Sternberg's youth was thus spent in painful poverty and rootlessness, now in Austria, now in New York. His formal education was equally spotty, with some high school in Queens, New York, but no diploma, much less a college degree. The teenage "Jo" Sternberg first got media-related work in New York and New Jersey film labs, before and during World War I, advancing from the most menial tasks to editor, assistant director, cameraman, and writer. These short-term jobs moved him from New Jersey to the Army Signal Corps, then to similar film and literary projects in England and on the Continent, and, from 1923, in Hollywood.

Here, still working his way in from the margins, he did manage to get more important assignments, including the direction of a couple of unsuccessful features, one of which, the self-financed *Salvation Hunters,* reveals the influence of von Stroheim — as does the new, more aristocratic name that he assumed at this time: "Josef von Sternberg." In compensation for his lack of academic degrees, Sternberg read widely throughout his life, began an impressive collection of twentieth-century European art and exotic antiques while still in his thirties, and broke into print as early as 1922 by translating an Austrian book of short stories into English.

Having paid his dues during a difficult third of a century, Sternberg at 33 suddenly put together the right combination at Paramount Studios, beginning in 1927, with the gangster blockbuster *Underworld,* and continuing through *Devil Is a Woman* (1935). This nine-year Paramount period yielded fourteen major films, a very successful combination of Sternberg's hard-earned technical expertise with strong box-office vehicles, fronted by Paramount's lineup of star performers (Jannings, Bancroft, Brook, Brent, etc.), whom Sternberg photographed to great advantage. Of the 14 major films, only one was produced outside the Paramount studio, and that was *Blue Angel* (1930, Germany, but financed and distributed by Paramount), which turned the unknown Marlene Dietrich into one of the greatest stars of world film history.

Sternberg has received much press coverage and critical analysis as one of the most important film directors in the world, thanks to his dazzling visual style, full of ornamentation and emotional flair; his misanthropic view of human relationships; and his personal image (variously regarded as misunderstood genius, aloof elitist, Continental dandy, and insufferable snob). His main collaborators were performer Dietrich (8 films), writer Jules Furthman (9), and designer Hans Dreier (12). Sternberg had no regular cameraman, preferring to control his own camera work, even maintaining membership in the American Society of Cinematographers, and taking two official camera credits himself for *Devil Is a Woman* and *Anatahan.*

At 41 he left Paramount and, seemingly, also lost his creative spark. In the next two decades he made only seven more features at various studios, only a couple of which display much of his personal expressivity: *Shanghai Gesture* and *Anatahan* (pronounced ah-nuh-tuh-HAHN in gazeteers). Other interests occupied his time, including teaching film courses at the University of Southern California (USC) and the University of California, Los Angeles (UCLA); writing an autobiography, *Fun in a Chinese Laundry* (1965); and traveling world-wide to lecture, rescreen his masterpieces, give interviews, and receive accolades at many international cinema conclaves (Locarno, 1960; Museum of Modern Art, 1965; Mannheim, 1966; Sydney, 1967; etc.). The quintessential outsider, Sternberg wound up with several commercial failures and no personal Academy Awards, although he was nominated as director of *Morocco* and of *Shanghai Express*. In fact, he was one of the first people to resign from the Motion Picture Academy in a squabble over whether to give awards competitively. He also did not appear in *Who's Who,* disdaining to fill in their questionnaire. On the other hand, he did accept a medal of honor from the Eastman House (1957) and an honorary membership in Berlin's Academy of Arts (1960).

Around 1926–1927, Sternberg married a teenage performer, Riza Royce (1908?–1980). The unhappy course of this marriage—a separation, reunion, second separation, and finally a formal divorce (1930)—probably helped to shape his jaundiced view of male/female relationships as reflected in his films. His second marriage (1943), to his young secretary Jeanne McBride (1922–   ), was equally short-lived. A mellow 54-year-old Sternberg married for a third and last time in 1948 to Meri (Ottis) Wilner (1920–   ), a young widow with a four-year-old daughter Catherine. In 1951 they had a son, Nicholas J., who has become a cameraman on independent and foreign films such as *Hospital Massacre* and *Pink Motel*. Meri von Sternberg, the niece of a Norwegian diplomat, taught art history (especially Asian art) at UCLA and USC. On December 22, 1969, Josef von Sternberg died of heart failure at Midway Hospital, Hollywood.

STERNBERG, THE DIRECTOR (24 FEATURES)

YR	PRO	FILM TITLE	SCRIPT, TITLES	CAMERA	DESIGN
25	UA	*Salvation Hunters*	Sternberg (JVS)	Gheller	(uncredited)
26	MGM	**Exquisite Sinner*	JVS, Miller, Farnham	Fabian	Gibbons, Wright
26	UA	*# Woman of the Sea*	JVS	Ivano	Hall
27	PAR	*Underworld*	+ Lee, Marion	Glennon	Dreier
28	PAR	*Last Command*	+ Goodrich, H. Mankiewicz	Glennon	Dreier
28	PAR	*Drag Net*	J. & C. Furthman, H. Mankiewicz	Rosson	Dreier
28	PAR	*Docks of New York*	J. Furthman, Johnson	Rosson	Dreier

YR	PRO	FILM TITLE	SCRIPT, TITLES	CAMERA	DESIGN
29	PAR	*Case of Lena Smith*	+ J. Furthman, Johnson	Rosson	Dreier, Porkay
29	PAR	*Thunderbolt*	+ J. & C. Furthman, H. & J. Mankiewicz	Gerrard	Dreier
30	GER	*Blue Angel*	+ Zuckmayer, Vollmoeller, Liebmann	Rittau, Schneeberger	Hunte, Hasler
30	PAR	*Morocco*	+ J. Furthman	Garmes, Ballard	Dreier
31	PAR	*Dishonored*	+ D. Rubin	Garmes	Dreier
31	PAR	*American Tragedy*	+ Hoffenstein	Garmes	Dreier
32	PAR	*Shanghai Express*	+ J. Furthman	Garmes	Dreier
32	PAR	*Blonde Venus*	+ J. Furthman, Lauren	Glennon	Ihnen
34	PAR	*Scarlet Empress*	+ Komroff	Glennon	Dreier, Ballbusch, Kollorsz
35	PAR	*Devil Is a Woman*	+ Dos Passos, Winston	JVS, Ballard	+ Dreier
35	COL	*Crime and Punishment*	Lauren, Anthony	Ballard	Goosson
36	COL	*King Steps Out*	Buchman	Ballard	Goosson
39	MGM	*Sergeant Madden*	Root	Seitz	Gibbons, Duell
42	UA	*Shanghai Gesture*	JVS, Herczeg, Vollmoeller, J. Furthman	Ivano	Leven, Bristol
52	RKO	**Macao*	Schoenfeld, J. Rubin	Wild	D'Agostino, Berger, Silvera, Miller
53	JPN	*Saga of Anatahan*	JVS, Asano	JVS, Okazaki	Kono, Watanabe
57	RKO	**Jet Pilot*	J. Furthman	Hoch, Cochran	D'Agostino, Gray, Silvera, Miller

+ Weinberg ascribes the credit to JVS, but most other sources cite "official" credits (as above).

WYLER BIOGRAPHY

William Wyler was born July 1, 1902, in the eastern French/southern German border city of Mulhouse (pronounced mew-LOOZ), a few miles from the Swiss border. Quite unlike the humble beginnings of Capra and Sternberg, Wyler came from a very comfortable, middle-class, cultured family. His Swiss father, Leopold Wyler (1864–1939; pronounced VÜ-ler), owned two haberdashery shops. Wyler's mother, Melanie (Auerbach, 1878–1955), the niece of a prolific German novelist, was herself well-educated, knowledgeable in French language and culture as well as German. She passed on those interests to her two famous sons, Robert (1900–1971, drama and film writer-producer, husband of performer Cathy O'Donnell), and William—who was probably officially registered as "Wilhelm" or "Guillaume," but known informally as "Willy" or "Willi" by everyone in Mulhouse.

After very undistinguished schooling and apprenticeship in Europe, the adventuresome, still immature Wyler came to the United States in 1920, sponsored by his mother's cousin. This cousin happened to be Carl Laemmle, head of Universal Pictures, where the teenage Wyler (Americanized pronunciation: WY-ler or WY-luh) was given a variety of back-office and behind-the-camera jobs, starting at the very bottom. Soon his superiors recognized a lifelong Wyler characteristic: the willingness to try anything and to apply his incredible energy until the job was finished. At age 23 he was promoted to short-subject director and quickly ground out an ultra-cheap series of at least 29 Western shorts and semifeatures (from *Pinnacle Rider, Ore Riders,* and *Thunder Riders* to *Ridin' for Love,* 1925–1927).

At 26 Wyler earned his chance to direct full-length, non-Western features, which he continued to do, creating higher-budgeted, more carefully made dramas and comedies almost without interruption for the next 43 years, one of the longest directing careers in U.S. history. Wyler did much of his work at two studios: Universal (from the start through 1934, 11 features) and Samuel Goldwyn (8 features, 1936–1946). His favorite cameraman (7 films) was the famous Gregg Toland, before the latter's early death.

Wyler's 36 features, most very successful commercially and critically, display the director's meticulous focusing of all the elements of a film—including photography composed in depth—on the story and the performers, not on directorial touches for their own sake. Under his guidance, performers such as Walter Huston, Bette Davis, Walter Brennan, Merle Oberon, Laurence Olivier, Gary Cooper, Audrey Hepburn, Gregory Peck, and many others, gave memorable performances, depicting characters originated by writers ranging from Emily Brontë, General Lew Wallace, Theodore Dreiser, Ferenc Molnar, and Henry James, to Somerset Maugham, Elmer Rice, Lillian Hellman, Sinclair Lewis, Edna Ferber, Jessamyn West, and John Fowles.

Wyler was often criticized by weary performers for retaking the same shot or scene over and over, but his exhaustive and exhausting approach resulted in dozens of acting and technical awards for his cast and crew. His actors, for instance, received a phenomenal total of 33 Oscar nominations and 14 Academy Awards. Wyler, the "actor's director," himself received 12 Oscar nominations for Best Director and won three times, for *Miniver, Best Years,* and *Ben-Hur.* In my statistical ratings of all U.S. directors, 1930–1959 (see Bibliography), Wyler ranked number one on the "popular films" scale and number two on the "artistic films" scale. (Capra ranked third in the popular and fourteenth on the artistic scale; Lubitsch and Sternberg were much lower down.) Wyler was awarded many other honors, including the Irving Thalberg Memorial Award and the D. W. Griffith Award (both 1966) and the AFI Life Achievement Award (1976)—

the presentation of which was telecast nationally. Another such tribute, telecast in 1986, was "Directed by William Wyler" in the PBS "American Masters" series.

An interesting reflection of Wyler's dedication to detail may be found in *Who's Who*. Unlike Capra, Lubitsch, and Sternberg, the meticulous Wyler answered every question. He listed every one of his feature film credits, mentioned his brief service in the National Guard as a youth, as well as the exact date in World War II when he won a medal, spelled out his daughter Catherine's middle name and his own political and religious affiliations ("Democrat, Jewish"), even revealed the street address of his home in Beverly Hills!

William Wyler became a U.S. citizen in 1928. His first marriage, to movie star Margaret Sullavan (1911–1960), lasted only from 1934 to 1936 and was childless. In 1938, he married beginning performer Margaret Tallichet (TAL-uh-shay, 1914–1991), and they had five children: Catherine (1939–), Judith (1942–), William, Jr. (1946–1949), Melanie (1950–), and David (1952–). Catherine produced both "Directed by William Wyler" and a 1990 feature remake of her father's World War II documentary *Memphis Belle*. William Wyler died in Beverly Hills after a heart attack on July 27, 1981.

WYLER, THE DIRECTOR (36 FEATURES)

YR	PRO	TITLE	SCRIPT, TITLES	CAMERA	DESIGN
28	UNV	*Anybody Here Seen Kelly?*	Clymer, Anthony, DeMond	Stumar	(uncredited)
29	UNV	*Shakedown*	Logue, Marks, DeMond	Stumar, Ash	(uncredited)
29	UNV	*Love Trap*	Clymer, Marks, Thompson, DeMond	Warrenton	(uncredited)
30	UNV	*Hell's Heroes*	Reed	Robinson	(uncredited)
30	UNV	*Storm*	Root, (Logue, Reed, Brown)	Wyckoff	(uncredited)
31	UNV	*House Divided*	Clymer, Van Every, Huston	Stumar	Hughes
32	UNV	*Tom Brown of Culver*	Buckingham, Green, Marks	Stumar	Hughes
33	UNV	*Her First Mate*	Snell, Marks, (Walker, Jarrett)	Robinson	Fleischer
33	UNV	*Counsellor at Law*	Rice	Brodine	Hall
34	UNV	*Glamour*	Anderson, Unger	Robinson	Hall
35	UNV	*Good Fairy*	Sturges	Brodine	Hall

YR	PRO	FILM TITLE	SCRIPT, TITLES	CAMERA	DESIGN
35	FOX	*Gay Deception*	Avery, Hartman, Richman	Valentine	Parker
36	GLD	*These Three*	Hellman	Toland	Day
36	GLD	*Dodsworth*	Howard	Mate	Day
36	GLD	**Come and Get It*	Murfin, Furthman	Toland, Mate	Day, Heron
37	GLD	*Dead End*	Hellman	Toland	Day, Heron
38	WB	*Jezebel*	Ripley, Finkel, Huston	Haller	Haas
39	GLD	*Wuthering Heights*	Hecht, MacArthur	Toland	Basevi, Heron
40	GLD	*Westerner*	Swerling, Busch	Toland	Basevi, Heron
40	WB	*Letter*	Koch	Gaudio	Weyl
41	GLD	*Little Foxes*	Hellman, Kober, Parker, Campbell	Toland	Goosson, Bristol
42	MGM	*Mrs. Miniver*	Wimperis, Froeschel, Hilton, C. West	Ruttenberg	Gibbons, McCleary, Willis
46	GLD	*Best Years of Our Lives*	Sherwood	Toland	Jenkins, Ferguson, Heron
49	PAR	*The Heiress*	R. & A. Goetz	Tover	Horner, Meehan, Kuri
51	PAR	*Detective Story*	Yordan, R. Wyler	Garmes	Pereira, Hedrick, Kuri
52	PAR	*Carrie*	R. & A. Goetz	Milner	Pereira, Anderson, Kuri
53	ITA	*Roman Holiday*	Trumbo, (Hunter), Dighton	Planer, Alekan	Pereira, Tyler
55	PAR	*Desperate Hours*	Jos. Hayes	Garmes	Pereira, Johnson, Comer, Gregory
56	AA	*Friendly Persuasion*	(Wilson, J. West, R. Wyler)	Fredericks	Haworth, Kish
58	UA	*Big Country*	Webb, Bartlett, Wilder	Planer	Hotaling, Boyle

YR	PRO	FILM TITLE	SCRIPT, TITLES	CAMERA	DESIGN
59	ITA	*Ben-Hur*	Tunberg, (Fry, Behrman, Vidal)	Surtees	Horning, Carfagno, Hunt
62	UA	*Children's Hour*	John Hayes	Planer	Carrere, Boyle
65	GB	*Collector*	Mann, Kohn	Surtees, Krasker	Stoll, Tuttle
66	FR	*How to Steal a Million*	Kurnitz	Lang	Trauner
68	COL	*Funny Girl*	Lennart	Stradling	Callahan, Luthardt, Kiernan
70	COL	*Liberation of L. B. Jones*	Silliphant, Ford	Surtees	Reid, Tuttle

BIBLIOGRAPHY

Affron, Charles. *Cinema and Sentiment*. Chicago: Univ. of Chicago Press, 1982.

————. *Star Acting: Gish, Garbo, Davis*. New York: E. P. Dutton, 1977.

Agel, Henri. *L'espace cinématographique*. Paris: Jean-Pierre DeLarge, 1978.

Anderegg, Michael A. *William Wyler*. Boston: Twayne, 1979.

Andrew, Dudley. *Film in the Aura of Art*. Princeton: Princeton Univ. Press, 1984.

Anobile, Richard, ed. *Ernst Lubitsch's "Ninotchka," Starring Greta Garbo, Melvyn Douglas*. New York: Universe Books, 1975.

Arnheim, Rudolf. *Film as Art*. Berkeley: Univ. of California Press, 1957.

————. *Toward a Psychology of Art: Collected Essays*. London: Faber and Faber, 1966.

————. *Visual Thinking*. London: Faber and Faber, 1970.

Ashcraft, Norman, and Albert E. Scheflen. *People Space: The Making and Breaking of Human Boundaries*. Garden City, N.Y.: Anchor/Doubleday, 1976.

Bachelard, Gaston. *The Poetics of Space*. Trans. Maria Jolas. New York: Orion, 1964.

Baxter, John. *The Cinema of Josef von Sternberg*. South Brunswick, N.J.: A. S. Barnes, 1971.

————. *Hollywood in the Thirties*. New York: A. S. Barnes, 1968.

Baxter, Peter. "*Blonde Venus*: Memory, Legend, and Desire." *CineAction!* 8 (1987): 42–50.

————, ed. *Sternberg*. London: British Film Institute, 1980.

Bazin, André. *What Is Cinema?*. 2 vols. Trans. Hugh Gray. Berkeley: Univ. of California Press, 1967.

Belenky, Mary Field, Blythe McVicker Clinchy, Nancy Rule Goldberger, and Jill Mattuck Tarule. *Women's Ways of Knowing: The Development of Self, Voice, and Mind*. New York: Basic Books, 1986.

Belton, John. "Dexterity in a Void: The Formalist Esthetics of Alfred Hitchcock." *Cineaste!* 10 (1980): 9–13.

Benson, Edward. "The Screen of History and the Construction of the Middle Class in the Best Years of Our Lives," unpublished essay.

Bergman, Andrew. *We're in the Money: Depression America and Its Films*. New York: New York Univ. Press, 1971.

Bergson, Henri. *Laughter: An Essay on the Meaning of the Comic*. Trans. Cloudesley Brereton and Fred Rothwell. New York: Macmillan, 1924.

Bogdanovich, Peter. *Pieces of Time*. New York: Arbor House, 1973.

Bond, Kirk. "Ernst Lubitsch." *Film Culture* 63–64 (1977): 139–153.

Bordwell, David, Janet Staiger, and Kristin Thompson. *The Classical Hollywood Cinema: Film Style and Mode of Production to 1960*. New York: Columbia Univ. Press, 1985.

Bourget, Jean-Loup. "Romantic Dramas of the Forties: An Analysis." *Film Comment* 10 (1974): 46–51.

Branigan, Edward. *Point of View in the Cinema: A Theory of Narration and Subjectivity in Classical Film*. Berlin: Mouton, 1984.

Braudy, Leo. "The Double Detachment of Ernst Lubitsch." *Modern Language Notes* 98 (1983): 1071–1084.

Browne, Nick. *The Rhetoric of Filmic Narration*. Ann Arbor, Mich.: UMI Research Press, 1982.

Bugental, James F. T., ed. *Challenges of Humanistic Psychology*. New York: McGraw-Hill, 1967.

Capra, Frank. *The Name Above the Title: An Autobiography*. New York: Macmillan, 1971.

Carey, Gary. "The Lady and the Director: Bette Davis and William Wyler." *Film Comment* 6 (1970): 18–24.

Carney, Raymond. *American Vision: The Films of Frank Capra*. Cambridge: Cambridge Univ. Press, 1986.

Carringer, Robert L., and Barry Sabath. *Ernst Lubitsch: A Guide to References and Resources*. Boston: G. K. Hall, 1978.

Carroll, John M. *Toward a Structural Psychology of Cinema*. The Hague: Mouton, 1980.

Casty, Alan. "On Approaching the Film as Art." *Film Comment* 1 (1963): 29–34.

Cawelti, John G. *Adventure, Mystery, and Romance: Formula Stories as Art and Popular Culture*. Chicago: Univ. of Chicago Press, 1976.

Chatman, Seymour. *Story and Discourse: Narrative Structure in Fiction and Film*. Ithaca: Cornell Univ. Press, 1978.

Corrigan, Robert W., ed. *Comedy: Meaning and Form*. New York: Harper and Row, 1981.

De Lauretis, Teresa. *Alice Doesn't: Feminism, Semiotics, Cinema*. Bloomington: Indiana Univ. Press, 1984.

Di Franco, Philip. "An Essay on Belief." *Cineaste!* 2 (1968): 7–9.

Durgnat, Raymond. *The Crazy Mirror: Hollywood Comedy and the American Image*. New York: Horizon, 1970.

Eisner, Lotte H. *The Haunted Screen: Expressionism in the German Cinema and the Influence of Max Reinhardt*. Trans. Roger Greaves. London: Thames and Hudson, 1969.

Erickson, Erik. *Toys and Reasons: Stages in the Realization of Experience*. New York: W. W. Norton, 1979.

Geist, Kenneth. *"Carrie." Film Comment* 6 (1970): 25–27.

Giedion, Sigfried. *Architecture and the Phenomena of Transition: The Three Space Conceptions in Architecture*. Cambridge: Harvard Univ. Press, 1971.

———. *Space, Time and Architecture: The Growth of a New Tradition*. Cambridge: Harvard Univ. Press, 1962.

Glatzer, Richard, and John Raeburn, eds. *Frank Capra: The Man and His Films*. Ann Arbor: Univ. of Michigan Press, 1975.

Goffman, Erving. *The Presentation of Self in Everyday Life*. Woodstock, N.Y.: Overlook Press, 1973.

Gombrich, E. H. *Art and Illusion: A Study in the Psychology of Pictorial Representation*. Princeton: Princeton Univ. Press, 1969.

Gombrich, E. H., Julian Hochberg, and Max Black. *Art, Perception, and Reality*. Baltimore: Johns Hopkins Univ. Press, 1972.

Griffith, Richard. *Frank Capra*. London: British Film Institute, 1950.

Hake, Sabine. "*So This Is Paris*: A Comedy of Misreading." *Journal of Film and Video* 40 (1988): 3–17.

Harbison, Robert. *Eccentric Spaces*. New York: Alfred A. Knopf, 1977.

Harrington, Curtis. *Index to the Films of Josef von Sternberg*. London: British Film Institute, 1949.

Haskell, Molly. *From Reverence to Rape: The Treatment of Women in the Movies*. New York: Holt, Rinehart and Winston, 1974.

Heilman, Robert. *Tragedy and Melodrama: Versions of Experience*. Seattle: Univ. of Washington Press, 1968.

Held, R. L. *Endless Innovations: Frederick Kiesler's Theory and Scenic Designs*. Ann Arbor, Mich.: UMI Research Press, 1977, 1982.

Hill, Steven P. "Confessions of a Swindler [Frank Capra]." *Focus Magazine* 1 (1982): 6–9.

———. "Evaluating the Directors." *Films in Review* 12 (1961): 7–13.

———. "The Popular Directors." *Films in Review* 13 (1962): 385–389.

Huff, Theodore. *Index to the Films of Ernst Lubitsch*. London: British Film Institute, 1947.

Huie, William O., Jr. "Style and Technology in *Trouble in Paradise*: Evidence of a Technicians' Lobby?" *Journal of Film and Video* 39 (1987): 37–51.

Husserl, Edmund. *Ideas: General Introduction to Pure Phenomenology*. Trans. W. R. Boyce. New York: Collier Books, 1962.

Isaacs, Neil D. "Lubitsch and the Filmed-Play Syndrome." *Literature/Film Quarterly* 3 (1975): 299–308.

Jacobowitz, Florence. "Power and the Masquerade: *The Devil Is a Woman*." *CineAction!* 8 (1987): 32–41.

Jacobs, Lea. "The Censorship of *Blonde Venus*: Textual Analysis and Historical Method." *Cinema Journal* 27 (1988): 21–31.

Jarvie, Ian. *Philosophy of the Film: Epistemology, Ontology, Aesthetics*. New York: Routledge and Kegan Paul, 1987.

Kaplan, E. Ann. *Women and Film: Both Sides of the Camera*. New York: Methuen, 1983.

Kawin, Bruce. "Authorial and Systematic Self-Consciousness in Literature and Film." *Literature and Film Quarterly* 10 (1982): 3–12.

———. *Mindscreen: Bergman, Godard, and First-Person Film*. Princeton, N.J.: Princeton Univ. Press, 1978.

Kern, Sharon. *William Wyler: A Guide to References and Resources*. Boston: G. K. Hall, 1984.

Kolker, Robert Phillip. *A Cinema of Loneliness: Penn, Kubrick, Coppola, Scorsese, Altman*. New York: Oxford Univ. Press, 1980.

Koszarski, Richard. *Hollywood Directors, 1941–1976.* New York: Oxford Univ. Press, 1977.

———. "On *Trouble in Paradise.*" *Film Comment* 7 (1970): 47–48.

LaFontaine, Jean S., ed. *The Interpretation of Ritual: Essays in Honour of I. A. Richards.* London: Tavistock, 1972.

Larson, Orville K., ed. *Scene Design for Stage and Screen.* East Lansing: Michigan State Univ. Press, 1961.

Lym, Glenn Robert. *A Psychology of Building: How We Shape and Experience Our Structural Spaces.* Englewood Cliffs, N.J.: Prentice-Hall, 1980.

Madsen, Axel. *William Wyler: The Authorized Biography.* New York: Thomas Y. Crowell, 1973.

Maland, Charles J. *American Visions: The Films of Chaplin, Ford, Capra and Welles, 1936–1941.* New York: Arno Press, 1977.

———. *Frank Capra.* Boston: Twayne, 1980.

Mast, Gerald. *The Comic Mind: Comedy and the Movies.* 2nd ed. Chicago: Univ. of Chicago Press, 1979.

Miller, Jean Baker. *Toward a New Psychology of Women.* Boston: Beacon Press, 1976.

Mordden, Ethan. *The Hollywood Studios: House Style in the Golden Age of the Movies.* New York: Alfred A. Knopf, 1988.

Mulvey, Laura, and Jon Halliday, eds. *Douglas Sirk.* New York: New York Zoetrope, 1972.

Nichols, Bill. "*Blonde Venus*: Playing with Performance." *Ideology and the Image,* pp. 104–132. Bloomington: Indiana Univ. Press, 1981.

Nichols, Bill, ed. *Movies and Methods: An Anthology.* Berkeley: Univ. of California Press, 1976.

Norberg-Schulz, Christian. *Existence, Space, and Architecture.* New York: Praeger, 1971.

Nordberg, Carl. "Greta Garbo's Secret." *Film Comment* 6 (1970): 26.

Paul, William. *Ernst Lubitsch's American Comedy.* New York: Columbia Univ. Press, 1983.

Percy, Walker. *The Message in the Bottle.* New York: Farrar, Straus and Giroux, 1975.

Perry, William Graves. *Forms of Intellectual and Ethical Development in the College Years: A Scheme.* New York: Holt, Rinehart and Winston, 1970.

Petri, Bruce. "George Stevens: Three Wartime Comedies." *Film Comment* 11 (1975): 52–56.

Petrie, Graham. "Theater Film Life." *Film Comment* 10 (1974): 38–43.

Piaget, Jean. *The Psychology of Intelligence.* Trans. Malcolm Piercy and D. E. Berlyne. London: Routledge and Kegan Paul, 1950.

Piaget, Jean, and Barbel Inhelder. *The Child's Conception of Space.* Trans. F. J. Langdon and J. L. Lunzer. London: Routledge and Kegan Paul, 1956.

Poague, Leland A. *The Cinema of Ernst Lubitsch.* South Brunswick, N.J.: A. S. Barnes, 1978.

———. *The Cinema of Frank Capra: An Approach to Film Comedy.* South Brunswick, N.J.: A. S. Barnes, 1975.

Quantrill, Malcolm. *Ritual and Response in Architecture.* London: Lund Humphries, 1974.

Quart, Leonard. "Frank Capra and the Popular Front." *Cineaste!* 8 (1977): 4–7.

Ray, Robert B. *A Certain Tendency of the Hollywood Cinema, 1930–1980.* Princeton, N.J.: Princeton Univ. Press, 1985.

Rose, Brian Geoffrey. *An Examination of Narrative Structure in Four Films of Frank Capra.* New York: Arno Press, 1980.

Sarris, Andrew. "All Talking! All Singing! All Lubitsch!: Ernst Lubitsch in the Thirties—Part II." *Film Comment* 8 (1972): 20–21.

———. *The American Cinema.* New York: E. P. Dutton, 1968.

———. *The Films of Josef von Sternberg.* New York: Museum of Modern Art, 1966.

———. "Lubitsch in the Thirties." *Film Comment* 7 (1971–72): 54–57.

———. "Preminger's Two Periods, Solo and Studio." *Film Comment* 3 (1965): 12–17.

———. "Reflections on Margaret Sullavan." *Film Comment* 13 (1977): 32–35.

Schechner, Richard, and Mady Schuman, eds. *Ritual, Play, and Performance: Readings in the Social Sciences/Theatre.* New York: Seabury Press, 1976.

Schickel, Richard. *The Men Who Made the Movies.* New York: Atheneum, 1975.

Schwartz, Nancy. "Lubitsch's *Widow*: The Meaning of a Waltz." *Film Comment* 11 (1975): 13–17.

Shibuk, Charles. *Index to the Films of William Wyler.* New York: Huff Film Society, 1957.

Smallman, Kirk. "Toward Visual Cinema." *Film Comment* 2 (1964): 44–45.

Sontag, Susan. *Styles of Radical Will.* New York: Farrar, Straus and Giroux, 1969.

Sternberg, Josef von. *Fun in a Chinese Laundry.* London: Secker and Warburg, 1966.

Studlar, Gaylyn. *In the Realm of Pleasure: Von Sternberg, Dietrich, and the Masochistic Aesthetic.* Urbana: Univ. of Illinois Press, 1988.

Trilling, Lionel. *The Liberal Imagination: Essays on Literature and Society.* London: Secker and Warburg, 1951.

Wald, Malvin. "Who Is the Film Author?" *Cineaste!* 2 (1968–69): 11–12.

Warshow, Robert. *The Immediate Experience: Movies, Comics, Theatre and Other Aspects of Popular Culture.* Garden City, N.Y.: Doubleday, 1962.

Weinberg, Herman. "Ernst Lubitsch: A Parallel to Georges Feydeau." *Film Comment* 6 (1970): 62.

———. *Josef von Sternberg: A Critical Study.* New York: E. P. Dutton, 1967.

———. *The Lubitsch Touch: A Critical Study.* 3rd ed. New York: Dover, 1968, 1977.

Willis, Donald C. *The Films of Frank Capra.* Metuchen, N.J.: Scarecrow Press, 1974.

Wolfe, Charles. *Frank Capra: A Guide to References and Resources.* Boston: G. K. Hall, 1987.

Wollenberg, H. H. "Two Masters: Ernst Lubitsch and Sergei M. Eisenstein." *Sight and Sound* 17 (1948): 46–48.

Wood, Michael. *America in the Movies.* New York: Dell, 1975.

Wood, Robin. "Acting Up." *Film Comment* 12 (1976): 20–25.

———. "Against Conclusions." *Film Comment* 11 (1975): 3–32.

———. "Ideology, Genre, Auteur: On *It's a Wonderful Life* and *Shadow of a Doubt*." *Film Comment* 13 (1977): 49.

———. "Sternberg's *Empress*: The Play of Light and Shade." *Film Comment* 11 (1975): 6–12.

———. "To Have (Written) and Have Not (Directed): Reflections on Authorship." *Film Comment* 9 (1973): 30–35.

———. "Venus de Marlene." *Film Comment* 14 (1978): 58–63.

Yamamoto, Akira Y. *Culture Spaces in Everyday Life.* Lawrence: Univ. of Kansas Press, 1979.

Zevi, Bruno. *Architecture as Space: How to Look at Architecture.* New York: Horizon, 1957, 1974.

Index

About the Author

BARBARA BOWMAN is Director of the Humanities Division and Professor of English at Illinois Wesleyan University, Bloomington, Illinois.